How to Grow
FRUIT
Berries & Nuts
in the Midwest and East
by Theodore James Jr.

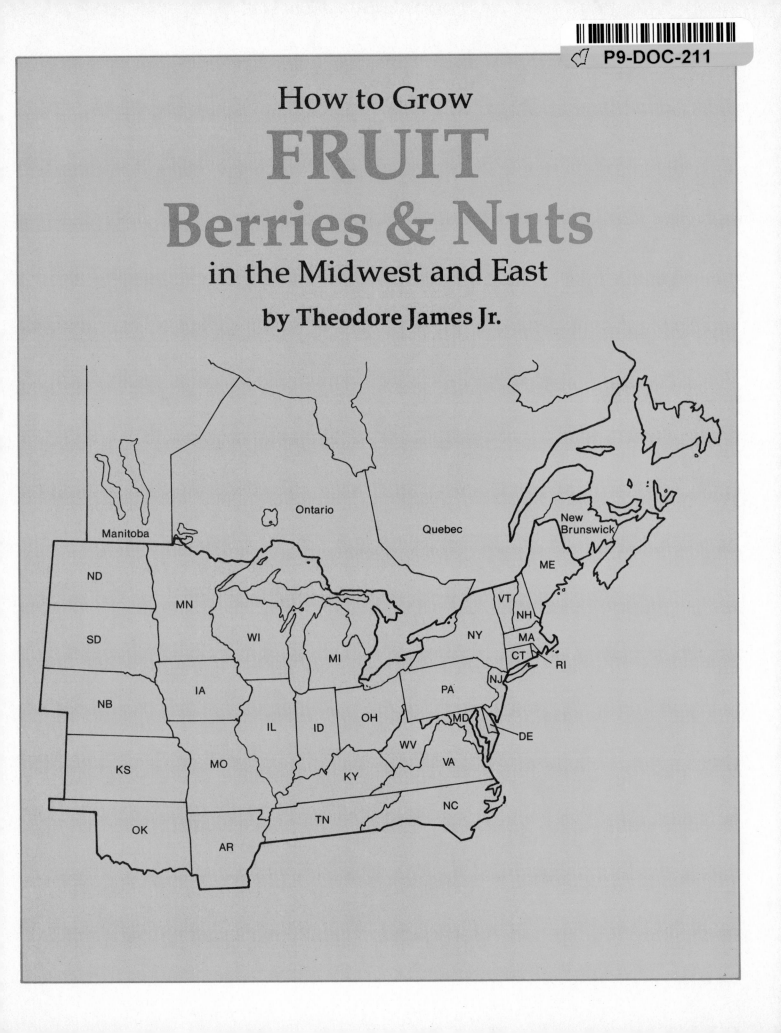

HPBooks

Publishers
Bill and Helen Fisher

Executive Editor
Rick Bailey

Editorial Director
Randy Summerlin

Editor
Scott Millard

Art Director
Don Burton

Book Design
Paul Fitzgerald

Illustrations
Black and white: Doug Burton
Color: Joan Frain

Major Photography
Harry Haralambou

Additional Photography
Muriel Orans

About the Author
Theodore James Jr. is a dedicated fruit gardener who grows vegetables and flowers as well. He is the author of 10 books, on subjects ranging from gourmet vegetable gardening to flower gardening. He has written several horticultural articles for the *New York Times* and for many major magazines. James gardens at his home on the north fork of Long Island, New York.

Acknowledgments
The contributions of the following individuals and organizations are greatly appreciated:

Theodore Averill Orchard, New Preston, CT
California Redwood Association, San Francisco, CA
Edgewood Orchard and Cider Mill, Cornwall, VT
Mr. Hinz, the Candyman, Orient, NY
Hargrave Vineyard, Cutchogue, NY
Dr. Jerome Hull, Department of Horticulture, Michigan State University
Henry Leuthardt, Henry Leuthardt Nurseries, Center Moriches, NY
Glenn Mays, North Carolina Travel and Tourism Division, Raleigh, NC
Riverhead New York Free Public Library, Riverhead, NY
Saxton River Orchard, Saxton River, VT
John Scheepers, Inc., New York, NY
Stark Bro's Nurseries and Orchard Co., Louisiana, MO
Paul Stoutenburg, Cutchogue, NY
Dr. John P. Tomkins, Extension Pomologist, Cornell University, Ithaca, NY
John Wickham, Wickham's Fruit Farm, Cutchogue, NY
Wilkinson Sword, Jackson Manufacturing Co., Harrisburg, PA

Special thanks to New York State Cooperative Extension and the many other State Cooperative Extension Services that helped provide information and research for this book.

About the Cover
From top left: 'Rome Beauty' apple, photo by Derek Fell; 'President' plum, photo by Muriel Orans; selected nut harvest, photo by Harry Haralambou; strawberries, photo by Derek Fell.

Published by HPBooks
P.O. Box 5367
Tucson, AZ 85703 602/888-2150
ISBN: 0-89586-223-9
Library of Congress Catalog Card Number: 83-80619
©1983 Fisher Publishing Inc.
Printed in U.S.A.

Contents

Growing Fruit in the Midwest & East

1

More and more people are discovering the joys of growing their own fruit, berries and nuts. It is difficult to surpass the satisfaction gained in harvesting fruit from plants you have selected, planted and nurtured yourself.

In addition to personal satisfaction, there is also the benefit of home-grown flavor. You can't buy fruit that tastes as flavorful as your own, picked fresh from tree or vine. Most supermarket produce, out of necessity, is picked green and shipped great distances. It ripens in railroad cars or in fruit bins at the market. Although the flavor can be good, it just can't equal that of fresh-picked fruit.

In addition, many kinds of fruit are not available at the market. If they are available, it may be for only a short time. Many kinds of berries perish quickly after they are harvested, and can't be shipped and stored on market shelves. You'll have to grow your own if you want to enjoy their special flavors.

Fruit for eating fresh is not the only value of a home fruit orchard. Homemade jams, jellies, juices, syrups and pies are a few of the ways to put your produce to use. When you make these with your own fruit, the flavor and quality is the best obtainable. Many tips for harvesting and use are included in these pages.

Growing fruit, berries and nuts is part of a trend in growing food-producing plants at home. Millions of people who have raised their own vegetables are growing fruit as well.

This trend is actually nothing new. Immigrants to the United States and Canada set about growing their own fruit, berries and nuts, just as their forefathers had done in Europe, Africa and Asia. When food shortages occurred during World War II, people replaced their lawns with food-producing plants.

WHY NOT GROW FRUIT?

It makes sense that growing fruit, berries and nuts appeals not only to the practical sense but to aesthetics as well. Many plants are *dual-purpose,* as attractive in the landscape as the most popular ornamentals. Consider the beauty and captivating fragrance of spring blossoms, cooling shade of trees in summer and colorful display of autumn leaves.

This book will tell you how to plant, establish and care for your own fruit garden. It will enable you to harvest fresh, delectable, tree-ripened fruit, berries and nuts. You can be a successful fruit gardener no matter where you live in Canada, the East, Midwest, Mid-Atlantic or upper Southern areas.

Left: Basket brimming with tree-ripened fruit is the goal of most gardeners. Above: Red currants are luscious, midsummer taste treat.

Right: Author Theodore James Jr. examines dwarf 'Bartlett' pear heavily laden with fruit. If you have little space for gardening, dwarf trees provide an easy way to grow fruit in a small area.

Below: Fruit trees provide much more than fruit. Many have beautiful blossoms and add a flush of color to the spring landscape. Here, yellow goldfinches contrast with vivid pink nectarine blossoms.

Left: Strawberries are a popular crop and easy to grow in most areas of the East and Midwest. Pick them when they are like this—bright red and juicy.
Below: In addition to fresh fruit from vine or tree, most tree fruit and berries can be canned or made into jellies and preserves. This saves on your food bill, and flavor is superior to store-bought products.

Planting & Care

2

A book cannot tell you *exactly* how to grow fruit. There are too many variables. But this chapter gives you principles to follow. Use it as a framework and guide to success. Read the other chapters in this book, paying close attention to the sections on individual fruit, berries and nuts. Look closely at the variety charts included in these sections. Note which cultivars do well in your area.

The section on climates and *microclimates,* small climates within a general climate, contains valuable information on the best locations for plants on your home lot. In some instances, plant placement can mean the difference between failure and success.

THE BASICS OF SUCCESSFUL GARDENING

Successful gardeners are not blessed with a "green thumb." They are simply aware of the basic needs of plants. They supply proper growing conditions and follow essential cultural practices so plants grow, stay

---

Left: Planting trees properly and in the right location are basic requirements for fruit-gardening success. Select site in full sun and plant in soil with good drainage.
Above: Don't be afraid to prune. Removing damaged and out-of-place branches during dormant season will help you obtain bountiful, high-quality harvests.

---

healthy and produce fruit. To be successful at growing plants—including fruit, berries and nuts—it is necessary to learn and apply these basics to your garden.
• Plant fruit that are adapted to your climate zone. Select varieties that are resistant to pests and diseases known to be active in your area. Doing this helps *avoid* problems and disappointments.
• Place plants in a good location. Most fruit-producing plants require exposure to full sun.
• Understand the kind of soil you have, and how it affects watering, fertilizing and even plant placement. In some instances you may want to improve your soil texture by adding organic matter.
• Realize that plants require certain amounts of essential nutrients. You may have to test your soil to see if these nutrients are available for plants.
• Learn to irrigate properly. Water deeply and infrequently. Sprinkling plants lightly causes roots to grow only in the upper soil level.
• Get to know what your plants look like when they are healthy. Then, if plant growth and appearance decline, you have a good chance of spotting the problem in its beginning stage. For example, look at leaf color and texture. Inspect leaves frequently, especially the undersides, for signs of insects and diseases.
• Learn to thin and prune properly. The quality of your fruit depends heavily on pruning practices.

SOIL, FERTILIZER AND WATER

Orchard irrigation.

Providing plants with good soil, regular amounts of fertilizer and water is necessary for proper growth. The following pages tell you how to supply plants with these basics.

SOIL AND PLANT GROWTH

Plants have three basic requirements for healthy root growth:
- Regular moisture.
- Air in the soil.
- Nutrients available in proper quantities.

Your soil type has a great influence on how these ingredients are made available to plants. Soil type also determines watering and fertilizing practices. Find out what kind of soil you have *before* you plant. Your soil may affect which fruit you can plant, or where and how they are planted on your lot.

BASIC SOIL TYPES

Clay Soil—This soil is particularly prevalent in parts of the Northeast and Mid-Atlantic areas. Small, mineral particles retain moisture and nutrients, leaving little space for air. To test your soil, pick up a moistened handful and squeeze. If the soil feels greasy and sticky and forms ribbons through your fingers, it is predominantly clay soil. Drainage is usually poor, so water sparingly, depending on the season, rainfall and age of plant. Because drainage is poor, water stays for a longer period in the soil around roots in place of air. Without air, roots can suffocate and die. Waterlogged conditions in the root zone also promote bacterial and fungal diseases, which prey on the air-deprived roots.

Avoid planting apricots, cherries, peaches, nectarines, Japanese plums and walnuts in slow-draining soil. Apples, European plums, quince and especially pears are somewhat more tolerant. For small-scale plantings such as berries, dig soil several inches deep and mix in large quantities of compost, peat moss or other organic matter. This improves aeration and drainage.

Waterlogged or Marshy Soil—This is soil that is constantly wet due to poor drainage conditions. You will have no difficulty in determining if this soil condition exists. If the soil makes a squishing sound when you walk on it, it is waterlogged.

To correct marshy soil, a major drainage project is required. Professional help may be necessary. A process called *ditching,* digging channels to collect and divert water, is helpful. Depending on the severity of the situation, this may or may not solve the problem. To determine if the soil drainage is poor, run a drainage test before you plant. Fill a hole with water and allow it to drain. Immediately following, fill with water again. If the hole has not drained in about 12 to 24 hours, it is best to plant your fruit trees elsewhere. Or plant in containers or raised beds.

Rocky Soil—Two types of rocky soil exist in the Midwest and East. One type is filled with rocks of various sizes. The second type has a thin layer of soil on top of solid or almost-solid rock. Because plant roots need soil space to support plants and absorb nutrients and water, rocky soil does not provide good growing conditions.

Both kinds of rocky soil require major work to correct. If soil is deep but rocky, it is simply a matter of removing as many rocks as possible when you prepare the planting holes. If soil is only a thin layer over solid rock, it is necessary to bring in topsoil to build up the soil depth. This method should allow you to grow most berries and some dwarf fruit trees, but it is expensive and time-consuming. It may be better to grow plants in containers or raised beds.

Sandy Soil—This soil is prevalent in many areas of the Mid-Atlantic and Southern coastal regions. It lies south of the rocky debris left by the glacial advance of pre-historic times. If a ball of moistened soil crumbles in your hand when you squeeze it, the soil is predominantly sandy.

Water and nutrient retention of sandy soil are generally poor, so watering and fertilizing must be done more frequently than with other soil types. Sandy soil has good drainage, and can be productive if plants are given regular care.

Add peat moss, compost, manure and shredded bark or other organic matter to sandy soil to improve its moisture- and nutrient-holding capacity. During hot, dry weather, water frequently. Fertilizer should be applied more often, but this depends on the plant's nutrient requirements.

Loam—This is the ideal soil. It has a balanced combination of sand, clay and organic matter. Like sandy soil, drainage is good, yet moisture and nutrients are retained longer in the root zone. This greatly benefits plants.

Maintain a loam soil by continuing to work in organic matter, compost, rotted manure and peat moss each spring. Using an organic mulch around plants is also beneficial.

SOIL pH

The letters *pH* refer to the alkaline and acid content of your soil. This is caused by the breakdown of water molecules in the soil into positive and negative ions. The mineral and organic materials in the soil affect this breakdown. For example, if limestone or calcium is present in the soil, it will be alkaline. Peat, sulfur and aluminum cause the soil to be more acid.

Soil pH affects the way a plant uses fertilizer. All plants have specific pH levels which allow them to use fertilizer. If the soil is too acid or too alkaline for a plant, nutrients and fertilizers in the soil will remain "tied up" so the plant cannot absorb them.

In most areas of the East and Midwest, soils register between 5.5 and 7.0 on the pH scale, at or near neutral. Seven is neutral. Below seven is acid. Above seven is alkaline. Most fruit, berries and nuts prefer a neutral or slightly acid soil. For example, plums and peaches thrive at 6.0, apples at 6.5, strawberries at 6.0. The only plant included in this book that requires decidedly acid soil is blueberry, which thrives in soil with a 5.0 to 5.5 pH.

To determine the pH of your soil, home testing kits are available in most garden centers. By following instructions you will be able to find out your soil's pH. For a complete test, most state cooperative extension services will test your soil for a fee. Mail or bring in a sample of your soil to their office.

How Soil Type Affects Plant Growth

Left: Clay soil is made up of small, dense, mineral particles that tend to cling together and become compacted. Drainage is slow and root growth can be impeded. Right: Loam soil is a balance of sand, silt, clay and organic matter. Spaces between the various-size particles allow good drainage, yet moisture and nutrients are retained in the root zone so plants can absorb them.

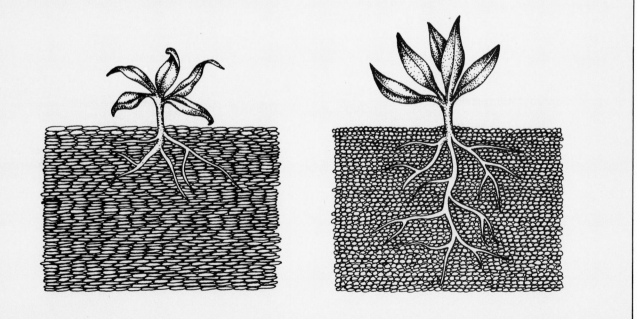

Modifying Soil pH—Because most soils in the Midwest and East are acidic, it is rarely necessary to lower the pH. If your soil is decidedly acid, 5.5 and below, it is easy to change it. To raise the pH one point, from 5.5 to 6.5, add lime at the rate of 10 pounds per 100 square feet of soil.

If your soil is decidedly alkaline, registering 8.0 or higher on the pH scale, add 3 pounds of sulfur per 100 square feet. This lowers the pH reading by approximately one point, resulting in a neutral soil with a reading of 7.0.

If you garden solely with organic methods, you can increase soil acidity by adding peat moss, composted oak leaves or by using a pine-needle mulch. Decrease soil acidity by adding wood ashes.

SOIL FERTILITY
Soil fertility refers to the amount of nutrients in the soil, and whether they are available to plants. To test your soil for necessary nutrients, it is best to have it done by a professional soil lab. If you do not want to test your soil, you can assume generally that your soil will need some additional nutrients. State universities in all states except Illinois and California will test your soil. Look in the white pages of your phone book under "County Extension Agent," or "Cooperative Extension Service."

BASIC NUTRIENTS FOR PLANT GROWTH
Carbon, oxygen and hydrogen, necessary for plant growth, are made available to plants by carbon dioxide present in the air and water in the soil. In addition, plants require three primary elements and 10 minor elements. These are:

Nitrogen—Required in the greatest amounts by most plants. If plants are healthy and vigorous, and if a yearly feeding is given, there is usually enough nitrogen available in the soil. Nitrogen is also the most common element to be deficient. Warning signs are new growth that is poor, yellowish foliage and small, poor-quality fruit.

Phosphorus—In most areas of the East and Midwest, phosphorus is present in the soil in sufficient amounts. It encourages lush, green leaves and firm, attractive, high-quality fruit. Signs of deficiency are rust-colored leaves in early fall, and fruit of poor quality.

Potassium (Potash)—This element is usually in adequate supply in Eastern and Midwestern soils. Signs of deficiency are when leaves wither and new shoots die back. Of all fruit, European plum is most subject to potassium deficiency.

Minor Elements—Generally, the trace elements—*boron, calcium, copper, chlorine, iron, magnesium, manganese, molybdenum, sulfur* and *zinc*—are present in the soil in sufficient quantities. Working compost or other organic matter into your soil usually supplies these elements.

CORRECTING NUTRIENT DEFICIENCIES
Check with your local cooperative extension service if you suspect your soil is lacking in nutrients. Have your soil tested and follow instructions for soil fertilization.

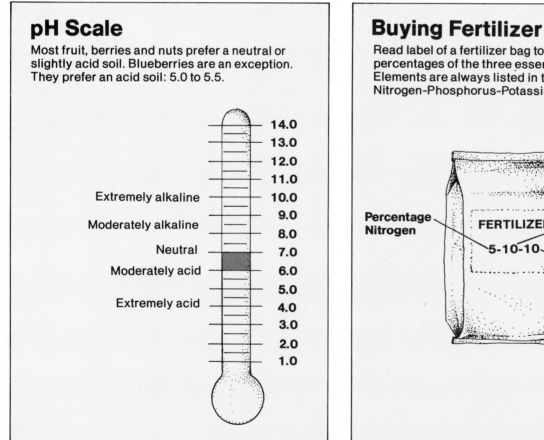

pH Scale
Most fruit, berries and nuts prefer a neutral or slightly acid soil. Blueberries are an exception. They prefer an acid soil: 5.0 to 5.5.

	14.0
	13.0
	12.0
	11.0
Extremely alkaline	10.0
	9.0
Moderately alkaline	8.0
Neutral	7.0
Moderately acid	6.0
	5.0
Extremely acid	4.0
	3.0
	2.0
	1.0

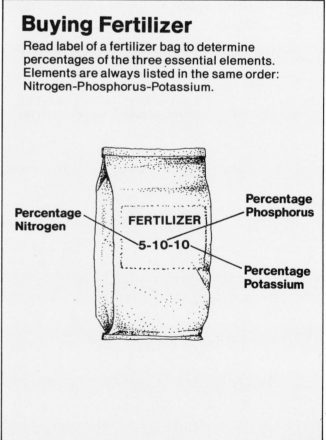

Buying Fertilizer
Read label of a fertilizer bag to determine percentages of the three essential elements. Elements are always listed in the same order: Nitrogen-Phosphorus-Potassium.

Percentage Nitrogen

FERTILIZER

Percentage Phosphorus

5-10-10

Percentage Potassium

Do not add large amounts of one element or another without seeking professional advice. You can destroy the soil's natural chemical balance, making it difficult or impossible to grow plants.

FERTILIZERS

Quantities of nitrogen, phosphorus and potassium contained in organic fertilizers differ from material to material. For example, dried cow or sheep manure is usually a 5-3-5 composition. This is 5% nitrogen, 3% phosphorus and 5% potassium. *Greensand,* material from ocean deposits, contains no nitrogen, 2% phosphorus and 6% potassium. Other materials such as compost, bone meal and rotted animal manure are often used as fertilizers and vary in composition.

Numbers appear on fertilizer bags to indicate the percentages of the three essential elements contained in the fertilizer. The elements are always listed in the same order: *nitrogen* first, *phosphorus* second and *potassium* last. Thus, 5-10-10 means the material contains approximately 5% nitrogen, 10% phosphorus and 10% potassium. A ratio of 15-10-10 means the fertilizer contains approximately 15% nitrogen, 10% phosphorus and 10% potassium.

There are two basic kinds of fertilizers: *natural organic* and *chemical inorganic.* Natural fertilizers include plant materials such as composted leaves and manure and animal byproducts. *Inorganic* or chemical fertilizers are composed of simple mineral salts such as sulfate of ammonia. One of the most commonly used chemical fertilizers is the all-purpose 5-10-10.

HOW TO FERTILIZE

Most experts recommend feeding plants in late winter or early spring, as soon as the ground thaws. After fertilizer is applied, spring rains slowly move the nutrients down to plant roots, where they can be absorbed. Spring is the time that plants make best use of nutrients. This is the time they are about to put forth their most profuse growth of the season. If you can't make applications of fertilizer in spring, the second-best time is in late fall, just before the ground freezes.

When you apply fertilizer, be aware of the root area of plants. Roots roughly encompass the same area below ground as plant branches do above ground, and are similar in size. That is, roots closest to the trunk are large and woody. Those farther away are small, hairy and fibrous. These small roots, the *feeder roots,* are the ones that absorb nutrients.

Spread fertilizer in a circle beginning about one or two feet away from the trunk, extending to beneath the outermost branches of the tree. Fertilizing too close to the trunk is most likely a waste, because feeder roots are too far away. If you mulch your trees, remove mulch before applying fertilizer. Replace it after making the application.

For trees 1 to 5 years old, fill a 1-pound coffee can with 5-10-10 fertilizer and spread around the tree. For trees older than 5 years, 1-1/2 to 2 cans may be required, depending on the vigor of the tree. Most commercial fertilizers give recommended amounts on the package label. Read and follow these directions for best results.

Fertilizing Properly

Apply fertilizer where it will be absorbed by the plant's *feeder roots.* These are fine, tiny, white roots that transport water and nutrients to the plant. Most are located in the top 3 feet of soil. Some gardeners dig into the soil around the *drip line,* an imaginary line from the outermost branches down to the ground, to see if the fine, white, feeder roots are present.

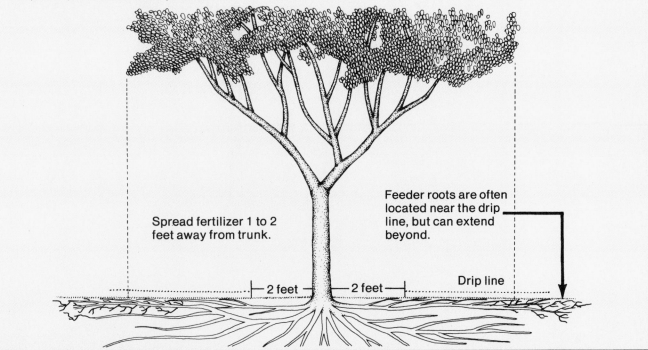

Spread fertilizer 1 to 2 feet away from trunk.

Feeder roots are often located near the drip line, but can extend beyond.

2 feet   2 feet

Drip line

If you use an organic fertilizer such as compost or rotted manure, spread material two inches deep from the trunk of the tree to the area beneath the outward spread of branches.

In either case, work the fertilizer into the top few inches of soil. Do not dig too deep or you will injure the feeder roots.

WATERING FRUIT PLANTS

How much and when to water depends on many factors such as climate, soil type, amount of rainfall and time of year. But one of the major factors is age of the plant. Newly planted stock requires regular attention. During the first growing season, it is important to keep soil moist, but not wet. This helps establish a strong root system and a healthy, vigorous plant resistant to diseases and pests.

As a general guide, water two or three times a week for about one month after planting, unless you receive a heavy rain. Be sure water reaches the root zone. Before watering, test the soil with a thin, stiff wire. If it slips into the soil easily, watering is probably not necessary.

If your soil is clay, watering twice a week is usually sufficient. For sandy soil, you may have to water three times or more per week. A month after planting, water plants about once a week. But don't follow a predetermined schedule. Check the soil for moisture before watering.

Established plants require a different approach. In areas receiving regular amounts of rainfall, watering may not be necessary, except during the warm summer months.

Soil type plays a major part in how often and how much to water. For example, sandy soil drains quickly, so you must water more frequently during periods without rain. Clay soil retains water, so you may not have to water at all if rainfall is sufficient. Check the soil with a stiff wire to determine if your trees need watering, or dig down with a shovel away from tree roots to see if soil is dry.

Watering is crucial during *fruit set*. This is the time after blossoms are fertilized, and the young fruit begin to form. If there is a drought during this period, irrigate thoroughly. Peaches, nectarines, plums, apricots, raspberries and strawberries are particularly susceptible to fruit drop if water is in short supply.

Use common sense and observation in deciding when and how much to water. If foliage appears limp and pale, the plant needs water. If your flower garden or broadleaved evergreens are drooping, your fruit trees probably need water. If rain has not fallen for several weeks, it is probably time to water.

Overwatering can damage or kill plants. If in doubt as to your plant's water needs, *don't* water. In most areas of the East and Midwest, spring and fall rains provide enough water for your plant's needs. Summer dry spells usually occur in July or August. This is the

Water Deeply

During periods without rainfall, it is necessary to irrigate plants. Left: Apply water slowly so it soaks deeply into the soil. Roots grow deep, giving plant a greater reservoir to draw on during drought. Right: Plants that are sprinkled frequently and lightly tend to have shallow roots. If upper layer of soil dries out, plant is unable to absorb water it needs to sustain growth and health.

period when you should be prepared to supplement rainfall with irrigation.

Watering Methods—Most of the primary roots of a fruit tree are located in the top 6 feet of soil. They spread out several feet beyond the branches. The area of soil beneath the tree's canopy is where water should be applied.

Under normal circumstances, water goes straight down into the soil. An inch of water applied over the soil surface moistens the soil about 6 inches deep.

When you water, apply enough so it soaks several inches into the soil. Deep, infrequent waterings are best. Plant roots penetrate deeply into the soil to absorb moisture. Sprinkling the soil around plants for 15 minutes does little or no good. In fact, it may eventually harm the tree. If water is appplied to the top few inches of soil, plant roots tend to stay shallow, growing where there is water. This creates a poor anchor for plants, and makes them susceptible to drying out.

MULCHING

A *mulch* is a layer of material placed over the soil surface. It can be *organic,* derived from living matter, or *inorganic,* derived from non-living matter—not animal or vegetable.

Organic materials include compost, cocoa shells, shredded bark, farm wastes, animal manure, hay, saw- dust, dried grass clippings, leaves, newspapers, dried evergreen needles, peat moss and wood chips. All of these decompose to improve the soil.

Inorganic materials include black and clear plastic, crushed rock or granite, flat rock or slate, marble or granite chips. These do not decompose.

Mulches are beneficial in several ways:
- Moisture is controlled by reducing evaporation.
- Earthworms often thrive in mulched soil, improving the soil through aeration.
- Rapid freezing and thawing of soil, which can *heave* plant roots out of the ground, is reduced.
- Valuable topsoil that can be washed away in rains or runoff is held in place.
- Weeds and grasses that rob soil of nutrients are reduced.
- Organic mulches gradually decompose, enriching the soil.

To mulch, spread a 2- to 6-inch layer of material over the soil around the base of plants. Keep moisture-retaining mulches such as sawdust or peat moss clear of trunks and stems, or they can promote disease.

If you have planted your fruit plants as part of your landscape, you won't want the visual clutter of old newspapers or farm waste scattered around as mulch. But it is simple to use these materials, then cover them with a layer of more attractive and often more expensive material.

Advantages of Mulching

Using a mulch helps plants in many ways. Soil evaporation is reduced, so less water is required. Soil remains cooler so plant roots can grow in the fertile upper layer. Weed growth is curtailed. Keep mulch 4 to 6 inches away from trunk or stem of plant. This eliminates hiding places for rodents, and prevents decay of plant stem or trunk from exposure to too much moisture.

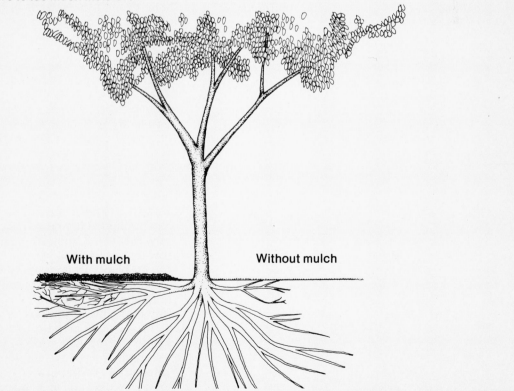

With mulch   Without mulch

PLANTING

When planting bare-root tree, be certain bud union is planted above soil level.

All fruit have two recommended planting times. One is during fall, just after leaves drop, when plants enter dormancy. The other is in spring, just before buds of new growth swell, while plants remain dormant.

The best time to plant depends on where you live. Fall or early spring is acceptable for fruit in Zones 6 and 7. If you live in areas with harsh winters, Zones 2 to 5, plant most stone fruit—apricots, nectarines, peaches and Japanese plums—in spring.

Apples, cherries, pears, quince and European plums can generally be planted in fall in warm areas of Zones 4 to 7. In cold areas of Zones 3 and 4, plant only in spring. See map, page 64.

Summer planting is not recommended. High temperatures put a strain on young plants. In addition, watering must be done frequently. It is best to wait until fall or spring.

BUYING PLANTS

Fruit-producing plants are normally sold in three different ways: *bare root, containers* and *balled and burlapped*. Each requires a slightly different planting procedure.

Bare Root—Most plants purchased through mail order are shipped *bare root*, that is, without soil on the roots. Roots are wrapped in plastic or other material that retains moisture. Growers of plant materials have lower production and handling costs with bare-root plants. Therefore, the retail cost of bare root is usually less compared to plants in containers or balled and burlapped.

Plants are usually dug in the fall, stored through the winter at proper temperature and humidity levels and shipped in early spring.

If you buy plants through a mail-order firm, it is important to take steps to ensure their health as soon as they arrive. Unwrap plants as soon as you receive them. Prune broken roots or branches. Place roots in a tub of water for several hours, but for no more than 24 hours. If possible, plant within a few hours after the soaking.

In Northern areas, Zones 2, 3 and 4, plants may arrive at your door on a cold day. The roots may be frozen. Allow roots to thaw slowly in a cool basement or garage, and then soak in water.

If planting must be delayed, it is recommended that you *heel-in* bare-root plants. Dig a trench in a shady location. Place the roots and about half the trunk inside the trench. Cover with soil or peat moss. Keep moist until you are able to plant. Plant as soon as possible, before root growth begins.

Container Planting—Plants sold in containers are usually shipped bare root to retail nurseries and potted at the nursery. Sometimes plants are left over from the previous year's stock.

Keep plants in containers well watered. Store in a sheltered-location until ready to plant. If plant is in a metal container, cut container with shears and gently remove the plant. Plastic containers can be difficult to cut. Water plant an hour or so before planting, and try to slide the rootball out. Do not bang the plant out of the container, because this will damage the rootball.

Balled and Burlapped (B & B)—Soil is retained around roots and they are wrapped and tied with burlap or other material.

Keep rootball moist and store in a sheltered location until ready to plant. Avoid bumping or breaking the rootball while handling. If you water the rootball lightly several hours before planting, it will be less likely to crumble. Untie and roll burlap down the sides of the rootball. You do not have to remove it; it will decay. Sometimes the rootball is bound with a synthetic material. If this is the case, remove before planting. After planting, be sure burlap is completely covered with soil.

For exact instructions on planting, see pages 18 to 21.

DIGGING THE PLANTING HOLE
When you dig a planting hole, it is important to keep an old adage in mind: "A $1 tree needs a $5 hole." This means to dig the hole larger than necessary to accommodate the roots or rootball of the fledgling tree. As a guide, hole should be about twice as wide and twice as deep as the rootball or roots. By digging a large planting hole, a sizeable area of soil is loosened, allowing roots to grow more easily than in hard-packed soil.

As you dig the planting hole, reserve the top layer of soil, the *topsoil*. This will be the *backfill*. Place it in a pile to the side. Use this soil to refill the hole. Save the lower layers of soil, the *subsoil,* for use in building a watering basin.

After you have dug the hole, check the condition of the backfill soil. Light, sandy soil or heavy clay soil usually benefit from the addition of organic matter. Make a mixture of about two-thirds backfill soil with one-third compost, rotted manure or other organic matter. Do not add any chemical fertilizer to the soil at this time, because it can burn the roots.

PRUNING NEWLY PLANTED TREES
During the process of digging, shipping and replanting young trees, some root damage is inevitable. To compensate for root loss, prune some of the top growth. Generally, remove one-third of the twig and branch growth. If root damage is severe, you may have to remove up to half of top growth. See page 26 for a step-by-step guide.

STAKING NEWLY PLANTED TREES
Although most young trees do not need support, staking is recommended in stormy, windy areas. This is particularly true of apricot trees, which have brittle trunks. Use two stakes driven into the ground. Place stakes so they are perpendicular to prevailing winds. If winds usually blow from west to east, place stakes facing north and south.

Lightly secure the tree to the stakes with rope fed through a piece of old garden hose or with strips of cloth. The tree should be free to move on its own so it will not become dependent on the stake for support. Check ties regularly to be sure they are not cutting into the bark, or they may *girdle* the tree, which can kill it.

PROTECTION FROM THE SUN
In areas of the Midwest and upper South, the summer sun can burn the bark of fledgling trees. This is particularly a problem with grafted trees—the graft is quite sensitive to strong sunlight. To avoid sunburn damage to a graft, plant tree so the outward curve of the bud union faces southwest—the most intense sun. The inward curve, the part most susceptible to sunburn, will face northeast, the direction of least sun intensity. You can also paint the trunk with white *latex* paint to protect against sunburn. Painting the trunk one or two inches below the soil line also discourages borer pests.

Tree wrap is available commercially at retail outlets. It is wrapped around the trunk to protect from sunburn, pests and bumps from mowers.

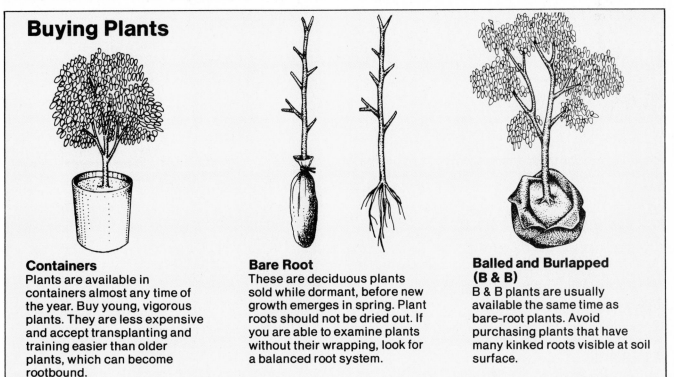

Buying Plants

Containers
Plants are available in containers almost any time of the year. Buy young, vigorous plants. They are less expensive and accept transplanting and training easier than older plants, which can become rootbound.

Bare Root
These are deciduous plants sold while dormant, before new growth emerges in spring. Plant roots should not be dried out. If you are able to examine plants without their wrapping, look for a balanced root system.

Balled and Burlapped (B & B)
B & B plants are usually available the same time as bare-root plants. Avoid purchasing plants that have many kinked roots visible at soil surface.

Planting Bare Root Step by Step

1. Select sunny location. Dig planting hole about twice as wide as spread of roots.

2. To be certain soil drains properly, fill hole with water. Allow to drain, then fill again. Water should drain in 12 to 24 hours.

5. Make cone-shaped mound of soil in center of planting hole. Spread roots over it. Bud union must be above ground level.

6. Fill planting hole with amended soil. Add soil in layers, firming around roots to eliminate air pockets.

3. If soil is mostly clay or sand, add some organic matter. Mix topsoil from planting hole with one-third peat moss, compost or similar material.

4. Prune dead, broken or twisted roots. Shorten long roots.

7. If you live in an area subject to strong winds, support tree with stakes. Place stakes on either side of tree, perpendicular to prevailing winds. Loosely tie tree to stakes.

8. Water to settle soil. Be sure tree is planted at same depth as it was previously grown. Build basin for irrigation unless you live in high-rainfall area. Apply mulch. See How to Prune a New Tree, page 26.

Planting from Containers Step by Step

1. Select sunny location. Dig planting hole approximately twice diameter of container. Check soil for drainage. See Step 2, page 18.

2. If soil is mostly clay or sand, add some organic matter. Mix topsoil from planting hole with one-third peat moss, compost or similar material and add to hole.

5. Fill in around rootball with amended soil. Firm soil in layers to eliminate air pockets.

6. Stake tree by loosely wrapping rope around stakes and trunk. Tree should be able to move on its own so it will not become dependent on stakes for support.

3. Remove rootball from container and place in hole. Metal containers can be cut at nursery, but only if you plant right away. Handle rootball gently.

4. Position rootball in planting hole. Plant at same depth as it was in the container. Place support stakes now so you won't drive them into rootball later. Place stakes on both sides of trunk, perpendicular to prevailing winds.

7. Make watering basin. If you live in high-rainfall area, be sure tree does not receive too much water. Keep soil moist but not soggy the first few weeks.

8. Water to settle soil. Check planting depth. Prune top growth of tree to compensate for root loss. See How to Prune a New Tree, page 26.

PRUNING

Long-handled loppers in action.

This section describes the basic principles of how to prune fruit-producing plants. Examine these techniques and modify them to suit your needs. No two trees grow in the same way, so use the instructions and illustrations as a general guide.

Pruning may seem complicated, but in truth it is not. Often, the most difficult problem is to overcome your reluctance to prune. Some gardeners feel they are hurting their trees by removing branches. But many positive things are accomplished when you prune:
● Dead, damaged and weak branches are removed, which improves the health and fruit-producing capacity of a tree.
● Fruit-bearing area of a tree is reduced. This reduces the number of fruit, but allows for larger fruit of better quality.
● Strong branches are developed that are able to sustain the weight of mature fruit without splitting.
● Basic tree shape is established and maintained, including development of strong, structural limbs.
● Tree is more likely to bear *annually,* every year, instead of *biennially,* every other year.
● Fruiting occurs earlier on young trees.
● Tree is shaped to manageable size and desirable shape to make harvesting and spraying easier.
● Central area of a tree is opened, increasing penetration of sunlight, air and sprays. This helps the tree produce better-quality fruit.

PRUNING TOOLS
Many types of pruning tools are available, but one piece of advice is certain—*buy quality.* Beware of bargains. They usually do not last as long, and become dull faster than quality tools. Invest in a good pair of shears and loppers. They will hold sharp edges longer. This eases pruning and reduces damage to your trees. Some tools can be purchased with gears, which increases leverage to make cutting slightly easier.

A sturdy ladder about 10 to 12 feet tall is useful for pruning standard or semidwarf trees. A three-legged or four-legged stepladder is safer than a two-legged ladder. Most dwarf trees can be pruned standing on a sturdy stepladder or a solid wooden box.

Keep your tools sharp. Sharpen them at least once a year with a file or electric knife sharpener or have them sharpened by a professional. Sharp tools make clean cuts. This reduces ragged bark near the edges of the cut. Exposed wood is smooth and flat. If you make a jagged cut, trim it with a knife, rasp or chisel.

THREE COMMON TRAINING SYSTEMS
Different fruit-producing plants adapt better to various methods of training. The following are the three most common. For step-by-step instructions on how to train plants to these methods, see the illustrations on pages 29 and 30.
Vase-Shape or Multiple-Leader Training—This system is commonly used to train apricots, nectarines, peaches, plums and sour cherries. Properly pruned to a vase-shape, a tree should resemble an upside-down umbrella. This shape allows maximum amounts of sunlight, air and sprays to penetrate the interior of the tree.

Central-Leader or Pyramid Training—This system is commonly used to train apples, sweet cherries, pears and quince. Vase-shape training is not recommended for these fruit. Trees grown close together shade each other's limbs. This slows and reduces fruit ripening. In addition, these trees tend to grow in a pyramid shape naturally.

Modified Central-Leader Training—This method is particularly useful for training nut trees such as walnut, butternut and hickory. Apples and pears can also be trained this way. Many of these trees are used as landscape specimens or shade trees. A spreading shape with the lowest branches high enough to walk under is desirable in these situations. However, the best system for producing shade is central-leader training.

PRUNING NEW FRUIT TREES

Most trees that you buy, whether bare root, in containers or balled and burlapped, are grown and dug at the nursery's planting fields. It is common practice for nursery employees to remove a substantial amount of the fledgling trees' root systems when preparing them for sale or shipping. Often, the reduced root system cannot support the top of the tree. For this reason, trees with 1-year-old tops grafted to 2-year-old roots usually grow and thrive after they are planted. Trees with tops 2 years or older are less likely to survive. Keep this in mind when ordering or buying your stock.

After planting, compensate for this root loss by removing one-third to one-half of top growth.

PRUNING YOUNG, BEARING TREES

After you have established your newly planted tree and initial training has begun, you must continue to prune. Proper pruning at this stage is particularly important to maintain a *balance of fruiting,* fruit production throughout the tree rather than on the upper, outer extremities, and proper air circulation.

Most important, *prune sparingly.* Heavy pruning at this stage causes prolific leaf growth, which reduces fruit production. See illustrations, page 26.

PRUNING MATURE TREES

If you prune your trees properly each year, you will be rewarded with a structurally sound tree of manageable size. A well-pruned tree produces quality fruit of good size that are evenly spaced throughout the tree.

A goal when pruning a mature tree is to enlarge the *zone of equilibrium.* This is the middle area of a tree where most of the fruit are produced. When a tree matures, the lower growth becomes spindly and yields little fruit, or fruit of poor quality. The upper growth is leafy, producing many stems. These two areas tend to enlarge, reducing the zone of equilibrium.

To enlarge this fruit-bearing zone, prune more drastically in the upper, outer reaches of the tree than in the middle and lower portion. Start pruning from the top. As you move down the tree, prune less and less as you get closer to the bottom. See illustration, page 27.

PRUNING OLD, NEGLECTED TREES

Old and neglected apples, pears or plums usually do not bear. If they do produce any fruit, it is sparse and of poor quality. But you can revive an old tree's fruit-producing capacities. This renovation project takes three years to complete, but in most instances the result is worth the time and effort. You will need pruning shears, loppers, saws and a sturdy ladder to do this job. See illustrations, page 28.

Pruning Tools

Hand-held pruning shears, sometimes called *snippers,* are used to prune small twigs and branches. Pruning shears are available in *blade-and-anvil* and *hook-and-curved-blade* models. Hook-and-curved-blade types are preferred over anvil types because they make cleaner cuts. *Long-handled lopping shears* are used for cutting branches up to 1 inch in diameter. They are also available in anvil-type or hook-and-blade type. A *bow saw* is recommended for large limbs, 3 or more inches in diameter. A smaller *folding saw* is best for medium-size limbs, 1 to 3 inches in diameter. When cutting large limbs with a saw, it helps to have a *rasp* handy for filing rough edges. A pair of *hedge shears* comes in handy when pruning large stands of cane fruit.

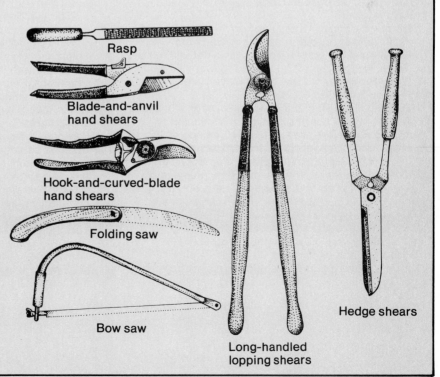

Rasp

Blade-and-anvil hand shears

Hook-and-curved-blade hand shears

Folding saw

Bow saw

Long-handled lopping shears

Hedge shears

Pruning Glossary

Apical Dominance—Characteristic of tree to produce *terminal buds*—those at the end of any shoot or branch. *Apical* is derived from the word *apex.* Terminal buds contain a hormone called *auxin,* which strongly inhibits the formation of side buds. By removing a terminal bud, apical dominance is also removed. Side buds can then begin to grow. Side buds produce shoots that eventually produce other terminal buds, restoring apical dominance.

Buds—Rows of small growths line the branches of plants. These contain the embryos of stems, leaves and blossoms. They are most easily seen during the dormant season.

Flower Bud—In their dormant stage, during fall and winter, flower buds are thin and green. In the spring, they are the first to increase in size and become plump.

Leaf Bud—Triangular buds that grow flat on the sides of branches. When you prune, cut above leaf buds that point outward from the trunk. Future growth will grow in this direction, away from trunk, enabling new branches to receive sufficient light and space.

Terminal Bud—Buds located at the tips of a branch. They regulate the mature length or height of that branch. If you remove a terminal bud, adjacent buds on the same stem will grow to replace it.

Central Leader—Main stem or trunk of a plant.

Cordon—Single stem that has short, stubby side shoots. Used in espalier training.

Crotch—Angle where two or more branches fork. Wide-angled crotches, 45° or more, are recommended. Narrow crotches are weak and split apart easily.

Deciduous—Plants that lose their leaves in fall and winter, as opposed to *evergreens* that are in leaf all year.

Dormant—Period when plants grow slowly, or not at all. Cold temperatures bring on dormancy.

Espalier—Method of training plants flat against a wall or supports, helpful in small-space gardens.

Evergreen—Plants that are in leaf all year.

Flower Bud—See Buds.

Fruiting Habit—Location of blossoms on a branch, and the age of bearing branches. Blossoms of apples and pears are located on the ends of branches. Blossoms of apricots, cherries, nectarines, peaches and plums are located on the sides of branches. Apples, cherries, plums and apricots bear on *spurs*—small, twiggy shoots that carry flower buds and fruit. Spurs can be one or two years old or several years old. Peaches and nectarines bear on the previous season's growth. Grapes bear on growth of the current season.

Growth Habit—Pattern and shape of a plant's growth, determined by its genetic makeup. It may be upright, semiupright, spreading, semidwarf, dwarf, prolific or sparse.

Head—Section of a tree that produces the scaffold-limb framework.

Heading—Pruning technique used to cut back the end of a branch. Heading usually increases branching and shortens and stiffens limbs.

Healing a Wound—Bark wounds are fed by leaves located around the wound. Because there are no leaves above a cut, large stubs will not heal over. When making a cut, prune close: but do not cut into the *branch collar,* the portion of the branch where it meets the trunk.

Leader—Stem or branch that grows more vigorously and stronger than others. A limb's direction of growth is determined by the leader. The terminal bud is at the end of the leader.

Leaf Bud—See Buds.

Nodes—These grow on leafy branches at the point where stems are attached. If you remove a leaf along with its stem, you will see a node just above the resulting scar. Growth enzymes are concentrated here.

Pinching—Pruning technique similar to heading, except new, tender growth is pinched off with thumb and finger.

Scaffold—Basic structure of a tree. Includes the main limbs that branch from the trunk. Prune limbs so they are widely spaced up and down the trunk. If limbs are not spaced widely, weak crotches may form and split apart at maturity.

Spreading—Artificially creating a larger crotch angle between a limb and the trunk of a tree. Thin, notched pieces of wood, clothespins and weights can be used to accomplish this. Spreading modifies apical dominance and strengthens crotches.

Spur—Small, twiggy shoot that carries flower buds and fruit. Common on apples, apricots, pears and plums. See Fruiting Habit.

Suckers or Root Suckers—Vigorous shoots that grow at the base of trees from the bud union or below. Remove at base as soon as they appear.

Terminal Bud—See Buds.

Thinning—Selective pruning technique. Entire branch is removed. Because no buds remain, no new shoot growth results.

Watersprout—Vigorous shoots that grow vertically from a dormant bud on an old branch. Sprouts usually appear after heavy pruning. Remove them from well-structured trees, cutting them off at the base.

Whip—Young tree with a single stem. Whips are commonly planted as espaliers.

Wood, New—Portion of each branch that grew during the previous season. It is smooth, has pale bark and sparse side growth.

Wood, Old—Wood from the season *before* the last season. It is dark in color, has rough bark and many twigs.

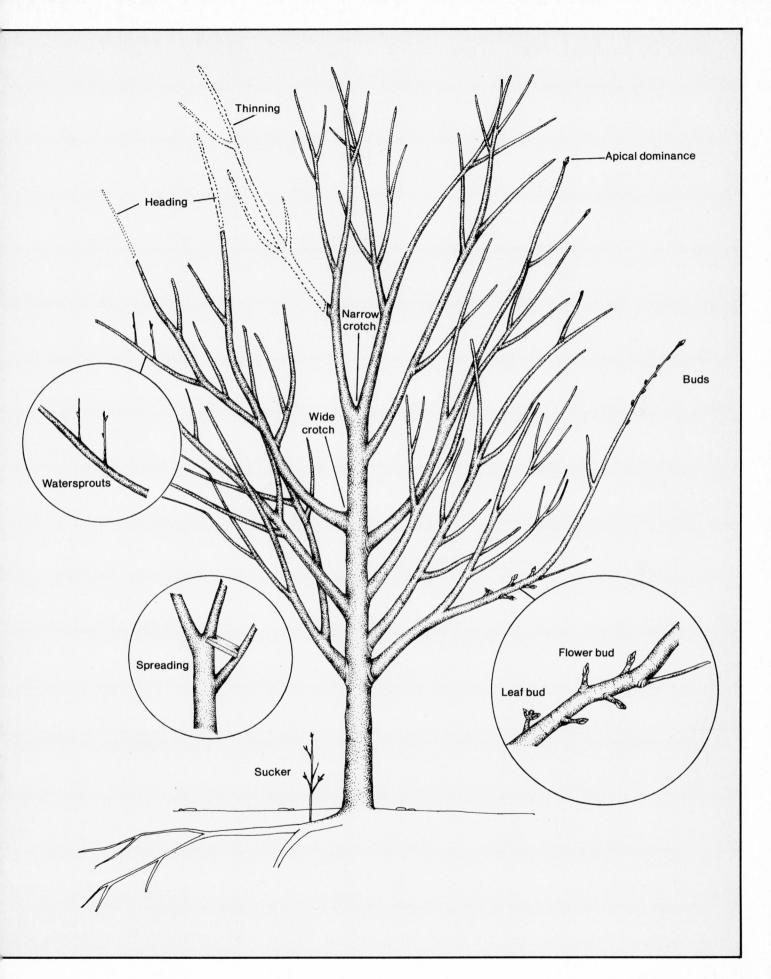

Thinning

Heading

Apical dominance

Narrow crotch

Buds

Wide crotch

Watersprouts

Spreading

Sucker

Flower bud

Leaf bud

How to Prune a New Tree

Bud union

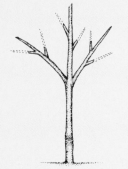

1. In early spring when you plant tree, compensate for root loss by heading trees about 2 feet above the ground. Do not cut below the *bud union,* the knobby wood near the base of the tree.

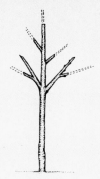

2. Head back well-placed side branches to an outward-pointing bud. Cut about 3 to 6 inches off top of main trunk.

3. During the first or second summer, select appropriate training system and train main scaffold limbs of tree. See following. Select well-placed, vigorous shoots. Pinch or remove unwanted shoots.

4. Insert spring-type clothespins to support wider angles. These scaffold limbs should be spaced 6 to 8 inches, up and around the trunk.

How to Prune a Young, Bearing Tree

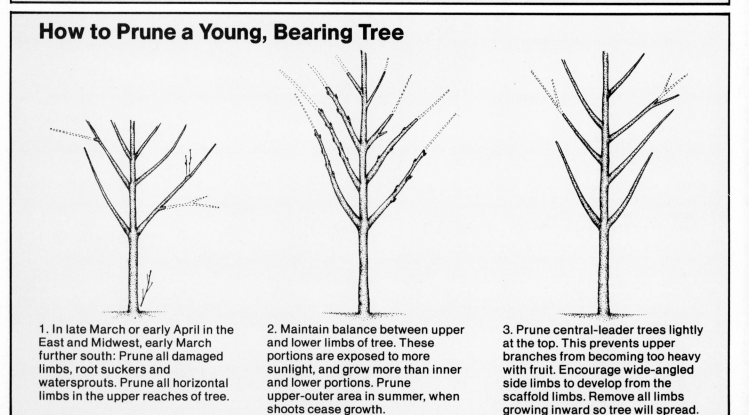

1. In late March or early April in the East and Midwest, early March further south: Prune all damaged limbs, root suckers and watersprouts. Prune all horizontal limbs in the upper reaches of tree.

2. Maintain balance between upper and lower limbs of tree. These portions are exposed to more sunlight, and grow more than inner and lower portions. Prune upper-outer area in summer, when shoots cease growth.

3. Prune central-leader trees lightly at the top. This prevents upper branches from becoming too heavy with fruit. Encourage wide-angled side limbs to develop from the scaffold limbs. Remove all limbs growing inward so tree will spread.

How to Prune a Mature Tree

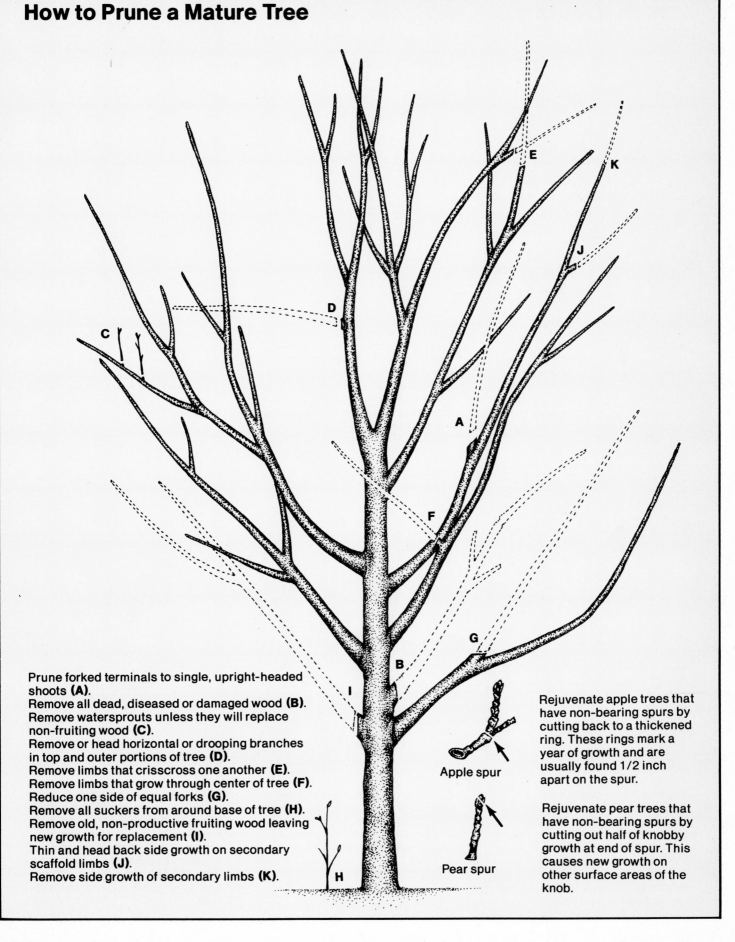

Prune forked terminals to single, upright-headed shoots **(A)**.
Remove all dead, diseased or damaged wood **(B)**.
Remove watersprouts unless they will replace non-fruiting wood **(C)**.
Remove or head horizontal or drooping branches in top and outer portions of tree **(D)**.
Remove limbs that crisscross one another **(E)**.
Remove limbs that grow through center of tree **(F)**.
Reduce one side of equal forks **(G)**.
Remove all suckers from around base of tree **(H)**.
Remove old, non-productive fruiting wood leaving new growth for replacement **(I)**.
Thin and head back side growth on secondary scaffold limbs **(J)**.
Remove side growth of secondary limbs **(K)**.

Apple spur

Pear spur

Rejuvenate apple trees that have non-bearing spurs by cutting back to a thickened ring. These rings mark a year of growth and are usually found 1/2 inch apart on the spur.

Rejuvenate pear trees that have non-bearing spurs by cutting out half of knobby growth at end of spur. This causes new growth on other surface areas of the knob.

How to Renovate an Old, Neglected Tree

 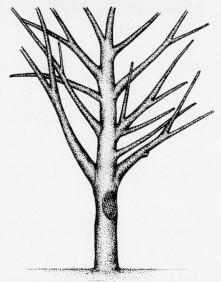 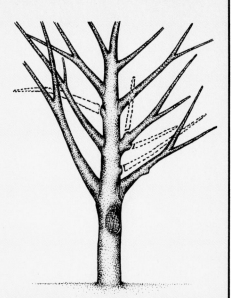

Follow this three-year plan:
1. First year: When tree is dormant, remove all brush, weed growth and brambles from beneath tree to the drip line. Remove dead wood, and scrape off loose bark with a mason's trowel. Remove decayed material from large holes to the green, living wood of tree. Fill holes with cement mixture. Deeply score outer face of the cement to absorb expansion and contraction stress.

2. Step back a few yards and examine height and form of tree. Ideally, a standard-size tree should be 18 to 25 feet tall. If it has grown taller, use pruning shears, loppers and a saw to remove some of the excess growth. The goal is to remove one-third to one-half of the excess growth over the three-year revitalization program.

3. Remove large branches on the inside of the tree. Remove the weaker of two branches that cross. Rake up and destroy all branches, bark and debris removed from the tree. Spray *all* parts of the tree with a heavy coat of dormant-oil spray.

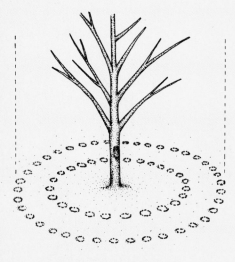

4. Using a bulb planter, cut out 6-inch-deep cores of soil in a ring around the tree. This ring should follow the tree's drip line, spaced 1 foot apart. Halfway toward the trunk, make another ring of 6-inch-deep cores. Place well-rotted manure into the holes created by the bulb planter.

5. During the summer of the first year, the tree will produce suckers to replace lost growth. Snip them off as they appear. Spray with an all-purpose spray every 10 days.

6. Second year: During the dormant period, repeat the entire process. Remove more of the tree's undesired top and side growth. Third year: Follow the same procedure. At the end of the third year, tree should be on the way to recovery and production of fruit.

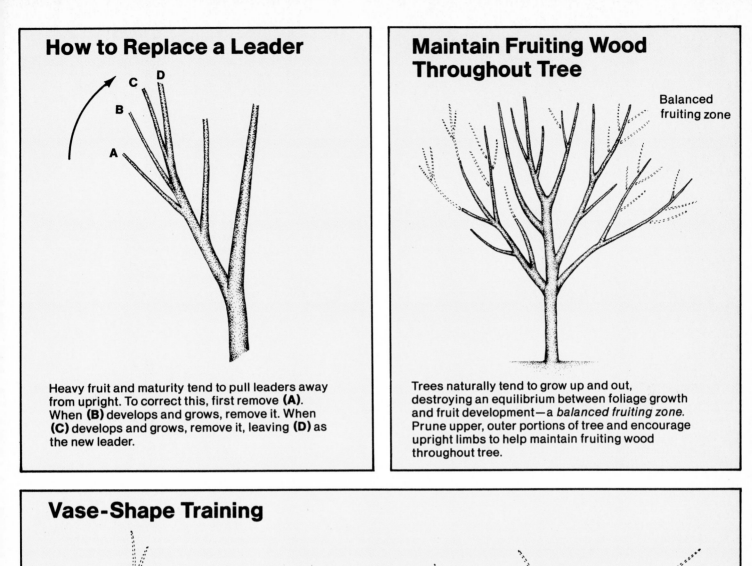

How to Replace a Leader

C D
B
A

Heavy fruit and maturity tend to pull leaders away from upright. To correct this, first remove **(A)**. When **(B)** develops and grows, remove it. When **(C)** develops and grows, remove it, leaving **(D)** as the new leader.

Maintain Fruiting Wood Throughout Tree

Balanced fruiting zone

Trees naturally tend to grow up and out, destroying an equilibrium between foliage growth and fruit development—a *balanced fruiting zone.* Prune upper, outer portions of tree and encourage upright limbs to help maintain fruiting wood throughout tree.

Vase-Shape Training

1. Plant tree, and remove all but three side branches. This will leave a basic framework. Branches can be spaced more closely than with central-leader training or modified-leader training. See next page.

2. Branches growing from the framework branches, *secondary framework branches,* should be located predominantly on the outside of the tree. This helps produce the vase effect. Remove those branches that grow toward the middle of the tree.

3. The next season, in late March in the East and Midwest, early March farther south, head back branches to about 2 feet from the crotch. Continue to train in this manner in subsequent years.

Central-Leader or Pyramid Training

1. Plant tree, and prune to 3 or 4 feet high. A large number of buds will begin growth. Let buds grow for one season.

2. In late winter of the following year, remove branches that compete and grow along with the central trunk.

3. Space 4 or 5 framework branches regularly up and down and around the trunk. Remove new shoots that will compete with the central leader and framework branches.

Whorl

4. Head back the top of the trunk or central leader to about 2 feet above the highest *whorl* of branches. Cut back to a well-placed bud or shoot.

5. To encourage strong side limbs, spread branches so they are at a 45° to 60° angle from the trunk. To do this, insert wooden splints between central leader and side branches.

6. As branches develop upward, tree assumes a pyramidal shape. If tree becomes too tall, re-train to a vase shape by removing part of the central leader each year over a period of years.

Modified Central-Leader Training

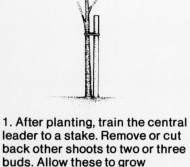

1. After planting, train the central leader to a stake. Remove or cut back other shoots to two or three buds. Allow these to grow through the year.

2. The following year, head back the central leader to 6 feet. Do this while the tree is dormant.

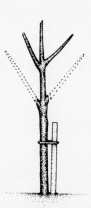

3. That summer, select scaffold branches near this 6-foot height. Remove all others. For remaining life of the tree, follow training methods as for central leader.

ESPALIERS

Pear trained as 4-armed palmette espalier.

An *espalier* is a plant trained to grow flat against a wall, framework or trellis. Espaliers can be formal or informal. Formal espaliers are often trained in intricate patterns. By pruning, pinching, bending and tying shoots and branches, they can be trained to grow along a trellis, fence, wall or other support.

An espalier is an efficient way to grow fruit trees in a limited space, as well as adding a unique focal point to the landscape.

Before you attempt to train trees to espalier patterns, there are several things you should know. Dwarf trees, preferably those with a *spur-type* growth habit, are normally best adapted to this training. Most successful are apples and pears. Peaches and nectarines can be espaliered but their growth habit is more vigorous. Careful attention to pruning is necessary. Damson plums, European plums and apricots are easier to train than Japanese plums, although results are not as successful as with apples and pears. Cherries will adapt, but crops will be small.

The best stock to plant for training is a 1-year-old *whip,* a single stem grafted to the rootstock. Specify that if you order plants from a mail-order source.

Do not use wire or nylon string when tying branches to supports, or they may girdle growth. Use strips of cloth, raffia or stretch plastic ties. For temporary fastening, spring-clip clothespins will hold the branch to the support.

Espaliered trees that have already been trained are available from Henry Leuthardt Nurseries. For information, write to Henry Leuthardt, Montauk Highway, East Moriches, New York 11940.

Many standard espalier forms have evolved through the centuries. Here are some of the best. Step-by-step methods of training these espalier forms are shown on pages 32 and 33.

Vertical Cordon—This is the most basic espalier shape. It consists of a single trunk trained to desired height, bearing leaves, spurs and fruit. Dwarf pears and apples adapt best to this treatment. Cherries, plums, peaches, nectarines and apricots are not suitable. Provide support such as a trellis or post.

Horizontal Cordon—This method is often used to create fences for property lines. Apples and pears are the best for this method.

Horizontal-T Cordon—The same principles apply as for a horizontal cordon. Dwarf apples are the only recommended plants for this method.

Single-U Espalier—This is one of the simpler forms. It bears fruit early and is more manageable than most of the other forms. This method is recommended for training dwarf peaches or nectarines as well as dwarf apples and pears. Provide a support such as a trellis.

There are many other espalier forms. They include Belgian fence, four-arm palmette-Verrier, six-arm palmette-Verrier, triple-U form, fan shapes and double- and triple-horizontal cordons. After you've mastered the basic espalier forms, you might want to experiment with some of these. For more on espaliers, refer to the HPBook, *Hedges, Screens and Espaliers.*

Single-U Espalier

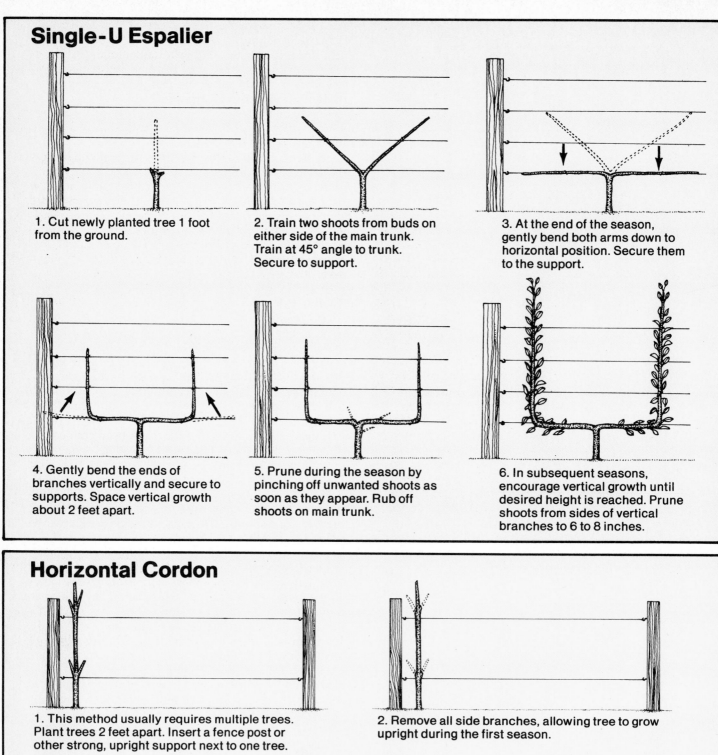

1. Cut newly planted tree 1 foot from the ground.

2. Train two shoots from buds on either side of the main trunk. Train at 45° angle to trunk. Secure to support.

3. At the end of the season, gently bend both arms down to horizontal position. Secure them to the support.

4. Gently bend the ends of branches vertically and secure to supports. Space vertical growth about 2 feet apart.

5. Prune during the season by pinching off unwanted shoots as soon as they appear. Rub off shoots on main trunk.

6. In subsequent seasons, encourage vertical growth until desired height is reached. Prune shoots from sides of vertical branches to 6 to 8 inches.

Horizontal Cordon

1. This method usually requires multiple trees. Plant trees 2 feet apart. Insert a fence post or other strong, upright support next to one tree.

2. Remove all side branches, allowing tree to grow upright during the first season.

3. At end of first season, tie tree trunk to the adjacent post at 6-inch, 10-inch and 14-inch levels. Run wires between and near the top of posts for support. Bend tree over so it is parallel with wire. Tie branches to wire.

4. During subsequent growing seasons, remove all shoots that are growing vertically. Retain those on bottom and sides of cordon.

Horizontal-T Cordon

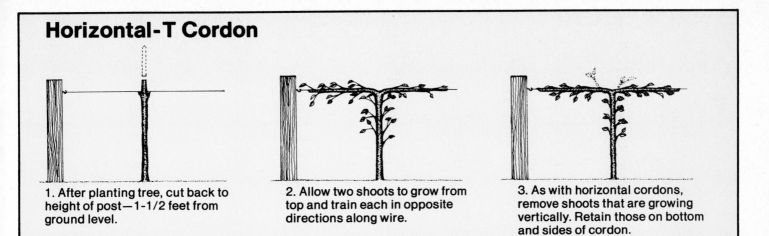

1. After planting tree, cut back to height of post—1-1/2 feet from ground level.

2. Allow two shoots to grow from top and train each in opposite directions along wire.

3. As with horizontal cordons, remove shoots that are growing vertically. Retain those on bottom and sides of cordon.

Vertical Cordon

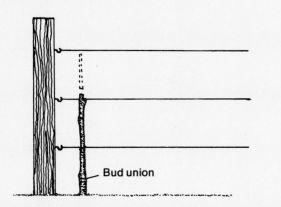

Bud union

1. Plant dwarfs only. Cut trunk back to a bud 1 foot above bud-union graft. Make cut just above a bud on left or right side. Usually, several vertical cordons are planted about 2 feet apart.

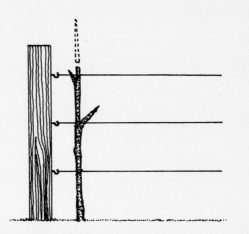

2. If you select a left-side bud the first year, head back to a right-side bud the second year. Do this during late winter.

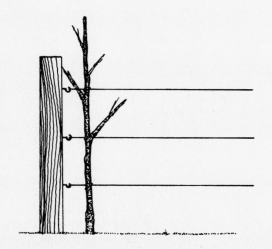

3. Each year, do alternate heading as Step 2 until desired height is attained.

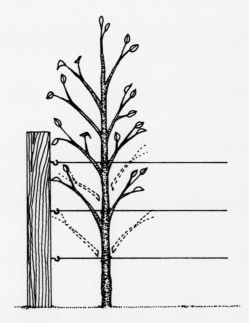

4. Prune during the season by pinching off unwanted shoots as they appear.

PROPAGATION

Making a cleft graft.

After you begin to establish your collection of fruit, berries and nuts, you will probably want to continue expanding your selection. *Propagation*—multiplying the number and variety of plants—is the answer to your needs. This section demonstrates the many ways you can expand your fruit garden.

The advantages of propagating your own varieties are many. They include:
- Growing old-fashioned varieties that are not available commercially.
- Growing two or more varieties on one tree. This is beneficial when space is limited and improves pollination in certain instances.
- Producing new plants to expand plantings that cannot be reproduced by other means.
- Changing the appearance or growth habit of an established plant.
- Repairing damaged trees and rejuvenating old neglected trees.

LAYERING
There are several different ways to layer to increase your planting stock. All are simple to do, and generally involve covering branches of plants with soil until they produce roots. *Simple layering* is used to propagate filberts, currants, gooseberries, quince, black raspberries and some grapes. You may also have success with blueberries, but they usually take several years to root. Other methods of layering include *tip layering,* used to propagate trailing blackberries and black raspberries, and *mound* or *stool layering,* used to propagate currants, gooseberries, quince and rootstock of dwarf apples. Step-by-step instructions on how to layer are given on page 38.

CUTTINGS
Most fruit trees are propagated by grafting or budding, but currants, figs, gooseberries, grapes and quince can be started from cuttings. Blueberries can sometimes be propagated from cuttings, but results are erratic.

There are two methods: *hardwood cuttings* and *root cuttings.* Hardwood cuttings must be taken in early spring while plants are dormant. The entire process—taking cuttings until healthy, rooted plants are ready for transplanting—takes one year. Step-by-step instructions on how to propagate from hardwood cuttings and root cuttings are shown on page 39.

Root cuttings should also be taken in early spring. A drawback to this method is that root cuttings require three years from start to finish.

RUNNERS
Strawberries send out *runners,* or long stems, to increase the number of plants. Runners have leaf rosettes on every other *node,* the knotlike swelling along the stem. Two methods of propagating by runners are shown on page 39. One method involves burying nodes in the soil. The other method uses flower pots placed in the ground near plants. Both should be done during the growing season when plants are actively producing runners.

Propagation Glossary

Budding—Attaching one plant to another by grafting a bud from the first plant to it.

Bud Union—Place on plant where scion is grafted to rootstock.

Cambium—Thin, moist layer of green or greenish-yellow tissue found just under the bark. It produces bark and wood.

Cutting—Piece of a stem or root taken from a plant. If it roots, it will grow into a duplicate of the original plant.

Graft—Union of two plants performed by attaching a live twig or scion of one plant to another plant.

Grafting Tape—Commercially available, moisture-proof tape used in grafting. Used instead of wax or as a supplement.

Grafting Wax—Composite wax material used to seal or weatherproof a graft.

Layering—Method of propagation. There are several ways to layer, including *simple layering, tip layering,* and *mound* or *stool layering.* All are described in the following pages.

Rootstock—Roots that serve as host to a grafted *scion*—top part of plant.

Scion—Shoot of a plant bearing buds that is grafted to rootstock of another plant.

Top-Working—Grafting or budding to a tree to alter the bearing variety or to add different varieties.

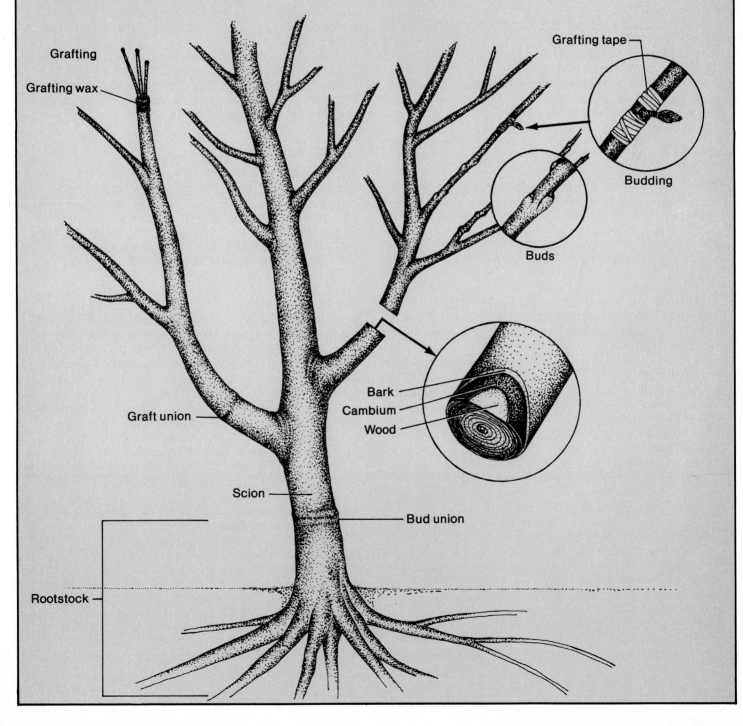

Grafting

Grafting wax

Grafting tape

Budding

Buds

Bark

Cambium

Wood

Graft union

Scion

Bud union

Rootstock

DIVISION

Fraise des bois and most other everbearing varieties of strawberry form few, if any, runners. They are best propagated by dividing existing plants. Dig and separate established plants in early April in the East and Midwest or late March farther south. Currants, gooseberries, blueberries, red raspberries and blackberries can also be propagated this way.

ROOT SUCKERS

Red raspberries and 'Stockton Morello' cherries produce suckers that grow from the roots of established plants. Suckers usually appear in early spring. At this time, dig and cut them with a spade and replant.

GRAFTING

Grafting is the joining of a branch or branches of one tree with those of another. It is a way of expanding your selection of fruit by adding one or more varieties to an existing tree. With some fruit, having different varieties on the same tree improves pollination.

All tools used in grafting should be clean and sterile before use to prevent possible disease infestations. Sterilize cutting surfaces of knives and shears by wiping them with 100% solution of alcohol or household bleach.

In the East, Midwest and farther south, grafting on deciduous trees is done when trees are dormant, in late winter or early spring. Consult the chart on page 37 for information about which varieties are compatible with one another.

Bark grafting is an easy way to *top-work,* changing the variety or adding other varieties to an existing tree. It is recommended for smaller trees. Do this in early spring when bark begins to *slip,* move easily on the branch. Cut shoots for grafting when they are dormant—during winter. Store them in a cool place such as the refrigerator until you are ready to graft. Keep them moist.

If you graft two or more scions to the stock, follow instructions on How to Protect Grafts. If you plan on top-working a larger, more mature tree, *cleft grafting* is recommended. Other grafting methods include *side-bark graft, whip graft* and *crown graft.* Crown grafting is primarily used to graft old grapevines, and is similar to cleft grafting. See photos, page 44.

Bud Grafting—Also called *budding,* this is a popular and easy way to propagate fruit trees and grapes. Essentially, budding consists of inserting a bud of one plant into a limb of another. The new bud grows from the host limb. This makes it possible to add a variety to an existing tree or to change the variety entirely.

Practice makes perfect. You will probably have to remove buds from budstock several times before you can do it successfully. Keep in mind that the *cambium,* the thin layer of tissue between bark and wood of each stock, *must* be in close contact for success. If a bud does not *take,* form a union with the stock, there is usually time left in the growing season to try again.

There are two budding methods based on the best times to bud: *spring budding* and *fall budding.* Fall budding is recommended in the East, Midwest and South. You can tell when it is time to bud by testing the bark.

If it *slips,* peels easily from the trunk, the time is right. This occurs right after most seasonal growth, around early August in the South, mid to late August in the East and Midwest and early September in the North. Timing will vary considerably according to seasonal and local conditions.

The first step in budding is to collect your budding material. Do this the same day you are going to bud. Select *scions,* the plant shoots bearing buds, of the current year's growth. These are the buds you will use when you bud graft. Each should have at least six *leaf* buds, not *flower* buds. Remove all leaves, but allow the leaf stems to remain on the plant. Place these scions in a shady spot while you prepare the receiving stock.

T- or shield budding is usually the most successful method and is recommended for all areas of the East, Midwest and South.

Other methods include *patch* or *flute bud, I- or modified H-bud* and *chip bud.* If you plan to bud walnuts, use the patch-bud method. It is the most successful. The tree's thick bark makes other methods impractical. Step-by-step instructions are shown on pages 40 and 41.

HOW TO PROTECT GRAFTS

Many products are available in garden centers or through mail-order nurseries that can be used to protect grafts. Take heed and use these products. You *must* protect grafts or your work will be in vain. All exposed wood must be completely covered with grafting wax or other material to keep it dry, protect it from sun and wind and guard against insect or disease infestation.

Grafting wax is the time-honored material used to protect grafts. Before use, it must be softened by placing it in warm water or holding it in the palm of your hand. While working with it, lightly cover your hands with cooking oil. The wax will slide in your hand, making softening easier. If you heat grafting wax to a semiliquid state, you can apply it with a brush. It hardens immediately and is waterproof.

Polyvinyl acetate-based plastic is another material used to protect grafts. It is easy to work with. After it has been applied and dried, it forms a slightly malleable yet durable covering that won't crack.

Plastic grafting tape is recommended as additional protection when used with grafting wax or grafting plastic.

Caution—Few grafts require more protection than mentioned above, but walnut trees are an exception. Because they are grafted in late spring, grafts are subject to higher temperatures and more intense sunshine than other trees. Place a ventilated paper bag or similar device over the grafted scions to provide shade, or cover with white latex paint.

Propagating Fruit, Berries and Nuts

Multiplying the number and variety of fruit plants can be done in a number of ways. Step-by-step instructions for the most common methods are provided in the following pages. Use this chart as a guide to the best method for the fruit, berry or nut you wish to propagate. Growing plants from seeds have special requirements. Seeds from hybrid plants produce unpredictable offspring. In many cases, it is better to use another method such as layering. In addition, some seeds will not germinate until they are exposed to a certain amount of cold temperatures. This is called *cold stratification,* listed in the heading below. Fulfill this natural requirement by keeping seeds in the refrigerator for the number of days listed.

	Seed	Cold Strati-fication Days Required	Hardwood Cuttings	Softwood Cuttings	Layering	Root Suckers	Remarks
TREE FRUIT							
Apple	Yes	60	Some varieties	No	Yes	Yes	Most apples, including dwarfs and rootstock-types, can be layered.
Apricot	Yes	80-90	No	No	No	No	Rootstocks can be grown from seeds.
Cherry, Sour	No	None	No	No	No	Yes	Rooted suckers are the most popular way to propagate rootstocks.
Cherry, Sweet	Yes	190	No	No	No	Yes	Rooted suckers are the most popular way to propagate rootstocks.
Crabapple	Yes. Depends on variety.	Yes	Yes	No	No	Yes	Days required for cold stratification depends on variety.
Fig	Yes	None	Yes	Yes	Yes	Yes	Year-old suckers from base of tree provide most vigorous rootstock. Hardwood cuttings should be from 2- to 3-year-old wood.
Peach	Yes	70-105	No	No	No	No	Growing from seeds is the method used for rootstocks with specified soil and climatic adaptations.
Pear	Yes	60-90	No	No	Mound	No	Grafting is recommended.
Plum and Prune	Yes	90-150	Yes	No	No	Yes	Prune suckers root easily. Japanese plums are commonly propagated from hardwood cuttings.
Quince	Yes	None	Yes	No	Yes	Yes	Hardwood cuttings are the most common method of propagation.
BERRIES							
Blackberry	No	None	No	No	Tip	Yes	Root cuttings from erect blackberries provide the greatest success rate.
Blueberry	Yes	None	Yes	No	No	Yes	Hardwood cuttings are not too successful.
Currant	Yes	90	Yes	No	Yes	No	Hardwood cuttings are the best method.
Gooseberry	Yes	90	Yes	No	Yes	No	Hardwood cuttings are the best method.
Grape	Yes	None	Yes	No	Yes	No	Seeds will not produce varieties true to parent.
Raspberry	Yes	None	No	No	Yes	Yes	Root cuttings are a successful method.
Strawberry	Yes	None	No	No	No	No	Transplant runners for more stock. Use disease-free specimens.
NUTS							
Chestnut	Yes	None	No	No	No	Yes	Usually grown from seeds, although may not grow true to type.
Hazelnut	Yes	60-180	No	No	Mound	Yes	Commonly propagated from suckers, which are profuse.
Walnut	Yes	30-156	No	No	No	No	Propagation from seeds is most common.

How to Simple Layer

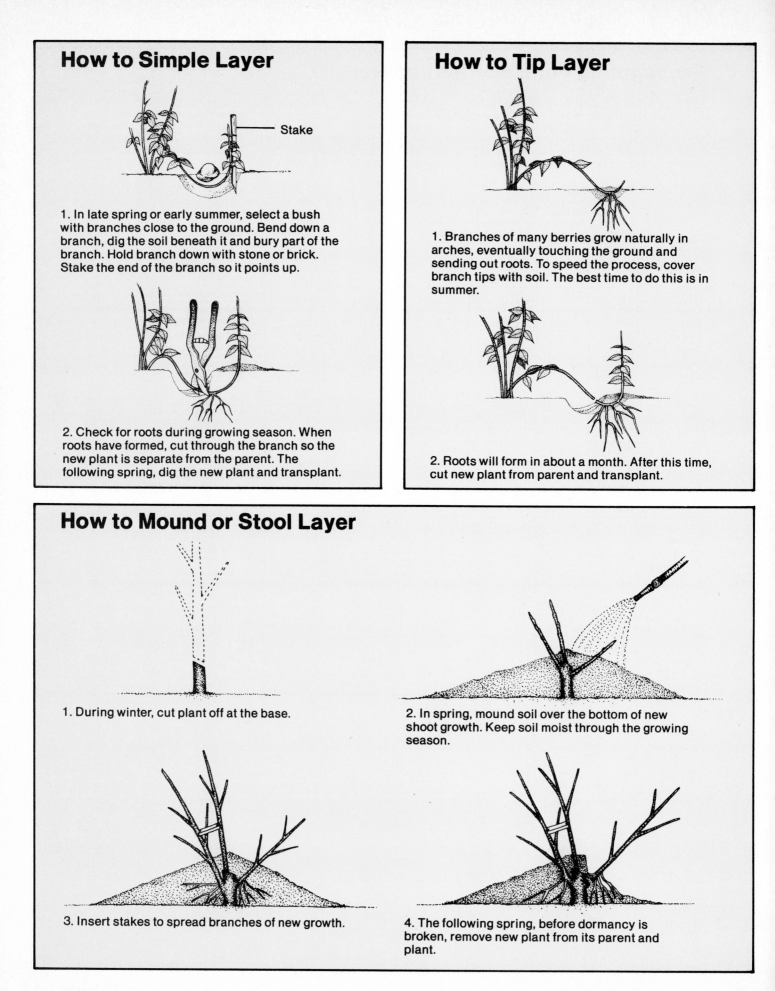

1. In late spring or early summer, select a bush with branches close to the ground. Bend down a branch, dig the soil beneath it and bury part of the branch. Hold branch down with stone or brick. Stake the end of the branch so it points up.

2. Check for roots during growing season. When roots have formed, cut through the branch so the new plant is separate from the parent. The following spring, dig the new plant and transplant.

How to Tip Layer

1. Branches of many berries grow naturally in arches, eventually touching the ground and sending out roots. To speed the process, cover branch tips with soil. The best time to do this is in summer.

2. Roots will form in about a month. After this time, cut new plant from parent and transplant.

How to Mound or Stool Layer

1. During winter, cut plant off at the base.

2. In spring, mound soil over the bottom of new shoot growth. Keep soil moist through the growing season.

3. Insert stakes to spread branches of new growth.

4. The following spring, before dormancy is broken, remove new plant from its parent and plant.

How to Propagate from Root Cuttings

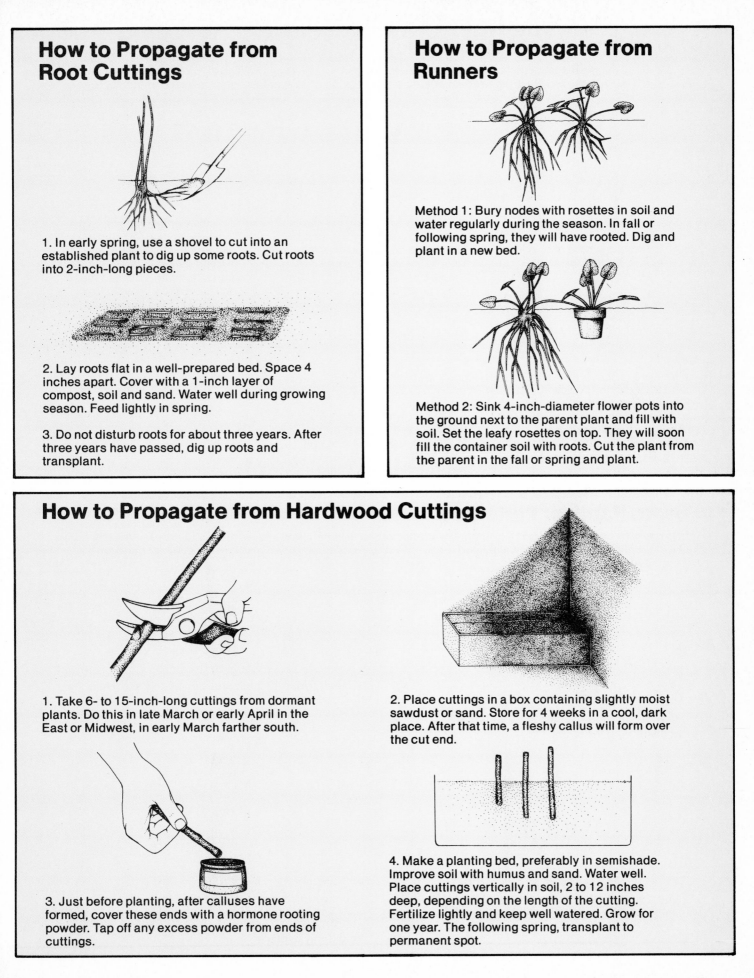

1. In early spring, use a shovel to cut into an established plant to dig up some roots. Cut roots into 2-inch-long pieces.

2. Lay roots flat in a well-prepared bed. Space 4 inches apart. Cover with a 1-inch layer of compost, soil and sand. Water well during growing season. Feed lightly in spring.

3. Do not disturb roots for about three years. After three years have passed, dig up roots and transplant.

How to Propagate from Runners

Method 1: Bury nodes with rosettes in soil and water regularly during the season. In fall or following spring, they will have rooted. Dig and plant in a new bed.

Method 2: Sink 4-inch-diameter flower pots into the ground next to the parent plant and fill with soil. Set the leafy rosettes on top. They will soon fill the container soil with roots. Cut the plant from the parent in the fall or spring and plant.

How to Propagate from Hardwood Cuttings

1. Take 6- to 15-inch-long cuttings from dormant plants. Do this in late March or early April in the East or Midwest, in early March farther south.

2. Place cuttings in a box containing slightly moist sawdust or sand. Store for 4 weeks in a cool, dark place. After that time, a fleshy callus will form over the cut end.

3. Just before planting, after calluses have formed, cover these ends with a hormone rooting powder. Tap off any excess powder from ends of cuttings.

4. Make a planting bed, preferably in semishade. Improve soil with humus and sand. Water well. Place cuttings vertically in soil, 2 to 12 inches deep, depending on the length of the cutting. Fertilize lightly and keep well watered. Grow for one year. The following spring, transplant to permanent spot.

How to T- or Shield Bud

This is usually the most successful budding method and is recommended for all areas of the East, Midwest and South. If you live in an area with intense summer sun, bud on the north side of the tree, or provide shade for the union.

1. Select a branch about 1/4 to 1/3 inches in diameter. Using a sharp knife, cut a T-shape incision in the bark of the stock.

2. Remove a bud from the scion by cutting a shield-shape piece. Retain the small leaf stem for a handle. Include a thin piece of the scion wood beneath bud. Do not touch cut edges.

3. Pull open the flaps of the T-shape incision on the stock. Holding the bud by the leaf handle, insert it into the stock. Be sure it is right-side up. Line up the top of the bud with the top of the T. Close the flaps.

4. Bind the graft with *cotton* string or plastic stretch tape. Leave the bud and stem handle exposed to air. The graft is a success when the stem handle falls off. Remove the string or tape.

5. The following spring, cut off the top of the tree or branch about 1/4 inch above the bud graft. Make a slanting cut so rain water will flow away from cut.

How to Patch or Flute Bud

This is the recommended method for budding walnuts. Because walnut trees have thick bark, the budwood is thicker, making it difficult to T- or shield bud. As with T- or shield budding, summer is the recommended time to do patch budding.

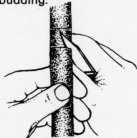

1. Select budstock the same as with T- or shield budding. Using a sharp knife, cut a square or rectangle around the bud.

2. Using your thumbs, press on opposite sides of the bud to remove it from the scion. A small piece of wood, essential for successful budding, should come off with the bud. It may require several attempts before successful removal of a bud.

3. Using a sharp knife, cut a piece out of the stock branch so that the budstock will fit snugly into it.

4. If the stock bark is thicker than the budstock bark and the fit is loose, shave off some of the stock bark. Bind with string or tape until the bud is held firmly in place.

How to Chip Bud

This system is used to bud grapes. It is done in late summer or early fall when grape buds are mature. You can also chip bud deciduous fruit.

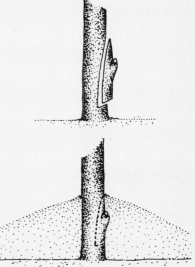

1. Select budstock as with T- or shield budding. With a sharp knife, remove bud by cutting into cane. First, cut downward about 1 inch below the bud at a 45° angle. Next, cut into cane about 1/8 inch deep, starting 1/2 inch above the bud. Cut straight down until the top and bottom cuts meet. With this cut, bud will come away from cane.

2. Make a cut in the stock near the soil line. Cut should be same size as budstock you just removed so budstock and stock will fit together snugly.

3. Secure budstock onto stock as with T- or shield budding. Mound 6 inches of moist soil over the bud graft. The following spring, if graft has taken, remove all growth to about 1-1/2 inches above graft. Train budstock to a stake and remove sucker growth.

How to Make an I- or Modified H-Bud

This is another method sometimes used for budding onto stock limbs with heavy bark.

1. Follow steps 1 and 2 of patch or flute budding, page 40.

2. Using a sharp knife, make 3 incisions in the shape of a letter "H" lying on its side.

3. Insert budstock beneath two flaps of stock. Continue steps 3 and 4 as in patch or flute budding.

How to Bark Graft

Cut *scions,* the shoots that you are grafting onto the existing tree, when they are dormant. Store them in the refrigerator until you are ready to graft. Keep them moist. They should be fully mature, about 1/2 to 3/4 inches in diameter, and 4 to 5 inches long. Be sure there are at least 6 buds on each scion. If you graft 2 or more scions onto the stock, follow instructions on How to Protect Grafts, page 36. If you plan on top-working a larger, more mature tree, cleft grafting is recommended. See page 44.

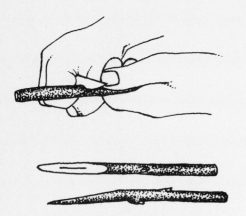

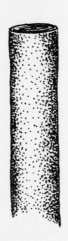

1. Prepare the scion. Cut at a sharp angle starting so scion tapers to a sloping point about 2 inches near the bottom.

2. Select stock—plant that will receive the scion—that is 2 or 3 inches in diameter. Cut off the trunk or stem of stock perpendicular to branch.

3. If stock has thin bark, use a sharp knife and make a 2-inch-long, vertical cut through the bark to the cambium. Gently pry up the bark with your knife on both sides of the slit so it will accept the scion.

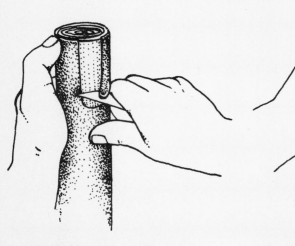

4. If the stock bark is too thick to be pried up, make two parallel, vertical cuts 2 inches long through the bark to the cambium. Cuts should be as wide as the scion. Remove old bark and peel new bark down, exposing cambium.

5. Carefully insert the scion, cut-side inward, until it is in close contact with cambium of the stock.

6. Position pointed end so it is snug under inner bark flap. If bark is too thick or too thin, secure scion to stock with nails or tie with cotton string or plastic tape. Seal all with grafting wax or grafting tape.

How to Side-Bark Graft

Side-bark grafting is done in early spring. It consists of uniting the scion to the side of the stock instead of to the top.

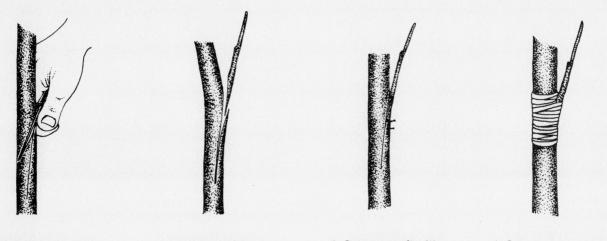
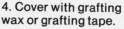

1. Select stock that is about 1 inch in diameter. Using sharp, heavy knife, make slanting cut at a 20° to 30° angle. Cut 1 inch deep into stock.

2. Prepare scion as in How to Bark Graft, page 42. Cambiums of scion and stock must be in close contact. Open cut slightly by bending it back to insert scion.

3. Secure graft with nails or tie with cotton string or plastic tape.

4. Cover with grafting wax or grafting tape.

How to Whip Graft

This system is used to top-work small trees or to graft together two branches similar in diameter. Branches to be grafted should be no more than 1/2 to 3/4 inch thick.

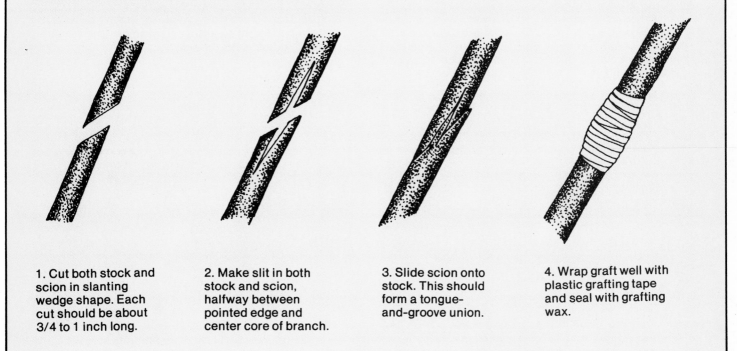

1. Cut both stock and scion in slanting wedge shape. Each cut should be about 3/4 to 1 inch long.

2. Make slit in both stock and scion, halfway between pointed edge and center core of branch.

3. Slide scion onto stock. This should form a tongue-and-groove union.

4. Wrap graft well with plastic grafting tape and seal with grafting wax.

Cleft Grafting Step by Step

1. Make horizontal cut across trunk or branch (stock) you wish to graft onto. Stock should be 2 to 4 inches in diameter.

2. Use heavy knife or hatchet to split stock lengthwise through center. Split should be about 3 inches long. Leave knife or wedge in cut to hold it open.

3. Select wood, *scion,* that is to be grafted onto stock. It should be about 5 inches long, 3/8 inch to 3/4 inch in diameter, and have at least two buds. Depending on size of stock, you may be able to graft more than one scion.

4. Make tapering cut on lower end of scion. Cut should be about 2 inches long, forming a wedge.

5. Place scion into split. Be sure *cambiums* of each are in close contact. Remove wedge from stock. Bind with tape and cover with grafting wax.

6. Label scion so you will have permanent record of grafted variety.

GROWING DWARF TREES

Dwarf 'Red Delicious' apple.

Fruit gardeners are discovering the benefits of growing dwarf fruit trees. This is not only true for backyard growers, but commercial orchardists as well. The primary advantage of growing dwarfs is obvious: They save space. A mature, standard-size apple tree requires about 30 square feet, but you can grow about a dozen dwarf trees in the same area.

ADVANTAGES OF DWARF TREES
Beyond the space-saving benefit, there are other advantages:
● Greater quantities of fruit in the same space as standard trees. Only the plant is dwarf. Fruit are the same size as fruit from standard trees.
● Smaller size of dwarfs allows you to grow several varieties with staggered maturity dates. A selection of fresh fruit is available for a longer period.
● Dwarf trees are cheaper to maintain. Because of their size, standard trees sometimes require expensive ladders and sprayers for regular maintenance chores. The small stature of dwarfs eliminates the need for this equipment.
● Harvesting, pruning and thinning are easier. With dwarfs, you usually do not have to climb a ladder to perform these tasks.
● Dwarfs come into bearing years sooner than standard varieties. Some bear the second year after planting.
● Most dwarfs are adapted to container culture. Fruit trees can be grown on city terraces, balconies or suburban patios. If existing soil conditions are poor, dwarfs can be grown in containers in improved soil.

GRAFTED DWARFS AND GENETIC DWARFS
Two kinds of dwarf fruit trees are available. One is created by forming a *grafted tree.* This is the most common method used to dwarf trees. They are produced by grafting, occasionally budding, the selected *scion,* the top part of the tree, to a particular dwarfing *rootstock.* The rootstock restricts growth of the top part of the tree that is grafted to it. Grafting is most successful with apples and pears. Through continued research and experimentation, more kinds of fruit are becoming available in this form.

Grafted trees are also produced by using an *interstem.* A small piece of rootstock is grafted between a standard rootstock and a scion of the selected variety. Depending on the variety, a stronger root system can result from this method.

Different rootstocks are used in the process of grafting. These result in trees that differ in their mature size. Dwarfing rootstocks produce mature trees ranging from 4 feet high to 15 to 20 feet high. Often, when you buy a tree, it is labeled only as "dwarf" or "semidwarf." No information about the rootstock is specified.

To allow space for the mature size of the tree you plan to purchase, you need to know what rootstock was used. Ask the seller, or specify which rootstock you want when you purchase a tree. Or do your own grafting, obtaining rootstock of a known quality.

Dwarfing Rootstocks—Two kinds of rootstocks are currently used to dwarf apple trees. They are called *Malling,* designated by the letter M., and *Merton-Malling,* designated by M.M.

The following are the most common rootstocks and the size of mature trees.

Rootstock	Maximum Height
M.27	4 feet
M.9	9 feet
M.26	12 feet
M.7	15 feet
M.M.106	18 feet

Size varies according to training method used.

Pears are most often grafted to 'Anger' quince rootstock. Sometimes *double grafting* is necessary because 'Anger' does not accept all varieties. In this case, a compatible variety of pear is grafted between the 'Anger' rootstock and the selected pear variety.

Peaches, nectarines, plums and apricots are usually budded to *Prunus besseyi* or *tomentosa* stock to produce a dwarf tree. Other stock can be used to grow larger trees.

Cherry trees are rarely dwarfed. Small trees do not produce enough volume of fruit for the home gardener. Semidwarf trees are more common. They can be produced by grafting an interstem of 'North Star' or 'Stockton Morello'.

Genetic Dwarfs—These are naturally compact varieties with dwarfed fruiting parts grafted to vigorous rootstocks. They tend to have a "lumpy" appearance because fruiting spurs and buds are spaced closely together. They usually overbear and require heavy thinning of fruit.

Spur-type apples, peach cultivars such as 'Bonanza', some nectarines, and sour cherries such as 'Meteor' and 'Northstar' are popular genetic-dwarf varieties.

Spur-type apples, called *sports* or *mutations,* are said to be created by a change in a gene or chromosome. It is speculated that this is caused when a cosmic ray comes in contact with a shoot of a tree. The result can be a new variety—different in color, taste, shape or growth habit. More often than not, the change is undesirable, but occasionally a tree will have improved flavor or fruiting habit. Because they grow slowly and are more compact than standard-size trees, spur-type apples require less pruning. They are not recommended for espalier pruning or training.

Some genetic dwarfs can grow 12 to 15 feet high, but usually grow to about 10 feet high. They are particularly well suited to container culture. Grown in containers, some grow to only 3 to 4 feet tall.

Genetic dwarfs tend to have vigorous rootstocks, and often send up many strong suckers. Remove these as soon as they are noticed.

FIVE-ON-ONE

You may have noticed mail-order catalogs promoting a fruit tree having several varieties on a single tree. Such trees are produced by grafting several different varieties to a single rootstock. These plants are useful when space is limited, or if more than one variety is required for cross-pollination.

Caring for these trees can be complicated. Different varieties often have different levels of vigor, making it difficult to prune plants. One or two vigorous varieties may dominate the tree, shading out the others. If in doubt, consult the variety charts in the sections on individual fruit for information on growth habits.

GROWING FRUIT IN CONTAINERS

If space is at a premium or if native soil is not workable, growing trees in containers can be a successful alternative. Trees tend to remain small because root growth is restricted.

Select a container made of a material that resists rot. Redwood is commonly recommended. Growing trees in containers requires using a soil with good drainage and aeration, or roots can suffocate.

The New York State Cooperative Extension Service recommends a soil mix of half loam and half peat moss. Ideally, the soil pH should be around 6.5. This mixture is recommended in the East, Midwest and upper South.

Watering—Soil in a container dries out faster than garden soil. Frequent watering is usually necessary, especially during warm summer months. Watering frequently leaches out many nutrients from the soil, especially nitrogen. To compensate, apply fertilizer more often but in smaller quantities than with trees in the ground.

A container measuring 2 to 2-1/2 feet in diameter should be fertilized as follows. When a tree is dormant in early spring, work in about 1/3 pound of 5-10-10 or equivalent organic fertilizer. Do the same in early June and again in early August.

Anatomy of a Dwarf Tree

By grafting the desired *scion,* top part of a tree, to a dwarfing rootstock, a smaller tree results. In some instances an *interstem* is grafted between the scion and a standard rootstock.

Standard tree

Standard tree

Interstem

Standard tree

Dwarfing rootstock

Standard rootstock

PEST AND DISEASE CONTROL

Red currants protected with netting.

A regular spray program sustained throughout the season is probably the most effective means of pest and disease control. Beginning at the time petals fall from plant blossoms, *petal fall,* spray fruit trees with an all-purpose fruit spray every 10 to 14 days. Be sure to read the label and heed instructions concerning the days between the last spray and fruit harvest.

Many gardeners are interested in returning to a more natural form of pest control, with fewer chemical sprays. They would rather rely on the balance of nature to maintain healthy plants. Instead of spraying at the first sign of infestation, they allow natural predators to reduce pests. They follow good cultural practices to keep their fruit-producing plants healthy.

Using only natural, organic methods sometimes results in less-than-perfect fruit, with occasional pest and disease infestations. But organic gardeners feel this is a small price to pay to harvest fruit free of chemical sprays. If you garden without sprays, you should know which insects are "friends of the garden." See page 50 for descriptions of beneficial insects.

10 STEPS TO PEST PREVENTION

1. Throughout the season, gather and dispose of fruit and leaves that have fallen to the ground. The area around trees should be clear of all fruit at the end of the harvest period. Many pests and diseases spend the winter in decaying fruit, and emerge in the spring to attack your trees.
2. Feed the birds during winter as well as in summer. Some birds take a few nibbles at your fruit, but when you consider how many insects they eat, the benefits outnumber the fruit they consume.
3. Scrape loose bark from trees to eliminate hiding places for insects during the winter.
4. Prune trees every year. Remove dead, broken or infected branches—places where trouble begins.
5. Thin interior of trees to provide air circulation. This reduces potential for fungus diseases.
6. Plan your orchard so that no two trees of one fruit variety are right next to one another. If a pest should attack one tree, chances are it will attack nearby trees of the same variety.
7. Make a weekly inspection tour of your fruit plants. Check plants closely to spot problems while they are minor.
8. Be aware of the climate and weather patterns of your area. If the summer is excessively wet or humid, be prepared to prevent a fungal attack.
9. Select disease- and pest-resistant varieties recommended for your area. See the variety charts included in the individual fruit descriptions.
10. Learn which visitors to your garden are friends. See the descriptions of beneficial insects on page 50.

THE CRUCIAL SPRAY—DORMANT OIL
Dormant-oil spray is so called because it is an oil sprayed on plants when they are dormant. It is actually the most important spray, and is a primary insect and disease preventive. The oil covers scale eggs and other pests that overwinter on the bark of trees, smothering them.

In the East and Midwest, apply this oil-and-water mixture in late March or early April, while trees are still dormant. Pick a day when the temperature is above 40F (5C) and is not likely to drop below 40F (5C) within 24 hours. Farther south, spray in early March, following the same temperature requirements as just mentioned. When you spray, drench all parts of the tree.

Even if you are an organic gardener, enduring occasional pests, do not neglect this simple spray. You can save yourself a great deal of trouble later in the season, eliminating problem pests before they have a chance to mature and attack your plants.

ALL-PURPOSE ORCHARD SPRAY

An *all-purpose* orchard spray, produced by many manufacturers and available in garden centers, destroys most insect pests. However, a few pests are not controlled by an all-purpose spray. They are:

Pear Psylla—If infestations are serious, control by spraying with a mixture of 4 tablespoons of imidan 12-1/2% *wettable powder*—powder that dissolves easily—to 1 gallon of water. Be sure to buy the 12-1/2% solution. Look on the product label for this percentage. Make first application when leaves show signs of browning and when small, yellow nymphs are noticed on leaves. Spray again 10 to 14 days later.

Peach-Tree Borer—This is particularly a problem in the Northeast. Prevent by drenching tree trunk with a solution of 20% lindane. See page 52 for additional control measures.

Apple Maggot—Spray with diazinon or carbaryl according to label directions. See page 52.

10 TIPS FOR SPRAYING EFFICIENTLY

1. Don't skip sprays. Insects and diseases don't take vacations.
2. Don't use herbicides and weed killers in the same sprayer used for insect- and disease-control sprays.
3. Spray shortly after a rain for disease control. Allow foliage to dry before spraying.
4. Mix a fresh batch of spray for each application. Use clean tap water when mixing. Do not save spray for a future application.
5. Follow label directions precisely when measuring products. Don't add in a little extra "just to be sure." You may injure your plants.
6. Stir the spray mixture or shake the sprayer frequently while spraying to keep the chemicals from settling.
7. Never spray an insecticide while plants are in bloom. Bees and other insects necessary for pollination may be killed. Without them, you will end up with little or no fruit. Fungicides are safe to use during bloom period.
8. Use the right spray for the pest or disease you wish to control. Consult with your nurseryman, and read the product label.
9. Spray in the right places—where the pests are hiding. Be sure to cover the *undersides* of branches and leaves.
10. Spray at the right time. Spray on windless days, and not during heat of the day. Do not spray when plants are hot or dry, such as after warm winds. Do not spray when foliage is wet.

When spraying fruit plants, be certain to cover *undersides* of leaves as well as top surfaces.

Pest and Disease Controls

These are some of the more readily available chemicals approved for use in home gardens. Use them with extreme care and follow all directions on product labels.

Generic Name	Trade Name	Uses	Remarks
Bacillus thuringiensis	Bactur, Dipel, Thuricide	Codling moth, peach-twig borer, leaf roller, Oriental fruit moth, red-humped caterpillar.	Biological control. Insects eat the spores of *Bacillus thuringiensis,* which kills them slowly, sometimes taking as long as 72 hours. Timing is crucial. Destroys only caterpillars and larvae. Apply when pests are young. Non-toxic to humans.
Benomyl	Benlate	Scab, brown rot, bacterial leaf spot, powdery mildew.	Often used with captan. Some diseases are beginning to show resistance and immunity. Alternate with different fungicide to prevent resistance buildup. Non-toxic to humans. Safe to handle. Spray can be applied right up to harvest.
Bordeaux—copper sulfate and lime	Many	Peach-leaf curl, bacterial leaf spot.	Mix with dormant-oil spray for early spring application. Can be used right up to harvest.
Captan	Orthocide, Captan	Scab, brown rot, bacterial leaf spot, cherry-leaf spot.	Non-toxic to humans. Can be used right up to harvest. Apply with wetting agent or spreader.
Carbaryl	Sevin	Pear slug, codling moth, gypsy moth, Oriental fruit moth, leaf roller.	Highly toxic to honeybees and beneficial mites. Moderately toxic to humans. Do not spray within 5 days of harvest.
Diazinon	Spectracide	Borers, pear slug, leaf hopper, scale, aphids, codling moth.	Can cause russeting on green and yellow varieties of apples. Toxic to humans. Do not spray within 20 days of harvest.
Dicofol	Kelthane	Spider mites.	A second spray 7 days after first spray is often required. Moderately toxic to humans and toxic to beneficial predatory mites. Do not spray within 14 days of harvest.
Dormant oil	Volk Oil	Leaf roller, scale, spider mites, aphids, codling moth.	Most important spray of the year. Low toxicity. Do not use on walnuts.
Fixed copper—copper sulfate	Many	Brown rot, peach-leaf curl, bacterial leaf spot.	Similar to Bordeaux mixture but more stable. Apply with wetting agent. May be harmful to some trees.
Lime-sulfur	Dormant Disease Control, Orthorix, Lime-Sulfur	Scab, peach-leaf curl, bacterial leaf spot, powdery mildew.	Excellent for peach-leaf curl disease. Do not use at the same time as dormant oil. Avoid getting spray on painted surfaces because chemical can discolor finish. Do not use during hot weather or on apricot trees.
Lindane	Kwell	Borers.	Has long, residual quality, controlling borers effectively. Highly toxic to humans. Do not spray within 60 days of harvest.
Malathion	Cythion	Pear slug, walnut-husk fly, leaf hopper, scale, aphids, codling moth.	Low toxicity to humans but highly toxic to beneficial insects such as honeybees and wasps. Do not spray within 1 week of harvest. Has injured 'McIntosh' and 'Cortland' apples, sweet cherries, some European grapes and 'Bosc' pear.
Methoxychlor	Marlate	Leaf hopper, codling moth, scale crawlers.	Low toxicity to humans but toxic to fish. Do not spray within 1 day of harvest.
Sulfur	Many	Brown rot, scab, powdery mildew, mites.	A widely used and well-known fungicide.

Beneficial Insects

Many insects are not damaging to plants. In fact, they prey on other insects that attack fruit. Learn to recognize the insects described here, and do not destroy them.

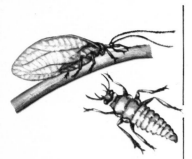

Aphid Lion, Lacewing
Description: Adults: Gauzy green wings, yellow eyes, fragile, hairlike antennae. Deposits eggs singly on hairlike stems, attached in clusters on the undersides of leaves.
Larvae have yellowish or mottled red or brown, long, narrow bodies that taper at both ends. Large, sickle-shape jaws, prominent, projecting hairs, about 3/8 inch long.
Benefit: Larvae feed on aphids, mealybugs, scales, thrips and mites.
Distribution: Continental United States and adjacent areas of Canada.

Assassin Bug
Description: Light brown, about 1/2 to 3/4 inch long, with long legs. Walks over plants ponderously. Holds forelegs in prayerlike position and uses them to capture prey.
Benefit: Feeds on immature insect pests.
Distribution: Continental United States and adjacent areas of Canada.

Damsel Bug
Description: Resembles assassin bug but is pale gray, about 3/8 inch long. Uses forelegs to capture prey.
Benefit: Feeds on aphids, leaf hoppers and small larvae of other insects.
Distribution: Continental United States and adjacent areas of Canada.

Ground Beetle
Description: Adults: Dull black or brown beetles with long, oval bodies and narrow heads. Usually found on ground under stones or loose trash. They hide during the day and are active at night. When disturbed, they scurry away. Larvae have slender, flattened bodies that taper slightly at the tail. They have two spines or bristles at tail end.
Benefit: Adults feed on caterpillars and other insects.
Distribution: Continental United States and adjacent areas of Canada.

Lady Bug
Description: Adults: Shiny red or tan. Some have black spots. Oval, about 1/4 inch long. Larvae are blue, orange or gray. Shaped like carrots and warty, about 1/16 to 1/4 inch long.
Benefit: Feed on aphids, spider mites, scales and mealybugs.
Distribution: Continental United States and adjacent areas of Canada.

Minute Pirate Bug
Description: Adults: Usually black beetles marked with white spots or streaks. Oval and flat, about 1/16 inch long. Nymphs are similar to adults, only yellowish brown. Found on flowers and under loose bark of trees.
Benefit: Feed on small insects and mites. Also eat eggs and larvae of many kinds of insects.
Distribution: Continental United States and adjacent areas of Canada.

Spiders and Mites
Description: Many kinds of spiders and mites can be found in the garden. They range in size from large, orb-weaving, black and yellow garden spiders to tiny mites. Some spiders have hairy bodies and legs. Others are smooth and shiny. They are black, brown, yellow and black or gray. Mites are gray or pinkish gray. Some spiders build webs for snaring prey. Others pursue and trap their victims.
Benefit: Large, web-spinning spiders prey on large insects that fly or crawl. Small, hunting spiders attack small insects such as flies, beetles, caterpillars, aphids and leaf hoppers. Mites feed on spider mites, cyclamen mites, aphids and thrips. They also eat larvae and eggs of many insects.
Distribution: Continental United States and adjacent areas of Canada.

Syrphid Fly
Description: Adults: Bright yellow and black, 1/4 to 3/8 inch long. They hover above flowers and plants.
Larvae resemble slugs and are brown, gray or mottled.
Benefit: Larvae eat insects. A single larva can eat one aphid per minute.
Distribution: Continental United States and adjacent areas of Canada.

Trichogamma Wasp
Description: Wide variance in size, color and body structure. Some are parasites. Others are predators.
Benefit: Tiny, parasitic wasps lay eggs in bodies of other insects. When larvae hatch from eggs, they eat their hosts. Large, predatory wasps sting caterpillars to paralyze them.
Distribution: Continental United States and adjacent areas of Canada.

Wildlife Pests

Birds
The three fruit most favored by birds are blueberries, cherries and currants. However, birds are often beneficial because they eat many insect pests. A good-size planting of raspberries usually provides enough fruit for you and the birds. If you want all the crop, cover trees or bushes with nets *before* fruit ripens. After harvest, remove nets.

Deer
If deer are a problem in your area, it is necessary to take steps to control them. If you don't, a hungry deer can eat your fruit trees right down to the trunk.

Few deterrents are completely effective. Human hair wrapped in nylon—a ball of hair about the size of a baseball in each tree—helps keep deer away. During spring, summer and early fall, placing dried blood or bone meal around trees helps reduce invasions. But these lose their odor and effectiveness when freezing temperatures occur in winter. Winter is also the time when food supplies for deer are low, which means they are more likely to visit your orchard. Other scare tactics such as blaring transistor radios or flashing lights work for a time. But soon, deer become accustomed to these distractions and ignore them.

Perhaps the best and only solution is a sturdily constructed deer fence. It must be at least 6-1/2 feet high for a small orchard, 9 feet high for a large orchard. Even then, deer have been known to jump over fences this high. A double row of fencing 9 feet high is about the surest way to prevent their entry.

Mice
Mice often live in the mulch or brush beneath trees. This gives them a place to hide while they gnaw at the bark. Remove mulch periodically and inspect for these rodents. In winter, apply mulch *after* the ground has frozen. Beyond that, control for mice is similar to rabbits.

Rabbits
Rabbits are probably your fruit tree's most serious enemies. They relish the bark of young trees and the tender new growth of old trees. Rabbits are most damaging during the winter. When they eat the bark, they usually girdle the tree. This may kill the branch or the entire tree.

Control by using *tree wrap,* available at nurseries, and 1/4-inch wire screen around trunk and low branches. Using both to encircle tree at planting time should prevent rodent damage. Replace the wire mesh periodically. As the tree grows, the wire may girdle the trunk.

In areas of deep snowfall, wrap aluminum foil around branches above snow level. This prevents rabbits from reaching and gnawing on limbs. Or remove heavy snow from beneath trees.

Raccoons
These animals can devour large quantities of ripe fruit right off the tree. Dogs may be able to chase them away, but this is sometimes impractical. In some areas, local leash laws make it illegal. The best solution is to set box traps. These traps do not harm animals. After a raccoon is trapped, you can release the animal in an undeveloped area, and hope he doesn't return.

Squirrels are a similar problem. As with raccoons, there is no reasonable solution except to use box traps and transport them to another locality. If it is your nut trees that you're trying to protect, it's a matter of first-come first-served. Harvest nuts before the squirrels strip your trees of their bounty.

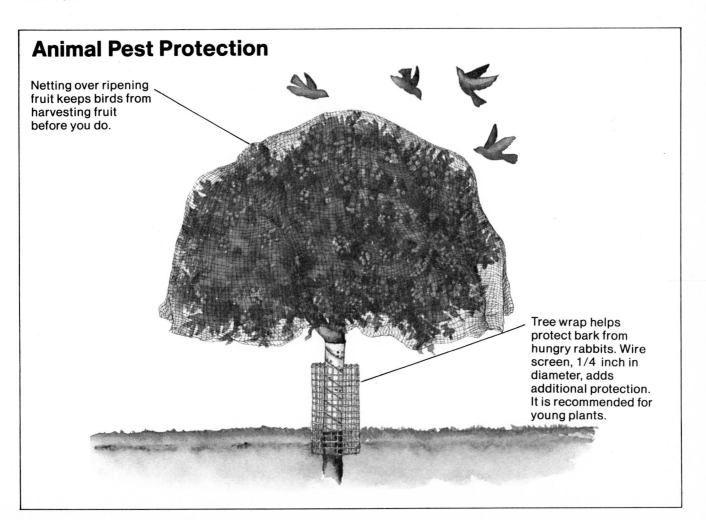

Animal Pest Protection

Netting over ripening fruit keeps birds from harvesting fruit before you do.

Tree wrap helps protect bark from hungry rabbits. Wire screen, 1/4 inch in diameter, adds additional protection. It is recommended for young plants.

Common Insect Pests

Aphids
Hosts: Apples, pears and plums.
Evidence: Tiny infestations of greenish or reddish bugs on bottom of leaves. They suck plant juices. Leaves may curl.
Description: Small and plump in various colors. Some aphids secrete a substance called *honeydew* that forms a black, sooty mold attracting ant colonies. Woolly apple aphids leave white, cottony puffs on twigs.
Control: Dormant-oil spray in early spring, plus regular program of general-purpose spray throughout the season. For severe infestations, apply a contact spray of malathion, carbaryl or diazinon. Follow instructions on package label.

Apple Maggot, Railroad Worm
Hosts: Apples, blueberries, cherries, plums and wild crabapples.
Evidence: Eggs hatch and tiny maggots tunnel through fruit flesh, leaving brown, winding channels. Fruit becomes dimpled and distorted at harvest time.

Description: Adult fly is black, slightly smaller than a housefly. It has three or four white bands on its body.
Control: A regular spray program throughout the season may not prevent infestations. If pests are noticed, spray with diazinon or carbaryl. Follow instructions on package label. Do not use diazinon within 14 days of harvest.

Cherry Fruit Fly
Host: Cherries.
Evidence: Maggots feed in fruit, making holes and causing contamination.
Description: Adult fly is black, smaller than a housefly. It has four black bands on its wings. Larvae are tiny, yellowish.
Control: Regular spray program throughout season. For severe infestation, spray with diazinon or other product registered for cherry fruit fly. Read product label. Spray as soon as you notice fly or maggot infestation at 7-day intervals. Do not spray diazinon within 14 days of harvest.

Codling Moth
Hosts: Apples, pears and quince. Occasionally attacks other fruit.

Evidence: Infested apples have holes from the side or blossom end to the core. *Frass,* insect-produced debris, often protrudes from these holes.
Description: Worms are about 3/4 inch long when fully grown. They overwinter as pinkish-white larvae with brown heads. Moths are gray with brown patches on tips of front wings. They have a wingspan of 1/2 to 3/4 inch.
Control: Regular spray program throughout the season. For severe infestations, spray with diazinon after petal fall. Continue at 7- to 10-day intervals throughout the season. Do not spray diazinon within 14 days of harvest.

Japanese Beetle
Hosts: Foliage of grapes and raspberries.
Evidence: Large holes in leaves, usually in sunny locations.
Description: Large, 1/2-inch-long insects with copper-colored bodies and metallic-green wing covers.
Control: If small in number, remove with gloved hand. Or use a beetle trap. Many kinds are available in garden centers. For severe infestations, apply spores of *Bacillus popilliae,* milky disease, to surrounding soil areas. It does a good job in reducing larvae. Or use carbaryl chemical spray.

Leaf Roller
Hosts: Apples and many other deciduous trees.
Evidence: Rolled leaves where insects feed, which are eventually skeletonized. They also burrow into fruit, making shallow, irregular channels.
Description: Adult has wingspan of 1/2 inch. Forewing is marked with a band that widens toward the edge.
Control: Regular spray program throughout the season. For severe infestation, spray with diazinon according to instructions on package label. Do not use diazinon within 14 days of harvest.

Peach-Tree Borer
Hosts: Nectarines, peaches, apricots, cherries and plums.
Evidence: A thick, gummy substance formed at the entrance to the bored hole. Fine, sawdustlike substance is evident.
Description: Worms have brown heads and cream-color bodies. They are about 1 inch long when mature. They tunnel into trunks near or beneath ground level.
Control: To eliminate pests by hand, remove soil from around base of tree to 6 inches deep. Inspect for tunnels. The best time to do this is spring or fall. If you locate a tunnel, push a length of flexible wire into it to kill worms, or dig worms out with a knife. Usually, 50 to 75%

of borers are found during the first examination. Repeat the process two weeks later. Fill in soil around trunk base after each examination.

To prevent infestations, treat in mid-September even if you don't see evidence of pests. Prepare a solution of 20% lindane. The product label will tell you its percentage. A sprinkling can is ideal for applying solution. Drench tree trunk from crotch down to ground level. Solution should soak into soil surrounding base of trunk. Apply at least 1 gallon of solution to and around each tree 6 inches or larger in diameter. For trees smaller than 6 inches in diameter, apply 1/2 gallon of solution.

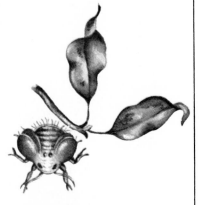

Pear Psylla
Host: Pear.
Evidence: Leaves turn brown, eventually dropping from tree. Pests can be seen gathered on undersides of leaves. Twigs, fruit and leaves may be coated with sticky substance called *honeydew*, on which a black fungus grows. Do not confuse the black substance on leaves with fireblight. The black fungus formed on honeydew can be washed off.
Description: Small, brownish, aphidlike insects suck plant juices.
Control: Dormant-oil spray early in spring and regular applications of general-purpose spray throughout the season. For severe infestations, apply imidan or malathion according to package instructions. Do not spray within 1 day of harvest.

Pear Slug
Hosts: Cherries, pears.
Evidence: Skeletonized leaves have lacy patch remaining.
Description: Small, moist, green worms. Mature pear slug resembles a housefly.
Control: Regular spray program throughout the season. For severe infestations, cultivate soil in early June and mid-August to kill emerging adults. For cherries and pears, spray malathion, diazinon or carbaryl at petal fall. Spray pears again at pre-harvest. Do not use diazinon within 14 days of harvest.

Plum Curculio
Hosts: Apples, apricots, cherries, crabapples, nectarines, peaches, pears and plums.
Evidence: Small holes in the skin of fruit where beetles have fed. Crescent-shape cuts with a small, round hole in skin of small fruit, caused when beetles lay eggs. When eggs hatch, young worms eat into fruit flesh.
Description: Adult is brownish gray, about 1/5 inch long, hard-shelled beetle with a snout. It has four pairs of bumps on upper surface of the body.
Control: A regular spray program throughout the season plus a dormant-oil spray in early spring. For severe infestation, spray with carbaryl or other product labeled for plum curculio control.

San Jose Scale
Hosts: Apples, apricots, currants, gooseberries, peaches, pears, plums, nectarines and sweet cherries.
Evidence: Scale insects can be seen on bark, foliage and fruit. They feed on fruit and foliage, causing small, reddish spots. Entire tree or limbs of tree may be killed. Infested fruit are inedible if scales are not controlled.
Description: Scales are shaped like discs, about 1/12 inch in diameter. They resemble tiny oyster shells. They encrust twigs and branches. When mature, legs emerge under the crusty shells and scales begin to crawl— *crawler stage.*
Control: Use dormant-oil spray in early spring before buds start to open. Essential to coat all parts of tree thoroughly. Spray only when temperatures are above 40F (5C) and when night temperatures will not fall below freezing. If infestation persists, spray with diazinon or malathion after crawlers hatch. Follow instructions on package label. Do not use diazinon within 14 days of harvest. Do not use malathion within one day of harvest.

Spider Mite
Hosts: Apples, plums, pears and other deciduous fruit.
Evidence: Leaves turn brown. Silvery webbing can be seen on the undersides of leaves.
Description: Tiny, red, spiderlike pests spin small, silver webs between leaf axils. Mites suck plant juices.

Control: Dormant-oil spray kills eggs in early spring. Mites thrive under dusty conditions, so wash foliage with jets of water during dry spells. Regular spray program throughout the season controls this pest. For severe infestation, use diazinon or malathion. Follow instructions on package label. Do not use diazinon within 14 days of harvest. Do not use malathion within 1 day of harvest.

Tent Caterpillar
Hosts: All fruit trees.
Evidence: Large webs in branches.
Description: Hairy caterpillars can be seen nesting in tentlike webbing, usually 20 or more in each tent. They emerge to eat leaves.
Control: Regular spray program throughout the season may prevent infestations. If they do occur, remove webbing from branches using a long stick with nails driven into it. Burn web and worms. Do not burn tents while they are on trees. You will damage branches worse than the caterpillars.

Walnut-Husk Fly
Host: Walnuts.
Evidence: Maggots of the husk fly feed on the husks of walnuts, producing a substance that penetrates the shell of the nut and stains the kernel. The kernels take on an off-color and flavor.
Description: Small, white worms blacken husks.
Control: Spray with malathion in early August, and again in late August when adult flies emerge.

Diseases

Bacterial Canker

Hosts: Apples, apricots, cherries, nectarines, peaches, pears and plums.
Evidence: Gummy cankers and damp-looking patches form on branches and trunk of tree. Blossoms and young fruit may appear infected.
Control: No spray is available to effectively treat this disease. Dormant copper sprays may help. Remove and destroy infected branches after leaf fall. Use sharp tools and disinfect with alcohol or household bleach after each cut. Cherries are particularly susceptible. If bacterial canker is a problem locally, avoid planting 'Bing', 'Lambert', 'Royal Ann' and 'Van'. 'Sam' is resistant to bacterial canker.

Bacterial Leaf Spot

Hosts: Apricots, cherries, nectarines, peaches and plums.
Evidence: Purplish spots develop on leaves. They turn brown and become holes. Fruit spurs can be attacked, causing fruit to drop.
Control: Spray at fruitlet stage with captan, Bordeaux, fixed copper or lime-sulfur product. Spray again at leaf fall. Follow instructions on package label.

Black Knot

Hosts: Cherries and plums.
Evidence: Elongated swellings on smaller twigs, as well as *galls*—hard, rough knots on larger branches. Knots may girdle branches and kill portions beyond. If not controlled, most branches are killed. Ultimately, the tree may die.
Control: Prune diseased branches in early spring or fall, cutting 4 to 5 inches in back of knot. Remove young swelling on twigs. Dispose of prunings. Spray with sulfur during *delayed dormant stage*— when a little green shows in the buds. Spray at the rate of 1 tablespoon to 1 gallon of water. Repeat 7 to 10 days later.

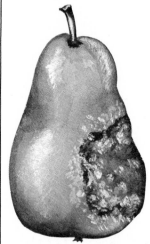

Brown Rot

Hosts: Apricots, cherries, nectarines, peaches and plums. Occasionally apples and pears.
Evidence: Small, firm, light-brown spot on fruit spreads over surface, mummifying it completely. Infected specimens look like shriveled, dried leather covered with a powdery substance. Most prevalent in cool, damp regions.

Control: Remove all dried mummies each year. Prune interior of tree to allow for maximum air circulation, and thorough spray penetration. For serious infestations, spray at colored-bud stage and again at pre-harvest stage. Use captan, sulfur, benomyl or fixed-copper products. If weather is wet for a long period, spray after rain.

Cedar Apple Rust

Hosts: Apples and quince, but red-cedar trees have to be nearby to complete life cycle of the disease.
Evidence: Bright-orange spots on leaves and fruit. Sometimes severe leaf drop.
Control: Regular spray program throughout season. For severe infestation, spray with sulfur. Follow application instructions on product label.

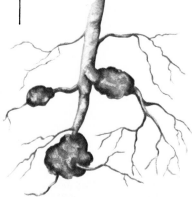

Crown Gall

Host: All fruit trees.
Evidence: Galls or swellings grow on crown and roots of tree. They eventually girdle and kill the tree.
Control: Sprays are available to prevent crown gall from infecting plants. Avoid disease by buying healthy stock from reliable nurseries. Avoid injuring stock during planting.

Seriously infected trees should be removed and destroyed.

Crown Rot

Hosts: Apples, pears.
Evidence: Late in the season, branch or branches can turn reddish. Foliage turns yellow or brown.
Control: Trunks that are constantly wet at the soil line are susceptible. Inspect bark at soil line to see if it is dead. If so, rake soil away to allow air circulation. If possible, plant higher and keep water from standing against trunk.

Dead Arm

Hosts: Grapes
Evidence: First attacks canes causing dark lesions to form. Leaves become small, crinkled and yellow. Untreated, it will girdle trunk and kill vine.
Control: This is a fungus disease. Treat with lime-sulfur, sulfur, captan, ferbam or benomyl.

Fireblight
Hosts: Pears, some apples, crabapples, quince, pyracantha and hawthorn.
Evidence: New spring growth suddenly wilts and dies. Pear branches appear as though they have been charred by fire. Apple leaves and shoots turn rusty brown. Cankers of various sizes sometimes develop.
Control: Plant resistant varieties. Beyond that, prune and destroy diseased twigs or branches at least 6 inches beyond edge of infection. Remove severely infected trees.

Check locally or with your county extension service to see if fireblight is common in your area. If it is prevalent, avoid planting the most susceptible pear varieties: 'Bartlett', 'Bosc', 'Clapp's Favorite' and 'Sheldon'. The least susceptible varieties are: 'Kieffer', 'Moonglow', 'Maxine' and 'Seckel'.

Susceptible apple varieties are: 'Gravenstein', 'Jonathan', 'Rome Beauty', 'Yellow Transparent' and 'Lodi'. Those somewhat resistant are: 'Golden Delicious', 'Red Delicious' and 'Winesap'.

Peach-Leaf Curl
Hosts: Nectarines and peaches.
Evidence: Leaves curl and twist and look as though they are infected with blisters.
Control: This disease is quite common but is easily controlled. Spray with protective fungicide such as ferbam, captan or benomyl. Spray before buds break in spring or shortly after leaf fall in autumn.

Powdery Mildew
Hosts: Apples, sometimes pears and cherries.
Evidence: A white, powdery growth appears on undersides of leaves and on young, terminal shoots, ultimately killing them. Growth is stunted and leaves turn yellow and drop.

This disease is particularly prevalent in areas with cool, damp summers. Plant in full sun and prune to encourage air circulation to avoid infection. Roses harbor mildew spores. Remove rose bushes near fruit orchard.
Control: Regular spray program throughout season. For severe infestation, spray with lime-sulfur, sulfur, karathane or benomyl at colored bud, petal fall and fruitlet stages. Do not use karathane on cherries.

Scab
Hosts: Apple, pears.
Evidence: Brown, corky patches first appear on leaves, then infect fruit.
Control: Disease overwinters on fallen leaves. Rake leaves and thoroughly clean around trees in fall. Trees grown in damp areas are especially susceptible. Prune to allow for maximum exposure to sunshine and air circulation. Spray with captan, lime-sulfur, sulfur or benomyl at colored bud, petal fall and fruitlet stages. Follow instructions on package label. If spring weather is particularly warm and wet, spray every 3 days. Spray soil underneath tree.

Verticillium Wilt
Hosts: All fruit trees, canes and small fruit such as raspberries, blackberries and strawberries.
Evidence: Branch dies suddenly, going from bottom to top. Fruit trees show black sapwood under bark. Small fruit wilt and turn grayish blue.
Control: Difficult to correct. Avoid planting near susceptible plants such as tomatoes and strawberries, or in same soil where they were once grown. Fortunately, if you remove infected plant parts, most plants recover. Disinfect pruning tools with bleach after each pruning cut.

Pest and Disease Timetable

The following includes seven basic stages in the seasonal life of a fruit tree. Learn to recognize each stage and how it effects the tree's growth. This will help you take the proper control steps at the right time, treating problems before they become serious.

Stage One: Dormant—Winter to Early Spring

At this stage, buds have not yet begun to swell in anticipation of breaking open. Now is the time for necessary action to prevent infestations of certain pests and diseases.

Maintenance: Throughout the Northeast and Midwest and farther south, plant bare-root, container-grown or balled-and-burlapped trees. In areas of the Midwest or the South where summer sun is intense, cover trunks with tree wrap to protect bark against sun scald. Wire mesh around trunks protects against rabbits. This is also the time to prune existing trees. Check bark carefully, inspecting loose areas where pests like to hide. Remove cocoons of codling moths.

Sanitation: Clean up and dispose of debris from under and near trees. Many diseases overwinter on fallen leaves. Remove mummified fruit, because they may be host to spores of brown rot.

Chemical: Now is the time for the most important spray of the year. Completely cover every tree with dormant-oil spray. Pick a day when the temperature will remain above 40F (5C) for 24 hours. This helps smother scale, mites, aphids and pear psylla eggs that overwinter on tree bark. Spray peaches and nectarines with lime-sulfur, sulfur, captan or benomyl fungicide to prevent peach-leaf curl.

Peach bud

Peach bud

Stage Two: Colored Bud or Pre-Pink—Early Spring

At this stage, blossom buds have not yet opened, but show about 3/4 inch of green, pink or white.

Maintenance: You can still plant new trees and prune existing stock, but don't wait any longer. After trees leaf out, you will not be able to see branches that are damaged.

Chemical: Apple trees are the only fruit that *may* need an all-purpose orchard spray. As a guide, spray only if apple scab, mites and aphids have been serious problems in your orchard in the past.

Biological: If you plan to release beneficial insects such as lady bugs or lacewings, do so now. Be aware that you must cease applying chemical sprays at this time. The poisons will kill the beneficial insects.

Plum

Stage Three: Full Bloom—Early Spring

This stage is one of nature's most glorious spectacles. Trees in full bloom fill the air with their fragrance. Bees, nature's pollinators, are doing their work, helping ensure a healthy fruit set.

Maintenance: In coastal areas of the Mid-Atlantic States, or anywhere having warm, wet spring weather, carefully inspect pear and apple trees for fireblight damage. Remove and dispose of any infected branches as soon as they are spotted.

Chemical: If brown rot has been a severe problem in prior seasons, spray peaches and nectarines now. If not, wait until petal fall. Do not spray any insecticide until *after* petal fall. If you do, you will kill bees necessary for pollination.

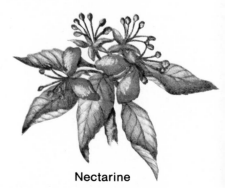

Nectarine

Stage Four: Petal Fall—Early Spring

By this time, most of the fruit has been set. Bees have pollinated blossoms, petals have fallen and tiny fruit, *fruitlets*, have formed. This is a crucial stage for pest and disease control.

Maintenance: Continue to be on the lookout for fireblight disease. Watch for signs of twig borers. Prune and dispose of infected twigs and branches.

Chemical: Dormant-oil spray during *dormant* stage, Stage One, is the most-important spray. An all-purpose orchard spray during petal fall is the second-most important spray of the season. Insects such as codling moth, leaf rollers and tiny aphids are active at this time. Eggs of other pests are also beginning to hatch. Be sure to cover every inch of tree with the spray.

Apple

Pear

Plum

Stage Five: Fruitlet—Spring
Fruitlets are beginning to develop into full-size fruit. This is another important phase of your pest-control program.
Maintenance: Keep weed growth clear of tree trunks. Apply a mulch around tree.
Chemical: Look for insects and larvae on fruitlets, new shoots and leaves. A second all-purpose orchard spray is recommended at this time.
Weather: If the season has been damp, inspect for fungal diseases such as powdery mildew, scab and others. If evident, spray with a fungicide. This spray is particularly important in coastal areas of the Atlantic and around the Great Lakes.

Peach

Stage Six: Pre-harvest—Summer and Fall
As the season progresses, fruit will grow larger and ripen. Continue to inspect trees for insect pests and diseases, particularly brown rot on peaches and nectarines.
Maintenance: Remove suckers and watersprouts. Thin fruit, gather and dispose of dropped fruit, cultivate, irrigate and weed. If you have been meticulous with your spray program, insects should be under control.
Chemical: Continue your all-purpose orchard spray program throughout the season, spraying every 10 to 14 days. As you near harvest, it is important to check the labels of the chemicals you use. With most sprays, you must wait a certain number of days after spraying before you can harvest fruit. In some cases, the label will instruct you to wait 7 days before harvesting. In others, you will be required to wait 10 to 14 days, depending on the fruit. When you pick fruit, always wash it before eating.
  If brown rot appears on peaches, nectarines and plums, spray with lime-sulfur, sulfur, benomyl or captan fungicide. This also helps to cut down on brown rot and other disease problems the following year.
Weather: Hot, dry weather in the Plains States or Mid-Atlantic areas may sunburn fruit and bark of trees. Protect branches and trunks with white latex paint. Spider mites thrive under dry, dusty conditions. Using a garden hose, direct strong sprays of water on the leaves. In coastal areas and near the Great Lakes, excessive humidity may promote fungal diseases. Be prepared to spray trees with fungicide.

Stage Seven: Leaf Fall—Fall
As leaves turn to autumn colors and drop, harvest should be complete. Trees prepare for winter by *hardening up*, gradually becoming acclimated to cold as temperatures drop.
Maintenance: Gather fallen leaves, fallen fruit and fruit remaining on trees. Bury in a compost pile. Clean area around trees so mice will not have winter cover. Examine trees carefully and remove diseased or damaged limbs.
  If you live in an area where snow accumulates on the ground, you will need to protect lower branches from hungry rabbits. Wrap branches within 18 inches of snow line with aluminum foil.
Chemical: Spray with fungicide if peach-leaf curl has been a problem during the season.

Encyclopedia of Fruit, Berries & Nuts

3

This chapter includes information on the fruit, berries and nuts that can be grown in Canada and the East, Midwest, Mid-Atlantic and areas of the upper South. The sections on individual plants will help you select the fruit and varieties suited to your needs and climate conditions.

Extensive charts of varieties are included with most of the individual fruit, berries and nuts. They provide information such as zone recommendations, time of bearing, growth habit, fruit size and color. Look closely at the column labeled Remarks. Included are the best ways to use the fruit: for eating fresh, canning, freezing or cooking. For example, some apples are best used for pies or sauce. Others are better when eaten fresh from the tree, but not for cooking.

Consult the boxed feature with each plant description for information regarding years to bearing, life expectancy, planting distance, height and spread at maturity and pollination requirements.

Gardener's Tips is an important feature included with most fruit. It contains information gleaned from years of experience from home and commercial fruit growers about picking, storing and preparing fruit.

Before you make your plant selections, realize that most fruit have varieties that bear at different times of the season: *early, midseason* or *late.* It pays in extended harvests to use these varied maturity dates to your advantage. For example, if you plant three peach trees, you could select an early bearing 'Redhaven', a midseason 'Cresthaven' and a late-bearing 'J. H. Hale'. This staggered harvesting approach can be applied to apples, apricots, nectarines, pears and European and Japanese plums.

If you live in a region that experiences adverse weather, the various maturity dates could mean the difference between failure and success. A *late-blooming* apricot may be able to succeed in a cold-climate area, where frost would destroy all the blossoms of an *early blooming* variety.

If you want to grow raspberries and strawberries, note that they are available in two basic bearing types: those that bear once during the season, and *everbearing,* which provide two crops during the year.

DWARFS AND GARDEN SPACE

Another factor that greatly influences plant selection is available garden space. Today, many residential lots are small, with little room for wide-spreading trees. Dwarf varieties are recommended for homes with small gardens. A 25-square-foot plot will accommodate nine dwarf trees, but is barely large enough to grow one standard-size tree.

Left: Apples can be grown successfully in most of the Midwest and East. These are 'Red Delicious'. Above: Spring blossoms of 'Golden Delicious' apple.

CLIMATES AND MICROCLIMATES

Apricots are among the first to bloom in spring, and are easily damaged by late frosts. It helps to understand climates and microclimates so you can select fruit adapted to your area and plant them in the best locations.

Climates exist on both large and small scales. Large-scale climates in the United States and Canada generally run in horizontal bands, largely determined by latitude. Zone 2 on the United States Department of Agriculture (USDA) map, page 64, is the most northerly zone discussed in this book. Temperatures here can drop to −50F (−45C) during winter. The *growing season,* number of days between spring frosts and fall frosts, is approximately 100 days or less.

Zone 7 is the most southerly zone covered in this book. Temperatures generally drop to 0F to 10F (−18C to −12C) during winter. The growing season is the longest, up to 230 days.

If you look closely at the USDA map, you will notice many irregularities in the horizontal pattern of climate zones. The area around Lake Erie and Lake Michigan lies in Zone 6 rather than Zone 4 or Zone 5. The waters of the lakes modify the climate. In summer, water evaporates and cools the surrounding air. In winter, water serves as a heat reservoir to warm temperatures.

A weather phenomenon common in the East, Midwest and upper South is the *ice storm.* Rain falls and freezes, covering everything with a coat of ice. The temperature is crucial in determining whether ice will form. If temperatures fall below 26F (−3C), the freezing rain usually turns to hail or snow. Temperatures between 26F and 32F (−3C to 0C) cause the rain to turn to ice. Planting in a protected, south-facing location helps lessen ice damage.

MICROCLIMATES
Elevation, exposure to sun, air drainage, fog, frost pockets, prevailing air currents, slope of land and proximity to bodies of water affect the climate of an area. These factors create small-scale climates called *microclimates.* The microclimate areas vary according to temperature extremes and length of growing season.

Microclimates range in size from an area the size of Eastern Long Island, warmed by the surrounding waters, to a garden wall with a southern exposure. Using them to the best advantage can affect which fruit you can grow successfully. The illustrations on the following pages show you how to put microclimates to work.

THE SUN AND MICROCLIMATES
The rays of the sun, called *solar radiation,* influence microclimates more than any other factor. Generally, this influence is confined to small spaces within an area.

It helps to understand some terms used in the explanation of solar radiation. They are:
- *Insolation*—The penetration of the earth's atmosphere by solar energy. This solar energy takes its form as heat or light rays (radiation).
- *Absorption*—Heat retained by any material after being struck by radiation.
- *Reflection*—Heat that bounces off any material struck by radiation.

SHORT WAVES AND LONG WAVES
The two kinds of radiation are *short wave* and *long wave.* Short-wave radiation occurs during the daylight hours. Radiation travels from the sun through the atmosphere, and is absorbed and reflected by the mate-

rials it hits. These materials include foliage, water, sides of buildings, streets and soil.

Long-wave radiation occurs after the sun has set. Short waves absorbed during daylight hours are released at night to warm the atmosphere. An example is a city street. During the day, short waves beat down on asphalt, concrete sidewalks and buildings. These materials absorb heat. During the night, the absorbed heat is slowly released to warm the surrounding area. Thus, the outdoor temperature in the city is likely to be slightly higher than the outdoor temperature in the nearby country, where there are fewer streets, sidewalks and buildings.

How can you use radiation to your advantage in growing fruit-producing plants? One of the simplest ways is to plant near the walls or sides of buildings around your property to take advantage of the extra heat. The color of the wall affects the radiation. White-colored walls *reflect* more short waves during the daytime. Fruit that require high heat to ripen—peaches, nectarines and Japanese plums—benefit by growing next to a light-colored surface. Dark-colored walls *absorb* heat in the daytime and release it slowly at night.

Often, varieties of fruit that are not recommended for an area because of cold temperatures can be grown successfully in a warm microclimate. For example, peaches not generally recommended for areas in northern Minnesota, Wisconsin, Maine, Vermont and New Hampshire have a better chance of surviving if grown against a dark wall or building with a southern exposure. Farther south, in central New England, northern Pennsylvania and other areas of Zone 5, chances of survival are even better.

A MICROCLIMATE AT WORK

A dramatic example of how a microclimate can be used is Alexander and Louisa Hargrave's vineyard in Long Island, New York. During the early 1970s, the Hargraves decided to raise *vinifera* grapes, *Vitus vinifera,* which are commonly grown in California and France. Except for an isolated instance during the 18th century, no one had ever grown vinifera grapes in the New York area. Most local experts said it could not be done.

To begin their vineyard project, they did extensive research of various climate areas in the United States. They concluded that the North Fork of Long Island, about 100 miles east of New York City, provided perfect growing conditions for their project. The area had always been agricultural. The soil was a deep, sandy loam.

Growing season of the North Fork region averages between 195 to 210 days, compared to 155 to 165 days in upstate New York. The longer season is necessary to ripen vinifera grapes.

Most important, the waters of Long Island Sound to the north and Peconic Bay to the south, both within a mile of the vineyard, modify temperatures. The thermometer rarely drops below 0F (−18C). Upstate, temperatures of −15F (−26C) which will kill vinifera vines are not uncommon.

In 1973, the Hargraves bought a potato farm and planted almost 50 acres of vinifera vines. In 1976, Hargrave Vineyard produced its first bottle of wine, deemed "excellent" by wine experts. In 1981, their Sauvignon Blanc was rated Top United States Wine at the International Food Show in New York City.

Using a Microclimate

A simple way to use a microclimate is to locate plants against a south-facing wall. Heat is accumulated during the day and released slowly at night. Overhang adds protection by radiating heat back toward plant.

Mrs. Louisa Hargrave, with harvest from her New York vineyard.

UNDERSTANDING EXPOSURE

The definition of *exposure* is the direction—east, west, north or south—that an object faces. In this case, we are interested in the exposure of your fruit plants. The following are general characteristics of each exposure.

• *Northern*—Little sunlight, the coolest exposure during the entire day.
• *Southern and western*—The most sunlight, with warm afternoon sun.
• *Eastern*—Sunlight in the morning, shade at midday and during the afternoon.

It is important to realize that the sun's exposure changes with the seasons. See the illustration below.

HOW BODIES OF WATER AFFECT CLIMATE

Oceans and lakes absorb 95% of the sunshine they receive, and release this heat slowly. This continuous release of warmth is fairly constant compared to land surfaces, which radiate faster. Because heat is released slowly, areas near bodies of water warm up later in the season compared to land surfaces. Blossoms, particularly those of early season apricots, emerge later in spring. Because they bloom later, they are less likely to be damaged by a late frost.

Areas near large bodies of water do not experience the extreme low temperatures of land areas located at the same latitude. Examples are Cape Cod, Massachusetts, the East End of Long Island and the shore area of Connecticut's Long Island Sound. Despite the northern latitude, the climate is tempered by the ocean. In these areas, climate is similar to that of Virginia and western North Carolina, far to the south.

THERMAL BELTS

The word *thermal* refers to heat. A *thermal belt* is an area where air is warmer than surrounding areas. Cold air is like water: It flows down hillsides, seeking the path of least resistance. If you have slopes or hills on your property, the lowest areas will be the coldest. An area on a hillside, about 100 feet above low ground, is substantially warmer than the lower area.

If you have hilly property, you may want to take advantage of thermal belts. If possible, plant trees in the upper areas on south-facing slopes rather than on valley floors.

If your property is in a valley, certain measures should be taken to avoid frost damage. As mentioned, cold air flows down slopes and hillsides. If it meets a solid, impenetrable object, it will dam up behind it, creating a *frost pocket*. To avoid this, provide good air drainage. Open up enclosed low spots so that cold air can flow out.

WIND AS A CLIMATE FACTOR

In some regions, particularly along the Atlantic Coast, the Plains States and areas along the Great Lakes, wind has a great influence on climate, lowering the air temperature. Almost everyone is familiar with the wind-chill factor included in the winter weather report each evening. The velocity of the wind can also be damaging, snapping tree limbs, damaging fruit and dessicating foliage.

If you live in an area subject to damaging winds, take steps to protect your fruit plants. Windbreaks that *diffuse* and *slow* the wind rather than *block* it are recommended. A solid wall will block the wind for a short dis-

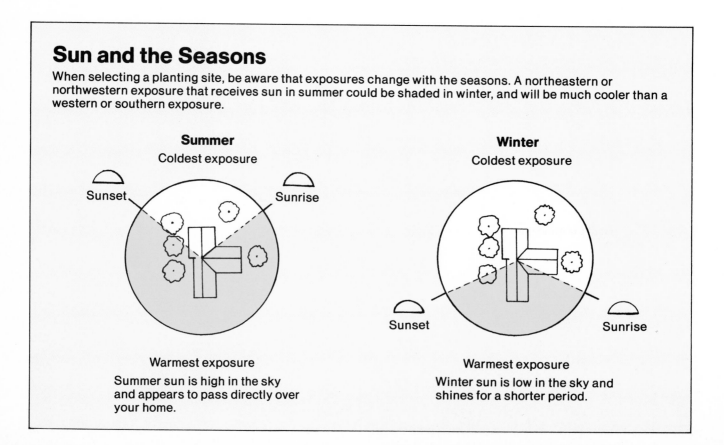

Sun and the Seasons

When selecting a planting site, be aware that exposures change with the seasons. A northeastern or northwestern exposure that receives sun in summer could be shaded in winter, and will be much cooler than a western or southern exposure.

Summer
Coldest exposure

Sunset   Sunrise

Warmest exposure
Summer sun is high in the sky and appears to pass directly over your home.

Winter
Coldest exposure

Sunset   Sunrise

Warmest exposure
Winter sun is low in the sky and shines for a shorter period.

tance, deflecting it upward. But after the wind passes over the wall, it comes down to earth with even greater force.

First, locate the direction of prevalent winds. During winter, most winds blow consistently from the same direction. Position the windbreak perpendicular to the wind. A windbreak can be man-made, such as lattice or fencing, but plantings of dense, evergreen trees and hedges are best. As a guide, the distance from the windbreak to the area where fruit plants are located should be *two to three times* the height of the windbreak. However, an area equal to 10 times the height of the break will be somewhat sheltered from wind.

PROTECTING PLANTS FROM COLD DAMAGE

All plants have an inherent tolerance of cold. If winter temperatures fall below these levels, roots will be damaged and plants will die. Blossom buds are first to be damaged, then wood. Some fruit trees are naturally more cold-hardy than others. Certain *varieties* of individual fruit are better able to withstand cold temperatures in winter.

Generally, damage to plant roots occurs as follows:
- Apricots, nectarines, peaches and Japanese plums: −15F (−26C).
- Pears, European plums, sweet cherries and quince: −20F (−29C).
- Apples and sour cherries: −30F (-34C).

Nature provides some protection in the form of heavy snow cover. Snow insulates plants from cold temperatures. Moist clay soil provides protection as well, because cold does not penetrate as easily as it does dry, sandy soil. You can provide further protection by mulching heavily with boughs from evergreens or leaves secured with chickenwire. Or plant grass as a cover crop around your trees.

Apricots, nectarines, peaches, sweet cherries and Japanese plums are not normally recommended in Zones 2 to 5. The subzero temperatures in winter can kill trees. But a more common problem is late-spring frosts, which kill the blossoms, thus eliminating crops.

Delaying Spring Bloom to Avoid Frost Damage—You can take steps to delay spring blooming. By slowing the bloom process, blossoms emerge after the last damaging frost has passed. The more blossoms that survive, the higher the potential for fruit crops.

If possible, plant next to dark, south-facing walls. They radiate heat at night to prevent blossom kill. Sprinkle trees with water each day to cool blossom buds, although this practice may decrease fruit set. If a late frost is predicted, water the afternoon before. The wet soil absorbs more heat than dry soil. This heat is released during the night, raising temperatures, perhaps enough to save the blossoms.

Slopes and Planting Sites

If your property is located in a hilly area, check out the contour of the land before you select a planting location. Cold air follows the path of least resistance, flowing down slopes like water, damming up behind obstacles to create cold pockets. In this site, the best planting location is the warm, south-facing slope that allows cold air to drain away.

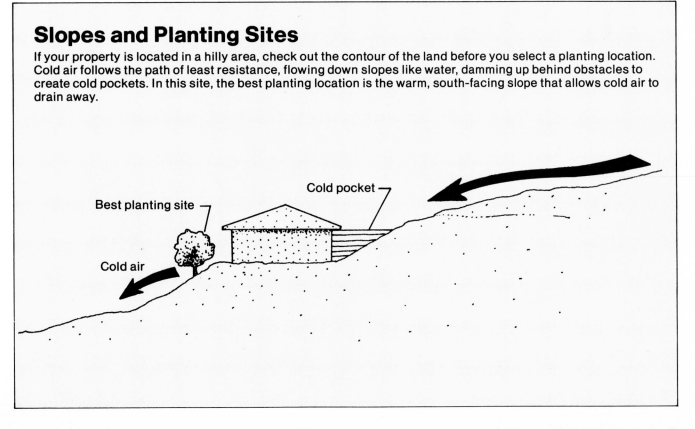

Best planting site

Cold pocket

Cold air

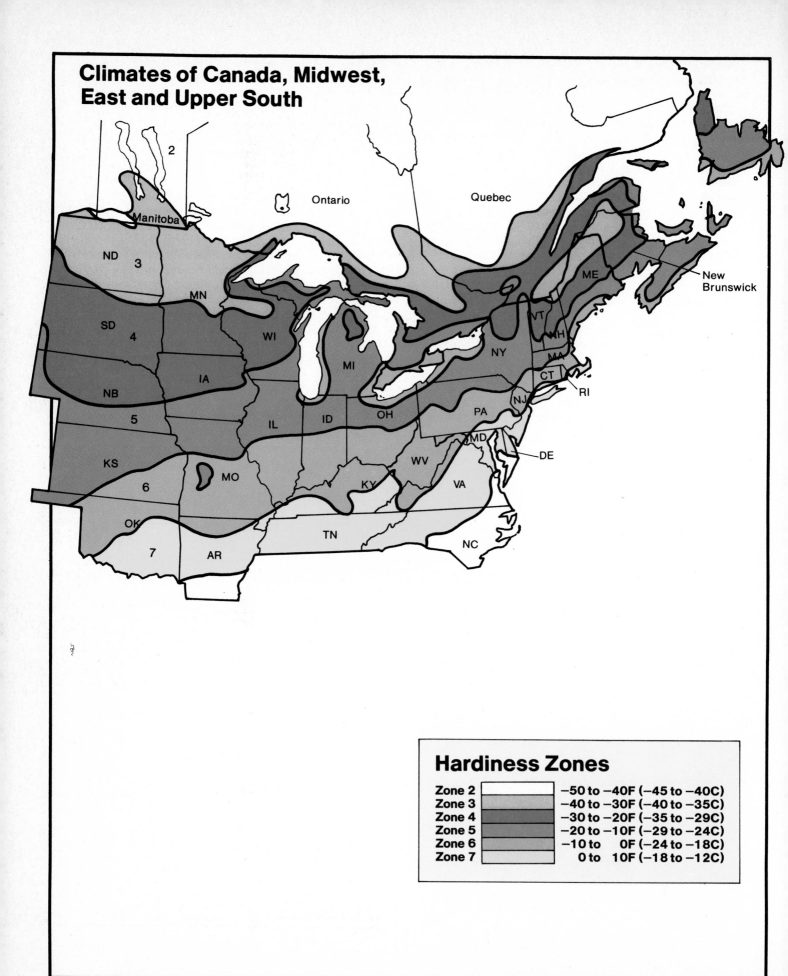

Climates of Canada, Midwest, East and Upper South

Hardiness Zones

Zone 2		−50 to −40F (−45 to −40C)
Zone 3		−40 to −30F (−40 to −35C)
Zone 4		−30 to −20F (−35 to −29C)
Zone 5		−20 to −10F (−29 to −24C)
Zone 6		−10 to 0F (−24 to −18C)
Zone 7		0 to 10F (−18 to −12C)

Looking at the map on page 64, you will see the United States Department of Agriculture (USDA) has divided the U.S. and Canada into plant-hardiness zones. These zones are determined by the approximate ranges of average, annual, minimum temperatures. In this book we are concerned with Zones 2 through 7.

In the Midwest and East, rainfall is fairly consistent. We do not have the extremes of the dry deserts of the Southwest, or the extremely wet, humid conditions in the Pacific Northwest.

Elevation extremes do not exist in the East and Midwest as compared to the West. Looking at the map, you will notice that the minimum temperature range in most of the Appalachian Mountain region is consistent with the latitude of the area. Only in the extreme northern areas of New England and in Minnesota does elevation seriously affect temperatures.

Atlantic coastal regions and areas immediately surrounding the Great Lakes are generally warmer than adjacent areas in the same latitude. This is because large bodies of water have a warming effect on climate. See page 62.

Other factors such as microclimates, cold-air pockets and late frosts can have a great effect on your gardening success. But generally speaking, annual *minimum temperature* is your best guide to plant adaptation. Keep this foremost in your mind when selecting fruit plants.

Many mail-order nursery catalogs carry zone-hardiness recommendations. They usually appear at the end of a fruit-variety description. For example, a description of a particular variety of apricot may read "Hardy from Zones 6 to 8." If you live in Zone 5, be wary of ordering this variety, unless experience has shown that the plant will be successful in your area. Local advice from experienced fruit gardeners is the best recommendation of all.

ZONE 2
This is the most northerly zone of concern in this book. It runs across Newfoundland, Quebec, Ontario and Manitoba. A small area of northern Minnesota is included. Temperatures drop to −40F to −50F (−40C to −45C). Only the most cold-hardy fruit should be planted. Even then, fruit production may be sporadic at best.

Apples and pears may bear every five years or so, depending on use of existing microclimates or harshness of winter weather. Sweet cherries, peaches, nectarines, plums, apricots and quince do not survive. Strawberries, early blueberries and raspberries are sometimes successful if substantial winter protection is provided. Sour cherries bear occasionally.

ZONE 3
This zone includes the far northern Green and White Mountain country of New England, parts of central Newfoundland, southern Quebec, Ontario and Manitoba, northern Wisconsin and Minnesota and most of North Dakota. Minimum temperatures range from −30F to −40F (−35C to −40C).

As with Zone 2, only the most cold-hardy varieties should be planted. Cold-hardy apples and pears may bear every other year.

Cold-hardy apples such as 'Hazan', 'Red Duchess', 'Dakota' and 'Lakeland', and cold-hardy plums such as 'Tecumseh', 'Redcoat' and 'Toka' are recommended.

Hardy pears such as 'Seckel' and Manchurian apricots can be planted, but results are chancy. Currants and gooseberries are cold-hardy in some of the warmer areas of the zone—those regions closest to Zone 4. The recommended grape cultivar is 'Beta'. Raspberries, early blueberries and some strawberries can be grown if substantial winter protection is provided.

Follow the same variety recommendations in northern New England and Canada.

ZONE 4
Zone 4 includes central New England, the Adirondack Mountains in New York, the St. Lawrence River Valley, areas adjacent to the northern shores of the Great Lakes and parts of Wisconsin, Michigan, southern Minnesota, northern Iowa, Nebraska and all of South Dakota. Minimum temperatures range from −20F to −30F (−29C to −35C) during the winter.

A few more options are available and practical to fruit growers in this zone, as compared to Zones 2 and 3. But only the most cold-hardy fruit, are recommended.

You may succeed with apples, pears, American plums, red and black raspberries, strawberries, currants, gooseberries and sour cherries. Peaches, nectarines, sweet cherries, European plums, Japanese plums and blackberries generally do not survive.

In eastern South Dakota, apricots should be planted only on a trial basis. They do not survive in central or western areas of the state. They may survive in northeastern Nebraska, northern Iowa and near the Great Lakes, if planted in a favorable microclimate.

ZONE 5
Zone 5 runs from east to west across Canada and the United States. Most of Nova Scotia, Newfoundland, southern Ontario and the northern parts of New York, Pennsylvania, Ohio, Indiana, Illinois and Missouri are located here. Temperatures dip to −10F to −20F (−24C to −29C). Many apples, pears, European plums and sour cherries are cold-hardy through most of this zone. Most bush and bramble fruit can be grown here as well. Blackberries need winter protection to be grown successfully.

Generally, Japanese plums, apricots, nectarines, peaches and sweet cherries are not recommended for planting. In some parts of central Illinois and Indiana, nectarines and peaches may survive. If you live in this area, select only the most cold-hardy varieties and plant in a sheltered location. See variety charts on pages 94 to 99 for further information on these fruit.

Because apricots bloom early in the spring, only cold-hardy varieties such as 'Alfred', 'Goldcot' and 'Veecot' are recommended. Even then, results may be chancy. If you live near the coast or another large body of water, you may have success with them.

Temperatures in the Berkshire Mountains of Massachusetts and northwestern Connecticut, the "icebox" district of northwestern New Jersey, and areas of the Appalachian Mountains in Pennsylvania and New York State, often fall below −15F (−26C). Peach and nectarine crops usually fail if temperatures drop this low. If temperatures fall much further, to −20F (−29C), trees usually die. In areas near water or near protected mountain foothills, the hardiest varieties may survive.

Fruit and nuts least likely to survive in sections of Kansas and Missouri that are located in Zone 5 are blueberry, apricot, sweet cherry and European filbert. Select the most cold-hardy peaches, nectarines and Japanese plums for these areas.

ZONE 6
Zone 6 has a minimum winter temperature range of −10F to 0F (−24C to −18C). Climate is favorable for growing most apples, pears, quince, European plums, sour cherries and small fruit. Blackberries are an exception, but they can be grown with some winter protection.

Peaches, nectarines, apricots and Japanese plums generally grow well here. Late frosts are always a possibility, so it is wise to select cold-hardy varieties of these fruit. Sweet cherries have uneven success in this zone, but are worth a try.

In New York, climatic conditions along Lake Ontario, the Finger Lakes and the Hudson River Valley are favorable for growing peaches and nectarines. However, during a particularly severe winter or if a late-spring frost occurs, you can expect substantial crop loss. Be safe and plant cold-hardy peaches such as 'Oriole', 'Reliance' and 'Lexington' in a favorable microclimate. Pears also do well in this area.

These same conditions are true for southern Pennsylvania, West Virginia, eastern Kentucky and southern sections of Ohio, Indiana, Illinois and Missouri, with the exceptions of the Ozark Mountain region, southern Kansas and northern Oklahoma. In southern Kansas, apricot blossoms are frequently killed by frost. Try 'Moorpark', 'Goldcot', 'Manchu' or 'Superb'. Blossoms of Japanese plums can also be damaged by late frost. Plant cold-hardy varieties such as 'Methley' or 'Ozark Premier'.

In northern Oklahoma, peach production can be erratic due to winter freezes, spring frosts and summer drought. 'Redskin' is recommended over 'Elberta', because it is more cold-hardy and can withstand some drought. Drought conditions can cause some apple varieties to drop their fruit prematurely. 'Lodi', 'Jonathan' and 'Golden Delicious' are recommended.

In Missouri, sweet cherries are not recommended. Plant sour cherries instead. Apricots are generally not successful. Pears are often plagued by fireblight disease. 'Seckel', 'Maxine', 'Duchess' and 'Keiffer' are resistant varieties.

In Kentucky, 'Mutsu' apples are particularly susceptible to bacterial blight. Fireblight is a serious problem here. Do not plant 'Bartlett' or 'Clapp's Favorite' pears, which are highly susceptible to the disease. Plant fireblight-resistant varieties only.

Although reliably cold-hardy, 'Reliance' peach attains poor flavor in Zone 6 in areas of Pennsylvania,

West Virginia, Ohio, Kentucky and westward.

'Darrow' is the only variety of blackberry recommended for planting in Zone 6 in Connecticut. Most other varieties require winter protection.

In southern Ohio, Indiana and Illinois, blossoms of apricots are frequently killed by frost. Trees bloom too early in the spring. If you want to grow apricots, 'Earli-Orange' and 'Superb' are recommended. Because of frost, expect only occasional crops of sweet cherries and Japanese plums.

In New Jersey, apricots are not recommended. Spring blossoms are commonly killed by frost. Pollination is poor, reducing fruit set. There is also a severe canker problem in the area. Birds can be a severe nuisance in this zone. Cherries are not recommended unless you cover fruit with netting.

Special mention should be made of the areas along the southern shores of Lake Michigan, Lake Erie and Lake Ontario. Despite the fact that this latitude is generally in Zone 5, the waters of the lakes temper the climate, making it possible to grow peaches, nectarines and Japanese plums.

ZONE 7
All fruit discussed in this book can be grown in Zone 7, the mildest zone. Winter temperatures usually dip to 0F to 10F (−18C to −12C).

A few, isolated exceptions to fruit adaptability exist. Apricots are not recommended for Maryland, Delaware or southern New Jersey. In Maryland, sweet cherries and sour cherries are satisfactory only in counties that border Pennsylvania.

In Tennessee, plant European plums, Japanese plums and apricots in protected sites to guard against late frosts, which often kill blossoms. Fireblight is a major problem here, so plant pear varieties that are disease resistant.

In Oklahoma, peach and nectarine production is sporadic because of winter freezes, spring frosts or summer drought. Oklahoma State University has developed 'Golden Rod' peach for these tough local conditions. Avoid planting late-ripening varieties because of summer drought.

In western Virginia and North Carolina, as well as in the mountain country of South Carolina, Georgia and Alabama, recommended peaches are 'Jerseyland' and 'Jersey Queen'. Fireblight is a problem, so select pear varieties that are resistant. Red raspberries thrive in upland areas of these states, but they do not thrive near the coast.

The northern and southern shores and the East End of Long Island, Cape Cod, Nantucket and Martha's Vineyard in Massachusetts, Block Island in Rhode Island and the western Long Island Sound shore of Connecticut are included in Zone 7. Their proximity to the Atlantic Ocean has a tempering effect on the climate. Grown in a sheltered location, camellias and pecans are known to flourish in these areas.

If you are interested in growing fruit in the western United States and western Canada, refer to the HPBook, *Western Fruit, Berries and Nuts,* by Lance Walheim and Robert L. Stebbins.

Climate Statistics

	Inches Annual Rain	Inches Rain July/Aug.	July % Sunshine	Dec. % Sunshine	July Days Above 90F	Mean Date Last 32F	Mean Date First 32F	Mean Days Freeze-Free Period
Zone 3								
Bismarck, ND	16	4.2	76	47	8	5/11	9/24	136
Duluth, MN	30	7.5	67	39	1	5/22	9/24	125
Fargo, ND	20	6.0	71	43	5	5/13	9/27	137
Williston, ND	14	3.6	75	47	8	5/14	9/23	132
Zone 4								
Burlington, VT	33	7.2	65	33	3	5/8	10/3	148
Greenville, ME	43	10.0	60	48	0	5/27	9/30	116
La Crosse, WI	29	6.5	69	46	6	5/1	10/8	161
Minneapolis, MN	26	6.7	71	40	7	4/30	10/13	166
Rapid City, SD	17	3.6	72	54	11	5/7	10/4	150
St. Cloud, MN	27	7.1	72	48	4	5/9	9/29	144
Sioux City, IA	26	6.2	76	51	10	4/28	10/12	167
Sioux Falls, SD	25	5.8	74	51	12	5/5	10/3	152
Zone 5								
Albany, NY	33	6.0	63	38	4	4/27	10/13	169
Akron-Canton, OH	35	6.5	62	31	11	4/29	10/20	173
Binghamton, NY	37	7.4	65	27	1	5/4	10/6	154
Concord, NH	36	6.0	62	47	5	5/11	9/30	142
Des Moines, IA	31	6.6	72	45	10	4/20	10/19	183
Dodge City, KS	21	5.7	79	65	22	4/22	10/24	184
Dubuque, IA	40	8.3	70	46	4	4/19	10/19	184
Grand Island, NB	23	5.5	78	60	18	4/29	10/6	160
Grand Rapids, MI	32	5.6	66	24	5	4/25	10/27	185
Lincoln, NB	29	6.9	74	52	18	4/20	10/17	180
Madison, WI	30	6.9	69	39	5	4/26	10/19	177
Marquette, MI	31	6.1	67	28	2	5/14	10/17	156
Milwaukee, WI	29	6.1	71	38	4	4/20	10/25	188
North Platte, NB	20	5.0	74	60	12	4/30	10/7	160
Peoria, IL	35	6.8	69	40	7	4/22	10/16	177
Pittsburgh, PA	36	6.9	53	23	6	4/20	10/23	187
South Bend, IN	36	6.9	72	37	4	5/3	10/16	165
Syracuse, NY	36	6.6	65	25	3	4/30	10/15	168
Zone 6								
Boston, MA	43	6.2	66	52	5	4/16	10/25	192
Buffalo, NY	36	6.5	69	27	1	4/30	10/25	179
Cairo, IL	47	6.7	75	45	17	3/23	11/11	233
Charleston, WV	41	8.1	60	39	7	4/18	10/28	193
Cincinnati, OH	40	7.0	68	38	10	4/15	10/25	192
Cleveland, OH	35	6.4	68	26	3	4/21	11/2	195
Columbia, MO	37	7.0	75	46	16	4/9	10/24	198
Detroit, MI	31	6.0	70	32	6	4/23	10/23	181
Evansville, IN	42	6.7	76	41	15	4/2	11/4	216
Harrisburg, PA	36	6.9	68	44	9	4/10	10/28	201
Hartford, CT	43	7.3	62	48	8	4/22	10/19	180
Indianapolis, IN	39	6.5	70	40	6	4/17	10/27	193
Kansas City, MO	37	8.2	82	59	19	4/5	10/31	210
Lexington, KY	44	8.2	70	42	6	4/13	10/28	198
Louisville, KY	43	6.7	66	40	9	4/1	11/7	220
Portland, ME	41	5.2	64	53	2	4/29	10/15	169
Providence, RI	43	6.7	60	51	3	4/13	10/27	197
Rochester, NY	31	5.8	69	31	4	4/28	10/21	176
St. Louis, MO	36	6.6	72	43	14	4/2	11/8	220
Springfield, IL	35	8.5	73	42	10	4/8	10/30	205
Topeka, KS	35	8.4	69	51	15	4/9	10/26	200
Wichita, KS	31	7.4	74	58	21	4/5	11/1	210
Zone 7								
Annapolis, MD	39	8.0	66	51	18	3/4	11/5	225
Asheville, NC	48	9.4	60	57	3	4/12	10/24	195
Baltimore, MD	40	8.3	65	48	11	3/28	11/17	234
Chattanooga, TN	52	8.3	61	42	16	3/26	11/10	229
Knoxville, TN	46	7.9	61	38	8	3/31	11/6	220
Little Rock, AR	49	6.4	71	48	22	3/16	11/15	244
Lynchburg, VA	38	8.1	62	52	7	4/6	10/27	205
Memphis, TN	49	6.9	73	50	21	3/20	11/12	237
New York City, NY	40	7.7	65	49	6	4/7	11/12	219
Philadelphia, PA	40	8.2	63	49	7	3/30	11/17	232
Roanoke, VA	39	7.9	61	41	9	4/20	10/24	187
Trenton, NJ	40	8.9	65	48	7	4/8	11/5	211
Tulsa, OK	37	6.4	72	54	23	3/31	11/2	216
Washington, DC	39	8.8	63	47	13	4/10	10/28	200

TREE FRUIT

'Redhaven' peach.

Zone Adaptation

	Zone 3	Zone 4	Zone 5	Zone 6	Zone 7
Apple	●*	●	●	●	●
Apricot		●*	●	●	●
Cherry, Sour		●*	●	●	●
Cherry, Sweet			●	●	●
Fig			●**	●**	●**
Nectarine			●	●	●
Peach			●	●	●
Pear		●*	●	●	●
Plum, European		●*	●	●	●
Plum, Japanese			●	●	●
Quince		●*	●	●	●

* See variety chart for cold-hardy varieties for this zone.
** Requires substantial winter protection.

'Winesap' apple.

Apple

No question about it, apple is the "king" of fruit. Apples can be grown in every section of the United States and Canada discussed in this book. In fact, apples are probably the most widely grown fruit in the world.

A wide range of apple varieties are available to the home fruit gardener. To make the selection process easier, an extensive variety chart is included later in this section. The chart includes old standbys, some recently developed hybrids and imports such as 'Granny Smith' from New Zealand and 'Mutsu' from Japan. Also included is a comprehensive chart of "old-fashioned" apple varieties, some of which have been in cultivation for centuries. These are rarely available in markets, but can often be obtained from growers in your area and through mail-order sources. If space allows, they are well worth your consideration.

When selecting varieties for your home orchard, you will need at least two different varieties for *cross-pollination*. If space is limited, you can graft other varieties to your tree to ensure pollination. See Propagation, pages 34 to 44.

In the southern areas of Zone 7, where temperatures are moderate, be sure to select apples that have a low *chilling requirement*. Some fruit, particularly apples, require a certain number of hours when temperatures

are below 45F (7C). The cold temperatures are necessary to bring trees out of their resting stage. See variety charts for recommendations.

SIZE CONTROL

A number of methods can be used to keep apple trees manageable in size. Dwarfing rootstocks produce dwarf trees. Genetic dwarfs or spur-type trees also limit tree size. Pruning will keep standard-size trees under control. See Growing Dwarf Trees, pages 45 and 46.

If space is at a premium in your garden, consider planting dwarf trees. Because of higher yields for space required, commercial growers are planting dwarfs instead of standard-size varieties. Dwarf stock is a little more expensive to buy, and some varieties require supports. But the advantages far outweigh the disadvantages.

In addition, dwarf trees can be trained to espalier patterns, used as garden dividers, screens and hedges or trained along a fence or wire. They are also well suited to containers.

POLLINATION

A few apple varieties set adequate fruit without a pollinator nearby. However, most require another, different variety for cross-pollination. Early ripening varieties usually bloom the same time as other early ripening varieties. Midseason varieties bloom with other midseason varieties. Many have overlapping bloom periods. Generally, if you plant three apple varieties, your trees will cross-pollinate.

Some varieties are not good pollinators. They do not transfer pollen well. These include 'Baldwin', 'Gravenstein', 'Mutsu', 'Rhode Island Greening', 'Spigold', 'Winesap', 'Stayman', 'Blaxstayman' and 'Staymanred'. To be safe, plant two other different varieties to ensure cross-pollination.

If you live where apples are commonly grown, you will usually have no problem with cross-pollination. Bees from nearby orchards will pollinate your trees.

If you do not have space for three or more trees, you can graft several varieties to one apple tree. This way a single tree provides its own cross-pollination.

Apple	Standard	Dwarf
Height at maturity (feet)		
Unpruned	40	*
Pruned	20	*
Spread at maturity with no competition (feet)	30-40	*
Recommended planting distance (feet)	20-40	10-16
Years to reach bearing age	4-8	3-4
Life expectancy (years)	60	60
Chilling requirement (hours)	900-1,000	900-1,000
Pollinator required	See text	
Good for espalier	Yes	Yes
Good for containers	No	Yes

*Various-size trees are available with the use of Malling rootstocks. Spur types and genetic dwarfs are also available.

Apple orchard in bloom.

Another method to provide for pollination is to cut several branches from another apple tree, and place them in a pail of water underneath your tree. The bees will visit branches in the pail and in the tree, cross-pollinating the flowers.

PRUNING
Most apple trees grafted to M. 27, M. 9, M. 26, and M. 7, as well as M.M. 106 rootstock, dwarf or semidwarf trees, should be trained as central leaders. See page 30. The natural growth habit of these trees is toward a central-leader form. Trained in this manner, they become established and bear sooner. In addition, trees grown close together do not shade adjacent limbs when trained in the same manner. Thinning, pruning, spraying and harvesting chores are easier when trees are trained this way.

Some apple varieties have especially vigorous growth habits, such as 'Golden Delicious' and its many offspring. Because of the tree's vigorous growth, it is best to train these trees to a multileader system. Central-leader training results in trees too tall to care for easily. When 'Golden Delicious' is grafted to M. 7 or M.M. 106 rootstock, the result is a semidwarf tree.

Some *tip-bearing* varieties send out long shoots. These bear fruit on the previous-season's growth as well as on some spurs. Many of these long shoots will not bear fruit, and should be *headed,* or pruned back. This will force branching and cause production of more bearing wood. 'Tydeman's Red' and 'Granny Smith' are tip-bearing varieties.

PRUNING BEARING TREES
Late March to early April is the best time to prune bearing trees in the Northwest and Midwest. Early to mid-March is the proper time farther south.

Spur Types—Many spur-type apple trees are now offered by mail-order nurseries. These are also called *sports* or *mutations.* They are presumed to be caused by a naturally occurring gene or chromosome change. 'Starkrimson Delicious' is one example.

Spur types produce fewer branches and limbs than non-spur trees, resulting in a somewhat smaller tree. Little annual pruning of limbs is necessary. At the same time, spur types tend to produce more fruit than a tree dwarfed by rootstock. Occasionally, too many fruit are produced. As a guide, remove about 10% of the spurs to ensure larger and finer-quality fruit. Eventually, usually after about eight years, spurs cease to bear fruit. They must be removed to allow for new spur growth. The best way to do this is to remove 1 out of every 10 spurs each spring.

Tip-Bearing Types—'Tydeman's Red', 'Rome Beauty' and 'Granny Smith' bear fruit on the end of shoots that grew the previous year, as well as on spurs. During the dormant season, remove some spurs and several of the fine shoots.

Tall Trees—Heading cuts are the only way to reduce the height of a tree. This can be tricky to do correctly. Never remove all of the tall branches in one season. Instead, do it over a period of three years, removing one or two branches each year when the tree is dormant. Most trees send up tall shoots to replace those re-

Gallery of Apples

'Cortland'

'Empire'

'Golden Delicious'

'Jerseymac'

'Macoun'

'Niagara'

'Red Delicious'

'Tydeman's Red'

'Winesap'

Late-afternoon light illuminates apples on tree in Connecticut orchard.

moved. These must be *headed* each spring. By reducing the size gradually over a period of years, you avoid disturbing the tree's natural balance of growth. If this balance is disturbed, *bitter pit,* a small indentation at the bottom of apples, may occur, causing fruit to be bitter. Should your fruit develop bitter pit, remove the most vigorous shoots, leaving weaker ones. The best time to do this is at the end of summer.

As with all fruit trees, prune dead, diseased and crossing branches each year. Remove root suckers and vertically growing watersprouts.

Old, Neglected Trees—This is best done as a three-year project. Do not prune an old tree severely in one year. First, remove all dead wood. Each succeeding year, remove several of the outer and upper limbs. This causes the tree to produce new, lower, inner wood, which will eventually bear fruit. Thin shoots. As new shoots grow, select strong shoots growing in a desirable location on the tree. Train these as you would a young tree.

Each year, feed the tree thoroughly with an all-purpose fertilizer. See Pruning, page 28, for more information on revitalizing old, neglected trees.

THINNING FRUIT
To produce large, quality fruit it is often necessary to *thin* your crop. Mother Nature's purpose in producing fruit is to produce seeds to create new apple trees, not quality fruit for your table. By selectively removing fruit when they are small and numerous, the remaining crop receives more energy from the tree, with more room to develop.

In the Northeast and Midwest, *June drop,* a natural dropping of fruitlets from the tree, is nature's way of thinning fruit. Farther south, this drop occurs in May. After June drop, thin remaining apples to about 8 inches apart. Many people are reluctant to thin, but if you don't, the following may occur.
• Fruit are small and of poor quality.
• Branches become so heavy with fruit they split or break off the tree.
• Trees may bear *biennially,* that is, bear fruit every other year.

The most important thing about thinning is how much fruit remains on the tree, not how much you remove. Generally, you will probably have to remove more than what will remain on the tree. Thin fruit when it is about the size of your thumbnail. When thinning, do not remove spurs. Thin all clusters to one fruit.

An exception to additional thinning after June drop is 'McIntosh'. If trees are pruned properly, nature's June drop usually takes care of thinning requirements. 'Yellow Transparent', 'Golden Delicious' and 'Wealthy' tend to overproduce. They must be thinned severely or trees will be short-lived.

Kids and apples seem to go together. Red and yellow varieties in galvanized tub create traditional scene.

Harvest Periods of Apple Varieties
Average picking dates for northeast Missouri.

Variety	July	Aug.	Sept.	Oct.
'Yellow Transparent'	▓			
'Lodi'	▓			
'Vista Bella'	▓			
'Jerseymac'		▓		
'Niagara'		▓		
'Paulared'		▓		
'Gravenstein'		▓		
'Akane'		▓		
'Tydeman's Red'		▓		
'Burgundy'		▓		
'Prima'		▓		
'Jonamac'		▓		
'State Fair'		▓		
'Priscilla'		▓		
'Summerland McIntosh'		▓		
'McIntosh'			▓	
'Jonathan'			▓	
'Hazen'			▓	
'Empire'			▓	
'Red Delicious'			▓	
'Sweet Sixteen'			▓	
'Winter Banana'			▓	
'Golden Delicious'			▓	
'Melrose'			▓	
'Gloster'			▓	
'Idared'			▓	
'Spigold'			▓	
'Keepsake'			▓	
'Jonagold'			▓	
'Regent'			▓	
'Winesap'			▓	
'Stark Blushing Golden'			▓	
'Mutsu'				▓
'Nittany'				▓
'Stayman'				▓
'Cortland'				▓
'Spartan'				▓
'Red Baron'				▓
'Macoun'				▓
'Honeygold'				▓
'Rome Beauty'				▓
'Granny Smith'				▓

HARVESTING AND STORAGE

For the majority of gardeners, harvesting your crop is what growing fruit is all about. Knowing the best time to pick is probably the most important phase of your annual program. After all, one of the great advantages in growing your own is picking tree-ripened fruit superior in quality to commercial versions.

Most people squeeze fruit to see if it is ripe. Do not do this, or you will bruise fruit. Pick by twisting the apple upward with a turning motion. Be careful not to damage the spur.

There are a number of ways to tell when apples are ripe.

Touch—When there is a waxy coat on the skin. This is the same wax that gives an apple its high gloss when polished.

Seeds—When seeds turn brown. They are white in unripe fruit.

Color—When apples change to mature color. Green to yellow for yellow apples. Dull-green undercolor to bright yellow and red for red apples.

Taste—This is your best indicator. Pick an apple and bite into it. When it is medium soft, juicy, tasty and sweet, it is ripe. If it is sour and brittle, it is not.

If you plan to store part of your apple crop, harvest the fruit before it is completely ripe. Store in a cool location such as a root cellar, storage shed or garage. Keep apples away from other fruit and vegetables be-cause they may pick up foreign tastes and odors. Put in boxes, and cover, or place in plastic bags and seal. Check periodically to see if any are rotting. One rotten apple can spoil the entire larder.

Apples also store well in plastic bags in the refrigerator at about 32F to 34F (0C to 1C). Many apples, particularly late-ripening varieties, can be stored this way until the following April or May. These include 'Golden Delicious', 'Rome', 'Mutsu', 'Idared' 'Empire' and 'Melrose'. Out-of-hand eating quality can deteriorate somewhat by that time, but apples can still be used for pies or applesauce.

APPLE CIDER

When harvest time arrives, you may have more apples than you can possibly use. One way to make use of them is to make apple cider. You will need a cider press. They are available ready-made or as kits from many mail-order companies. Occasionally, old presses turn up at auctions or yard sales.

Cider can be consumed as soon as you press it, and can also be frozen. If you allow it to stand at room temperature, it will turn into *applejack,* an alcoholic beverage. After several months, it turns to cider vinegar, useful in cooking.

The best cider is a blend of three or four different apples with different taste characteristics. The United States Department of Agriculture, Farmer's Bulletin No. 2125, *Making and Preserving Apple Cider,* suggests selecting one variety from each of the following groups.

Sweet Group—'Baldwin', 'Hubbardston Nonesuch', 'Rome Beauty', 'Stark', 'Red Delicious', 'Grimes' and 'Cortland'.

Mildly Acid to Slightly Tart Group—'Winesap', 'Stayman', 'Jonathan', 'Northern Spy', 'York Imperial', 'Wealthy', 'Rhode Island Greening' and 'Newtown Pippin'.

Aromatic Group—'Red Delicious', 'Golden Delicious', 'Winter Banana', 'Ribston' and 'McIntosh'.

Astringent Group—'Florence Hibernal', 'Red Siberian' (crab), 'Transcendant' (crab) and 'Martha'.

Many apple combinations make excellent cider. Experiment with different blends to see what works best for you.

PESTS AND DISEASES

Apples are popular hosts for many pests and diseases. However, if you spray with dormant oil in late March to early April in the Northeast and Midwest, slightly earlier farther south, problems should be minimal. Spraying with all-purpose orchard spray after petal drop and at the fruitlet stage reduces potential problems.

The codling moth is perhaps the most common insect pest to attack apples. It is a brownish-gray moth with a wingspread of less than 1 inch. It lays tiny white eggs on leaves. These eggs hatch into pink worms, which burrow and feed on apples for three weeks, then move on. Control with an all-purpose spray.

Scab and powdery mildew are fungi that can be controlled with an all-purpose spray. Some varieties are resistant to scab. They are 'Liberty', 'Priscilla', 'Prima', 'Redfree' and 'Sir Prize'.

Aphids, leaf rollers and apple maggots are other prominent pests. See pages 52 to 55 for control guidelines.

Crabapple fruit.

Crabapple

An entire species of apples, called *crabapple,* is available to the home orchardist. Generally, any apple smaller than 2 inches in diameter is considered a crabapple. Many crabapple cultivars are used exclusively as ornamentals. Their spring blossoms are strikingly beautiful. Many do not produce fruit.

A number of crabapples have beautiful displays of spring flowers, in addition to delicious fruit. The fruit are used for making tasty jellies and for pickling.

Varieties adapted to the warmer regions of Zones 2 and 3 include 'Dolgo', 'Osman' and 'Red Siberian'. 'Chestnut', 'Florence', 'Hyslop', 'Montreal Beauty', 'Transcendant', 'Whitney' and 'Young America' do well in Zones 4 to 7.

'Barbara Ann', 'Katharine', 'Profusion' and 'Siberian Crab' are prized for their ornamental value.

GARDENER'S TIPS

● Apples most commonly recommended and with the widest adaptation are 'Golden Delicious', 'Gravenstein', 'Lodi', 'Delicious', 'Rome Beauty', 'McIntosh', 'Winesap' and 'Jonathan'.

● Dual-purpose apples, those recommended for both eating and baking, include 'Gravenstein', 'Newtown', 'Melrose', 'Cortland', 'Winesap', 'Stayman Winesap', 'Jonagold', 'Mutsu' and 'Golden Delicious'.

● Apples stored over the winter and into spring develop a *caramelized* flavor, a rich, heady taste, retaining most of the apple essence. At this stage they can be used to make superior deep-dish apple pies and cobblers.

● A cool cellar or garage where temperature is maintained at slightly above freezing is a good place to store apples for the winter.

Blossoms and fruit of 'Golden Delicious'.

Apples

Variety	Origin	Zones	Harvest Season	Fruit and Tree	Remarks
'AKANE'	Tohuku, Japan, 1970	6, 7	Midseason	Fruit small to medium, round, flat. Pronounced crown resembles 'Jonathan'. Skin solid bright red. Flesh firm, crisp, juicy, white, slightly coarse. Flavor slightly acid. Tree naturally semidwarf. Less than moderate vigor. Tends to develop weak crotches.	Excellent quality for eating fresh. Bears early with light crops. No pre-harvest drop. Holds well on tree but does not store well.
'BURGUNDY'	Geneva, New York, 1974	5-7	Midseason	Fruit large, round. Skin almost blackish red, solid blush without stripes, smooth, glossy. Flesh crisp, low acid. Tree medium height, moderately vigorous.	Good eating quality. Fruit hangs for three weeks after ripe. Storage life is short, no more than a month.
'CORTLAND'	Geneva, New York, 1915	4-7	Midseason to late	Fruit large, roundish to flat. Skin solid red. Flesh white, crisp, tender, juicy. Flavor slightly acid. Tree vigorous. Tends to spread and droop.	Non-browning flesh. Use for salads or for eating fresh. Resembles 'McIntosh'. Tree susceptible to powdery mildew. Fruit hangs well on tree. Bears annually. Stores well.
'EMPIRE'	Geneva, New York, 1966	5-7	Midseason to late	Fruit uniformly medium. Skin dark red with a heavy, waxy bloom. Distinctly striped. Flesh cream-colored, crisp, juicy, slightly tart with good aroma. Tree large, upright, spreading, productive annually.	Use as dessert apple but not for cooking. Keeps longer when refrigerated than 'McIntosh'. Highly productive. Fast becoming one of the most widely grown apples.
'GLOSTER'	Germany, 1969	4-7	Late	Fruit large, conic shape with shoulder bumps at calyx end. Skin fully red. Flesh crisp, slightly tart. Resembles highly colored 'Delicious'. Tree vigorous, productive.	Often compared to 'Red Delicious' but ripens later. Not as good quality as 'Red Delicious'.
'GOLDEN DELICIOUS'	West Virginia, 1916	5-8	Late	Fruit medium to large, conic shape with shoulder bumps at calyx end like 'Delicious'. Skin golden yellow, occasionally with pink blush. Flesh crisp, firm, juicy, sweet and aromatic. Tree medium height, moderately vigorous, upright, bushy. Bears young.	Use for eating fresh and for cooking. Tends to bear biennially unless thinned. Spur-type form has same qualities except fruit are rougher and tree has more compact growth habit. Does not store well—shrivels.
'GRANNY SMITH'	New Zealand	6, 7	Late	Fruit medium to large, round, slightly elongated. Skin bright green with white flecks. Flesh tart, juicy. Tree vigorous, upright and spreading with much bare wood.	Use for eating fresh, cooking and sauces. Tree bears annually on ends of shoots. Requires long growing season. Susceptible to mildew. Good keeper. Becomes sweeter in storage.

Thinning apples, before and after. Thin when fruitlets are about the size of your thumbnail.

Apples

Variety	Origin	Zones	Harvest Season	Fruit and Tree	Remarks
'GRAVENSTEIN'	Germany	3-7	Early	Fruit large, with roundish, irregular shape. Skin light green with red stripes. Flesh creamy white, fine texture, crisp, firm, juicy. Tree vigorous, upright, spreading.	Use for eating fresh and for cooking. Tree tends to bear biennially unless thinned. Pollen sterile, requires pollinator. Slow to begin bearing. Similar to 'Red Gravenstein', but has better flavor.
'HAZEN'	North Dakota, 1980	3-5	Midseason	Fruit large, up to 3-inch diameter. Skin 90% dark red. Flesh creamy white, sweet, aromatic. Tree vigorous, cold-hardy. Natural semidwarf.	Early ripening 'Red Delicious' type. Recommended for cold, Northern regions.
'HONEYGOLD'	Minnesota	3-5	Late	Fruit medium, round. Skin yellow, sometimes has red blush. Flesh crisp, juicy, with tart flavor. Tree vigorous and cold-hardy.	Use for eating fresh, for pies and sauce. Recommended for cold regions of the North.
'IDARED'	Idaho, 1942	5-7	Late	Fruit medium to large, uniform in shape, nearly round. Skin solid red over faint yellow. Flesh white, crisp, juicy, fine grained, aromatic. Tree medium to small with moderately vigorous upright growth.	Use for cooking and desserts. Blooms early. Prolonged period of ripening. Bears annually and heavily. Subject to stem cracking. Excellent keeper, flavor improves with storage.
'JERSEYMAC'	Rutgers, New Jersey, 1971	5-7	Early	Fruit medium to large, standard and conic shape. Skin yellow with strong red blush. Flesh yellow-white, slightly tart. Tree strong, upright, spreading growth.	Use for eating fresh, for desserts. A 'McIntosh' type. Heavy producer, bears annually at an early age. Poor keeper. Fruit shows bruises easily.
'JONAGOLD'	Geneva, New York, 1968	4-7	Late	Fruit large, round or elongated. Skin scarlet stripes over bright yellow-green. Flesh yellow-white, crisp, medium-firm, juicy, slightly coarse. Tree sturdy, productive, with wide crotches.	Use for desserts and cooking. Tree not too vigorous. Pollen sterile so supply a pollinator. Good keeper.
'JONAMAC'	Geneva, New York, 1968	5-7	Midseason	Fruit medium. Skin brilliant red. Flesh crisp, juicy, slightly tart. Tree medium, very productive.	Use for desserts. Superior quality when ripened on tree. Susceptible to scab and especially to mildew. Superior to 'Jonathan' and 'McIntosh' parentage. Bears annually. Good keeper.
'JONATHAN'	New York	5-7	Midseason	Fruit medium, round to elongated. Skin washed red and yellow. Flesh firm, crisp, juicy, white, slightly acidic. Tree small, low vigor.	Use for eating fresh, salads, desserts. Tree susceptible to mildew. 'Jonamac' and 'Jonagold' are generally considered better choices.

Mature 'Red Gravenstein', loaded with fruit.

Apples

Variety	Origin	Zones	Harvest Season	Fruit and Tree	Remarks
'KEEPSAKE'	Minnesota, 1979	4-7	Late	Fruit medium to large. Skin 90% red. Flesh light yellow, fine grained, firm, crisp, juicy, strongly aromatic. Tree moderately vigorous, spreading.	Use for eating fresh, desserts, salads, cooking. Tree ideal for home garden because of long keeping in storage. Cold-hardy, recommended for colder zones.
'LODI'	Geneva, New York, 1924	4-7	Early	Fruit large. Skin bright yellow, dotted with brown. Flesh white, moderately soft and crisp, tart. Tree large and cold-hardy.	Good quality for summer apple. Use for desserts, cooking, sauces. Tends to bear biennially. Thin fruit to prevent this. Resistant to fireblight disease.
'McINTOSH'	Ontario, Canada, c. 1800	3-5	Midseason	Fruit medium, almost round. Skin yellow with red stripes. Flesh white, sweet, juicy, tender, medium soft. Tree vigorous.	Use for eating fresh and desserts. Somewhat prone to diseases. Requires pollinator if isolated. Heavy pre-harvest fruit drop. Spur-type form also available.
'MACOUN'	Geneva, New York, 1923	4-6	Late	Fruit similar to 'McIntosh' but smaller. Skin dark red. Flesh white, richly flavored, crisp, aromatic. Tree upright with long, lanky branches.	Excellent dessert fruit. Tends to bear biennially unless thinned. Fruit drop as they ripen. Keeps well. Not recommended for cooking. Because of excellent fresh-eating qualities, this apple has received much interest.
'MELROSE'	Ohio	5-7	Late	Fruit large, somewhat flat. Skin yellow with bright-red blush. Flesh white, juicy, crisp, firm, slightly tart. Tree medium height and vigor, upright with spreading tendency.	Use for desserts and cooking. Susceptible to scab and mildew. Resembles 'Jonathan' in color and shape. Does not polish like 'Red Delicious'. Good keeper.
'MUTSU'	Japan, 1948	5-7	Midseason	Fruit large to very large, oblong. Green skin develops yellow color when ripe. Occasionally has orange blush. Flesh yellow-white, firm, coarse texture, juicy, slightly tart. Tree large, vigorous with strong crotch development.	Use for cooking, baking or eating fresh. Bears annually and heavily. Less tendency to overset than 'Golden Delicious'. Large fruit tend to have bitter pits. Pollen sterile. Needs pollinator in isolated position. Keeps well. Does not shrivel as much when stored like 'Golden Delicious'.
'NIAGARA'	Geneva, New York	4-6	Early	Fruit of 'McIntosh' parentage, resembles it in appearance and flavor. Tree strong with vigorous growth habit.	Use fresh, in sauce or for cooking. Tree bears annually.
'NITTANY'	Pennsylvania, 1978	5-7	Late	Fruit large. Skin 90% red striped. Flesh firm, crisp, juicy, slightly tart. Tree vigorous.	Use for eating fresh, desserts, cooking. Tree bears early. Outstanding storage quality. Keeps six months under refrigeration.

Harvest time is something that can involve the whole family.

Apples

Variety	Origin	Zones	Harvest Season	Fruit and Tree	Remarks
'PAULARED'	Michigan, 1967	5-7	Midseason	Fruit medium, roundish. Skin red blush over bright-yellow base. Flesh white to cream, non-browning, firm, slightly acid taste. Tree upright with good branch structure.	Use for eating fresh, in sauce and pies. Pick when almost mature. Annual bearer, fruit holds well on tree. Keeps well.
'PRIMA'	Northeast United States, 1945	5-7	Midseason	Fruit medium to large, roundish. Skin medium dark red over yellow. Flesh greenish white to yellow, medium-firm, juicy, fine grained. Tree vigorous and spreading.	Use for eating fresh or cooking. Bears good crop annually. Fruit may hang on tree and become overripe. Resists scab. Fruit tend to have bitter pit in early life of tree.
'PRISCILLA'	United States, c. 1955	5-7	Midseason	Fruit large and roundish. Skin bright-red blush on yellow. Flesh greenish white in color, crisp, medium texture. Tree moderately vigorous.	Use for eating fresh. Scab resistant. A good partner for 'Prima', because it serves as adequate pollinator. Good keeper—up to three months.
'RED ASTRACHAN'	Russia	4-7	Early	Fruit medium, roundish. Skin yellow splashed with dark red. Flesh white, tinged with crimson, crisp, soft, juicy, tart. Tree medium, upright, spreading.	Use for eating fresh, desserts, salads but only when ripe. Good for cooking. Does not keep well. Perishable fruit. Recommended for warm-climate areas. Tree bears young, moderately.
'RED BARON'	Minnesota	3-5	Late	Fruit medium to large. Skin yellow-orange to yellow-green. Flesh yellow, crisp, tender, juicy. Tree moderately vigorous, but cold-hardy.	Use for eating fresh, in pies and sauce. Recommended for colder regions.
'RED DELICIOUS'	Iowa, 1872	5-7	Midseason	Fruit medium, elongated, tapered. Skin striped or solid red with with yellow tinge. Flesh juicy, aromatic, sweet taste. Tree large, upright, spreading.	The most widely grown apple in the world. Requires pollinator if isolated. Susceptible to scab. Responds to heavy feeding.
'REGENT'	Minnesota	3-5	Late	Fruit medium, roundish. Skin red. Flesh creamy white, juicy, crisp. Tree vigorous, bears annually.	Use for cooking or for eating fresh. Good keeper. Cold hardy, recommended for colder regions.
'ROME BEAUTY'	Ohio	5-7	Late	Fruit large, round, has long stem. Skin red. Flesh white with green tinge, medium texture, crisp, firm. Tree small to medium, moderately vigorous.	Use for baking. Bears annually at an early age on tips of shoots. Budsports are numerous. Recommended for areas with late frosts, because bloom is late.
'SPARTAN'	Summerland, British Columbia, Canada, 1936	4-7	Late	Fruit medium, uniform, symmetrical. Skin solid mahogany-red. Flesh light yellow, firm, tender, juicy, crisp. Tree strong, moderately vigorous, heavy producer.	Use for eating fresh, for salads and desserts. Bears annually if thinned. Some pre-harvest drop. Good keeper. Not good for cooking. Watercore soft, watery flesh, sometimes a problem.
'SPIGOLD'	Geneva, New York, 1962	4-6	Late	Fruit large. Skin 75% red striped. Flesh firm, crisp, juicy, sweet. Tree vigorous.	No value in pollinating other varieties. Mostly used as processing apple. Pits tend to have bitterness on young trees.

'Yellow Transparent'

Apples

Variety	Origin	Zones	Harvest Season	Fruit and Tree	Remarks
'STARK BLUSHING GOLDEN'	Missouri	5-8	Late	Fruit large, 2-1/2 to 3 inches in diameter, shaped like 'Golden Delicious'. Tree vigorous.	Great for eating fresh, for desserts or for cooking. Excellent keeper, up to 8 months.
'STATE FAIR'	Minnesota, 1978	3-5	Midseason	Fruit medium, attractive, conic shape. Skin 90% red. Flesh cream color, more firm than most midseason varieties. Tree moderately vigorous.	Use for eating fresh, in salads or desserts. Cold-hardy, recommended for colder regions.
'STAYMAN'	Kansas, c. 1860	5-7	Late	Fruit large, conic shape, roundish. Skin yellow-green with red blush freckled with dots. Flesh crisp, fine texture with zest. Tree medium, moderately vigorous.	Better flavor than 'Winesap'. Use for eating fresh, salads, desserts. Bears annually. Requires pollinator if isolated. Pollen sterile. Budsports: 'Improved Black Stayman', 'Scarlet Stayman', 'Blaxstayman', 'Acme' and others.
'SUMMERLAND McINTOSH'	Summerland, British Columbia, Canada, 1929	5-7	Midseason	Fruit blushed with red color pattern with little striping. Otherwise, identical to 'McIntosh'.	See 'McIntosh'.
'SWEET SIXTEEN'	Minnesota, 1978	4-6	Late	Fruit medium, conic shape. Skin red on yellow. Flesh cream color, crisp, firm, high sugar content, medium-acid, with nutty flavor. Tree vigorous and easily managed.	Use for cooking. Fruit fully colored. Tree resistant to fireblight disease.
'TYDEMAN'S RED'	England	5-7	Early	Fruit large, shaped like 'McIntosh'. Skin brilliant scarlet at an early stage. Flesh white, fine texture, moderately firm. Tree grows straggly with long, lanky branches. Can be controlled by pruning.	Best quality early season apple. Use for eating fresh and for cooking. 'McIntosh'-type, ripens four weeks earlier than its parent. Bears annually on tips of shoots. Tends to drop fruit. Poor pollinator.
'VISTA BELLA'	Rutgers, New Jersey, 1974	5-7	Early	Fruit medium. Skin glossy, dark red. Flesh creamy white, medium-firm, juicy, sweet. Tree moderately vigorous.	Firmer, better eating quality than most early summer varieties. Watercore, poor, soft watery flesh, sometimes a problem.
'WINESAP'	New York	5-7	Late	Fruit medium, round or slightly oblong. Skin red, occasionally has red stripes over yellow when ripe. Flesh yellow, crisp, coarse, juicy, firm, slightly acid. Tree vigorous.	Excellent dessert apple, also used for cider. Thought to have been formerly called 'Wine Sop'. Good keeper. Requires pollinator if isolated. Sterile pollen.
'WINTER BANANA'	Europe	5-7	Late	Fruit medium to large. Skin pale yellow with pink blush, waxy texture. Flesh tender, juicy, aromatic with zest. Tree vigorous.	Use for eating fresh or for cooking. Tree thrives in areas with mild winters. Will support a graft of 'Bartlett' pear. Requires pollinator if isolated. Spur-type is same but with compact growth habit.
'YELLOW TRANSPARENT'	Russia, c. 1880	4-7	Early	Fruit medium. Skin clear yellow, fine texture, tender, smooth. Flesh white, tender, slightly tart. Tree tall, vigorous, upright.	Use for cooking when greenish yellow. Bruises easily, fruit drop when ripe. Poor keeper. Cold hardy.

Old Apples

Variety	Origin	Zones	Harvest Season	Fruit	Remarks
'AMERICAN BEAUTY'	Sterling, Massachusetts	5-7	Late	Dark color, fine aroma.	Excellent quality. Slightly tart. Use for desserts.
'ARKANSAS BLACK'	Benton County, Arkansas	5-7	Late	Fruit small to medium, burgundy-red on yellow. Flesh hard, crisp, yellowish.	Use for applesauce.
'BALDWIN WOODPECKER'	Wilmington, Massachusetts, about 1740	5-7	Late	Fruit red stripes on yellow or green. Flesh yellow, firm, crisp, juicy.	Use for sauce, jam or jelly. Good for freezing.
'BEN DAVIS'	Tennessee, Kentucky or Virginia, early 1800	5-7	Late	Fruit medium to large, bright red or red striped. Flesh firm, white, crisp, slightly tart.	Use for drying. Poor for eating, fair for cooking. Stores well.
'BLACK GILLIFLOWER' 'SHEEPNOSE'	Connecticut, early 1800	5-7	Midseason to late	Fruit medium to large, red to dark purple. Flesh whitish or slight yellow.	Use for baking, eating fresh. Too dry and not tart enough for cooking.
'BLUE PEARMAIN'	United States, about 1800	5-7	Midseason to late	Fruit medium to large, yellow, washed with red. Flesh firm coarse, yellow tinged and juicy.	Use for cider, desserts or salad. Fair for cooking.
'CHENANGO STRAWBERRY'	New York, about 1850	5-7	Midseason	Fruit medium to large, yellow and white skin striped red. Flesh white, firm, tender, aromatic, juicy.	Use for cooking and eating fresh. Does not keep. Requires 4 to 6 years before first crop.
'COX ORANGE'	Bucks, England, about 1830	5-7	Midseason to late	Fruit medium, red and yellow. Flesh yellow, firm, crisp, tender.	Use for desserts and processing. Does not do well in Northeast.
'DUCHESS OF OLDENBURG'	Russia, early 1800	5-7	Early	Fruit medium, red stripes shaded with crimson. Flesh medium-firm, tart with good aroma.	Use for cooking. Too acidic for desserts.
'EARLY HARVEST'	Unknown, before 1800	5-7	Early	Fruit medium, nearly round, pale yellow, smooth, waxy skin. Flesh soft, fine, tender to crisp with good aroma.	Good for cooking or eating fresh, for salads and desserts. Requires 4 to 6 years to produce first crop.
'ESOPUS SPITZENBURG'	Ulster County, New York, 1800 or before	5-7	Late	Fruit medium to large, bright red with yellow dots. Flesh firm, crisp, tender. Slightly tart taste.	Excellent all-around apple. A dessert treat.
'FAMEUSE' 'SNOW APPLE'	France, before 1730	5-7	Midseason to late	Fruit medium, bright red skin. Flesh white, sometimes streaked with crimson. Crisp, good aroma, juicy.	Use for eating fresh and desserts, not for cooking. Does well at high elevations.
'GOLDEN RUSSET'	Unknown, before 1870	5-7	Midseason to late	Fruit round, golden russet with bronze blush. Flesh crisp and tender. Juice sugary.	Use for eating fresh or for desserts. Excellent keeper.
'GRIMES GOLDEN'	West Virginia, before 1800	5-7	Late	Fruit small, rich, golden yellow. Flesh tender, crisp, juicy, good aroma.	Use for eating fresh and for freezing. Poor for baking.
'HUBBARDSTON NONESUCH'	Massachusetts, early 1800	5-7	Midseason to late	Fruit medium to large, mostly red. Flesh firm, crisp, fine grain.	Use for eating fresh. Does not cook well. Good keeper.
'HUNT RUSSET' (RUSSET PEARMAIN)	Massachusetts	5-7	Late	Fruit medium, gold on russet blushed with red-russet.	Use for sauce, pies, jam, jelly, cider, juice or eating fresh.

Old Apples

Variety	Origin	Zones	Harvest Season	Fruit	Remarks
'LADY'	France, before 1628	5-7	Late	Fruit small, flat, red and yellow. Flesh tender, white, crisp, juicy with good aroma.	Use for dessert and at Christmas for decoration. Dwarf growth habit.
'MAIDEN'S BLUSH'	Unknown, early 1800	5-7	Midseason to late	Fruit medium, pale, lemon-yellow with crimson blush. Flesh fine to moderately crisp, slightly tart.	Use for drying or eating fresh. Doesn't keep well. Requires 4 to 6 years to produce first crop.
'MOTHER'	Boston, Massachusetts, early 1800	5-7	Midseason	Fruit bright red with golden blush. Flesh cream color, sweet, juicy, good aroma.	Use as dessert apple.
'NORTHERN SPY'	East Bloomfield New York, about 1800	5-7	Late	Fruit large, round, striped, bright scarlet. Flesh firm, juicy and tender.	Use for cooking and dessert. Grown in many areas as a commercial crop.
'PALMER GREENING'	Sterling, Massachusetts	5-7	Midseason	Fruit medium, yellow with red blush, waxy. Flesh white with yellow cast, crisp, firm and juicy.	Use for eating fresh.
'PORTER'	Sherburne, Massachusetts, 1800	5-7	Midseason to late	Fruit large, bright yellow blushed with red. Flesh white, fine, crisp with good aroma.	Use for cooking and desserts.
'POUND SWEET' 'PUMPKIN SWEET'	Manchester, Connecticut	5-7	Late	Fruit large, light and dark green with white cast. Particular flavor.	Use for baking and canning.
'RED JUNE'	North Carolina	5-7	Early to midseason	Fruit small, deep red over yellow or green skin. Flesh fine and tender.	Use for eating fresh or in desserts.
'ROXBURY RUSSET'	Massachusetts	5-7	Late	Fruit medium to large, green to russet. Flesh white with yellow cast, firm, coarse, juicy.	Use for cider. Keeps well in storage. Bears annually.
'SMOKEHOUSE'	Lancaster, Pennsylvania	5-7	Late	Fruit medium to large, yellow or green mottled with dull red. Flesh white with yellow cast, firm, good aroma.	Use for eating fresh, desserts and salads.
'SUMMER RAMBO'	France	5-7	Early to midseason	Fruit large and flat, greenish yellow striped with red. Flesh tender, juicy.	Use for eating fresh or sauce.
'TOLMAN SWEET'	Dorchester, Massachusetts	5-7	Late	Fruit medium to large, pale-yellow skin. Flesh white, firm, sweet.	Use for eating fresh and for baking. Fruit damaged easily. Bears biennially.
'TWENTY OUNCE'	Massachusetts	5-7	Midseason	Fruit large. Skin green, turns yellow with red blush upon ripening. Flesh white, coarse, juicy.	Use for cooking, sauce, baking, eating fresh.
'WESTFIELD-SEEK-NO-FURTHER'	Massachusetts	5-7	Midseason to late	Fruit medium, deep yellow or green with red blush. Flesh creamy yellow, firm, medium grain, crisp.	Use fresh, in desserts or salads. Do not use for cooking.
'WOLF RIVER'	Wisconsin	5-7	Midseason to late	Fruit large, yellow striped red. Flesh firm, tender, moderately coarse.	Use for cooking.
'YELLOW BELLFLOWER'	New Jersey	5-7	Midseason to late	Fruit medium, attractive yellow with pink blush. Flesh white with yellow tinge, firm, crisp.	Use fresh, for desserts and salads. Good for pies.

'Moorpark', like most apricots, is a midseason variety.

Apricot

One of the most desirable of all home-garden fruit trees is the apricot. Not only is the fruit delectable and versatile, the trees are easily managed, attractive and vigorous. They resemble handsome plum trees with roundish, glossy green leaves. The delicate, white spring blossoms are lovely. Their heady, seductive scent is comparable to that of gardenia and other sweet-scented flowers.

Apricots, by their nature, bloom early in spring. Areas where late-spring frosts are common are usually not suited to their culture. However, cross-breeding of apricots with Manchurian apricots has produced trees that are more cold-hardy and better adapted to Northern regions. Check the variety chart for specific recommendations.

CULTURAL REQUIREMENTS

Apricots thrive in various soil types, except those that are constantly wet. They do best in sandy soil. During dry spells, water regularly or fruit will be small.

POLLINATION

Most apricots are *self-fruitful.* This means they have both male and female flowers on each tree. If you live in Zone 4 or Zone 5, it is best to plant a second variety. This encourages a heavier fruit set, which is beneficial because late frosts often destroy a substantial number of young fruit. Be aware that not just any other variety will act as a pollinator. Consult the variety chart for requirements and for recommendations.

PRUNING

When you plant a new apricot tree, train it to a vase shape. See page 29. Select three branches spaced around the trunk at about the same height. Cut them back to 2 to 4 inches, leaving one to two buds on each

branch. Prune the top of the trunk back to 1 or 2 inches above the highest remaining branch. Remove all other branches.

Apricots are vigorous growers and require yearly pruning. As you prune, keep in mind that apricots bear fruit on spurs that produce for about three years. Part of the purpose of pruning is to induce the tree to develop new spurs. Branches require exposure to sunlight. Removing inside branches provides better exposure to the sun's rays. Remove older branches that bend down or head back to the point where they grow upward.

If the tree grows too tall, remove vertical branches to a lateral at the desired height. If the tree is too dense in the center, remove center branches. Little fruit will form at the interior of the tree if the wood is shaded.

THINNING FRUIT

Apricots usually set more fruit than the tree can ripen to maturity. Fruit drop normally occurs in late spring. This is late May in the Northeast and Midwest, early May farther south. After this natural fruit drop, thin remaining fruit to 4 inches apart.

HARVESTING AND STORAGE

When you pick apricots, take the fruit in your hand and twist lightly. If fruit is ripe enough to pick, it will separate easily from the stem.

Two schools of thought exist concerning the proper time to harvest apricots. Some experts say that fruit is most flavorful when allowed to ripen fully on the tree. Others say fruit should be picked before it is fully ripe, and allowed to ripen in a cool room. Try both methods and decide for yourself which way is best.

Apricots keep for about three weeks if stored in a cool place, about 40F to 50F (5C to 10C).

PESTS AND DISEASES

Brown rot and bacterial gumming are two serious diseases that strike apricots. Insect attacks are normally not a problem. Codling moth, scale, twig borers and plum curculio may attack trees in some areas. Wet soils cause roots to be susceptible to oak-root fungus, unless trees are grown on plum rootstock. Verticillium wilt can also be a problem. Avoid planting in soil that has been used in the previous five years to grow rasp-

Apricot		
	Standard	**Dwarf**
Height at maturity (feet)		
Unpruned	30	8-10
Pruned	15	6-8
Spread at maturity with		
no competition (feet)	30	6-8
Recommended planting		
distance (feet)	24-30	8-12
Years to reach bearing age	3-4	3-4
Life expectancy (years)	75	75
Chilling requirement (hours)	350-900	350-900
Pollinator required	See chart, pages 84 to 85.	
Good for espalier	Informal only	
Good for containers	No	Yes
Comments: Genetic dwarfs are available.		

berries, strawberries, tomatoes, potatoes, peppers or melons—crops that can harbor the disease. For more information, see page 55.

GARDENER'S TIPS
• Apricots grow fast, so be careful when applying fertilizer. If a tree sends out branches 6 feet or longer in a year, you are feeding it too much. Reduce amount of fertilizer by half.
• 'Moongold', 'Sungold' and 'Manchu' are the most cold-hardy varieties.
• To can, cook or preserve apricots, pick them before they are fully ripe. Handle fruit gently, although they do not bruise easily.
• Apricot preserves are used by pastry chefs to glaze a wide variety of pastries.
• Because of summer humidity in the East and Midwest, drying apricots outdoors is not recommended. Here is one recommended procedure if you decide to dry them.

Split fruit in halves and remove stones. Pour boiling water over fruit and steep for 20 minutes. Drain off water and place halves on a cookie sheet, cavity side up. Dry for 12 to 30 hours in the oven. Begin at 125F (34C) for 4 hours, then at 155 F (51C) for 6 hours. Lower to 125 F (34C) for the last 2 hours. After this period, apricots should feel like soft leather. Store them in plastic bags in a cool room. Dried properly, they should keep for over a year. For more information, refer to the HPBook, *How to Dry Foods*.

Apricots can be harvested when fully ripe, or just prior to peak ripeness. Try both ways and do a taste-test to see which you prefer.

Homemade preserves is reason enough to grow apricots.

Be cautious when selecting planting site for apricots. They are among the first fruit to bloom in spring. Late frost may damage blossoms, especially in Zones 4 and 5.

Apricots

Variety	Origin	Zones	Harvest Season	Fruit	Remarks
'ALFRED'	Geneva, New York	5-7	Midseason	Fruit medium, roundish. Skin bright orange with slight blush. Flesh freestone, medium-firm, fine grain, juicy, sweet and rich flavor. Tree vigorous.	Use for eating fresh or for cooking. Early bloomer but resists frost injury. Regular bearer. Self-fruitful.
'EARLY GOLDEN'	New York	5-7	Midseason	Fruit medium to large. Skin orange with red blush. Flesh freestone, firm, with good flavor.	Use for eating fresh and cooking.
'GOLDCOT'	South Haven, Michigan	5-7	Midseason	Fruit medium to large, roundish. Skin thick and golden. Flesh firm, medium orange. Tree strong with horizontal scaffolds.	Use for eating fresh or for cooking. Tendency to darken when canned. Oversets alternate years unless thinned.
'GOLDEN GIANT'	Hamburg, Iowa	5-7	Midseason	Fruit large. Skin golden orange with light-pink blush. Flesh firm, juicy, excellent flavor. Tree cold-hardy.	Bears heavily. Adapted to colder areas of Zones 5 to 7.
'HARCOT'	Harrow, Ontario, Canada, 1977	5-7	Midseason	Fruit medium to large, oval. Skin orange with slight red blush. Flesh orange, firm, smooth and usually freestone. Texture and flavor good. Tree vigorous and cold-hardy.	Use for eating fresh or for cooking. Resists perennial canker, bacterial spot and brown rot. Adapted to cold areas.
'HARDY IOWA'	Glenwood, Iowa	5-7	Midseason	Fruit small. Skin thin, pale yellow. Flesh sweet. Tree flowers late, often escaping frost. Bears heavily.	Use for eating fresh, for pies or preserves. Adapted to cold areas.
'HARGRAND'	Harrow, Ontario, Canada, 1980	5-7	Midseason	Fruit large, up to 2-1/2 inches in diameter. Skin orange with speckled blush. Flesh freestone, firm, orange. Good texture and flavor. Tree vigorous, cold-hardy, productive.	Use for eating fresh or for cooking. Trees tolerant of bacterial spot and brown rot.
'HARLAYNE'	Harrow, Ontario, Canada, 1980	5-7	Midseason	Fruit medium. Skin moderate red blush on orange. Flesh freestone, orange, firm, good texture and flavor. Tree cold-hardy, productive.	Use for eating fresh or for home canning. Tree resists perennial canker, brown rot and bacterial spot. Adapted to cold areas.
'HAROGEM'	Harrow, Ontario, Canada, 1980	5-7	Midseason	Fruit small to medium, very attractive. Skin glossy with bright-red blush on orange. Flesh freestone, orange, firm. Texture and flavor good. Tree vigorous, productive.	Use for eating fresh or for cooking. Tree resists perennial canker and brown rot. Moderately susceptible to bacterial spot. Adapted to cold areas.

Apricots ready for harvest.

Apricots

Variety	Origin	Zones	Harvest Season	Fruit	Remarks
'HENDERSON'	Geneva, New York	5-7	Midseason	Fruit large, roundish. Skin yellow with lighter yellow blush. Flesh freestone, thick, yellow, sweet and of good quality. Tree vigorous.	Use for eating fresh or for cooking. Attractive landscape specimen as leaves are glossy. Bloom is soft pink.
'HUNGARIAN'	Geneva, New York	6, 7	Midseason	Fruit medium, round to oval. Skin solid gold. Flesh firm with fine flavor. Tree not as cold-hardy as others listed here.	Use for eating fresh or for cooking. Does not overbear. May fail in zones receiving late-spring frosts.
'MANCHU'	Brookings, South Dakota	Warm areas of Zone 4, 5-7	Midseason	Fruit large. Skin yellow. Flesh orange, firm. Tree large and prolific.	Use for eating fresh or for cooking. Seedling of native Manchurian apricot. Adapted to cold areas.
'MOONGOLD'	Excelsior, Minnesota	Warm areas of Zone 4, 5-7	Midseason	Fruit medium. Skin orange and tough. Flesh yellow-orange, excellent quality. Tree medium, spreading.	Use for eating fresh or for cooking. Must be planted with 'Sungold' for cross-pollination. Recommended for cold areas.
'MOORPARK'	Hertford, England, 1760	5-7	Midseason	Fruit large. Skin orange with deep blush, at times dotted with brown and red. Flesh orange, good flavor and aroma. Tree cold-hardy and vigorous except in extreme north.	Use for eating fresh or for preserves. Not recommended for canning. Harvest when entire fruit is dead-ripe. Fruit ripens unevenly, with half green while other half is ripe. An old standby and often a standard by which new varieties are judged.
'NEW YORK'	Geneva, New York	5-7	Midseason	Fruit medium, oval. Skin deep orange with slight red blush. Flesh freestone, deep orange, firm, juicy and smooth, with sweet, rich flavor. Tree as cold-hardy as 'Alfred'.	Use for eating fresh or for canning.
'SUNDROP'	Summerland, British Columbia, Canada, 1975	5-7	Midseason	Fruit roundish to slightly oval. Skin bright orange with slight red blush. Flesh orange, medium-firm, juicy, smooth, sweet and mild. Tree vigorous.	Use for eating fresh and for cooking. Pits cling in some years.
'SUNGOLD'	Excelsior, Minnesota	Warm areas of Zone 4, 5-7	Midseason	Fruit medium, round. Skin golden blushed with orange. Flesh tender, mild, sweet flavor. Tree medium, vigorous, upright.	Use for eating fresh or for preserves. Must be planted with 'Moongold' for cross-pollination.
'VEECOT'	Ontario, Canada, 1954	5-7	Midseason	Fruit medium to large, round. Skin deep orange, flesh freestone, firm, smooth texture and slightly juicy. Tree moderately vigorous.	Excellent for canning. Tree productive, but not as cold-hardy as 'Alfred'.

'Bing' sweet cherry.

Cherry

Cherries are one of the most universally grown fruit trees. They are well suited to most of the growing areas included in this book. The trees are handsome, with dazzling displays of blossoms in spring. Trees usually produce fruit the first year they are planted.

Three types of cherries are available: *sweet cherries, sour cherries* and *Duke cherries.* Sweet cherries are cold-hardy, but not as hardy as other varieties of stone fruit. They do not accept blistering summer heat, so are not adapted to southern and southwestern areas of the United States. In fact, the bark of trees becomes sunburned under such conditions.

Extreme humidity and fog during the growing season are not good for growth of sweet cherries. 'Sam' is probably most tolerant of these conditions.

Of the three types, sour cherries are the easiest to grow. They survive hot summers, fog and cold winter temperatures. Some varieties are available as genetic dwarfs or semidwarfs.

Duke cherries are sometimes available in nurseries. They are an old-fashioned variety produced by crossing sweet cherries and sour cherries. But in the past few decades, many advances have been made in developing sweeter-tasting sour cherries, and sweet cherries that are more cold-hardy. Duke cherries are no longer recommended for cultivation in the Midwest and East because of these newer and better varieties.

Cherries grow to about 8 feet wide to 15 to 20 feet high. Home gardeners with limited space should consider growing genetic dwarfs, which grow to about 8 feet high. See variety charts for more information.

POLLINATION

All sweet cherries except 'Stella' require another variety nearby for pollination. But sweet cherries are particular about which variety will pollinate another. Do not depend on a semidwarf tree to pollinate a standard tree or vice versa. Plant semidwarfs to pollinate semidwarfs and standards to pollinate standards. See variety charts for information on which varieties are recommended as pollinators.

Sour cherries are self-pollinating.

CULTURAL REQUIREMENTS

Of all fruit, cherries are perhaps the most fussy about proper watering. Drought is particularly devastating to sweet cherries. Water deeply and regularly during summer dry spells.

Sour cherries are somewhat more tolerant of drought. As with all fruit trees, waterlogged soil can cause root diseases and eventually death of the tree. Be sure soil has good drainage.

PRUNING

Because sweet cherries grow naturally in a pyramidal shape, train to a central leader. See page 30. Sour cherries do best trained to a vase shape. If you plant semidwarfs, central-leader training is preferred because of increased penetration of sunlight, and reduced space requirements.

A problem you may encounter with sweet cherries is

Sour Cherry	Standard	Dwarf
Height at maturity (feet)		
Unpruned	20	10
Pruned	15	6-8
Spread at maturity with		
no competition (feet)	30	8-10
Recommended planting		
distance (feet)	18-24	8-10
Years to reach bearing age	5	3
Life expectancy (years)	30-35	30-35
Chilling requirement (hours)	800-1,200	800-1,200
Pollinator required	No	No
Good for espalier	Yes	Yes
Good for containers	No	Yes
Comments: Height varies by variety.		

Sweet Cherry	Standard	Dwarf
Height at maturity (feet)		
Unpruned	40	6-12
Pruned	25	6-8
Spread at maturity with		
no competition (feet)	30	4-8
Recommended planting		
distance (feet)	35-45	4-8
Years to reach bearing age	4-6	3-4
Life expectancy (years)	30-35	30-35
Chilling requirement (hours)	800-1,200	800-1,200
Pollinator required	Yes	No
Good for espalier	No	Yes
Good for containers	No	Yes

their tendency to sport vertical branches rather than horizontal laterals. 'Black Tartarian' and 'Lambert' are particularly prone to this. To remedy, cut back to a lateral-growing twig or bud during the dormant season. Repeat this process every year. After three years, your tree should attain proper form.

After trees mature, little pruning is usually necessary. Sweet cherries bear on spurs that produce for 10 years or more. Sour cherries bear on spurs that are 2 to 5 years old. Keep the tree healthy and productive by pruning out interior wood. Shorten long, fruiting branches.

HARVESTING
Pick fruit only when completely ripe. Sweet cherries become firm when ripe. Sour cherries part easily from the stem when ripe. When picking, leave the stem on the fruit, unless you plan on cooking or preserving them immediately. Fruit have a better keeping quality if stems are attached.

PESTS AND DISEASES
Scale, plum curculio, mites, aphids, slugs, fruit flies and fruit worms are known to attack cherry trees. Brown rot may occur, as well as bacterial gummosis. Late-spring rains may cause fruit to crack. *Doubling* of fruit, where two fruit are joined together, occurs at pollination. This is not a serious problem. Despite this long list of pests, most are easily controlled with three or four sprays during the season. See pests and diseases, pages 47 to 57.

Understandably, these sweet morsels are gourmet fare for birds. If you want any cherries for yourself, place netting, available at garden centers, over your trees as soon as the fruit ripens.

GARDENER'S TIPS
• After picking, cherries can be piled in large containers without fear of bruising.
• Fruit can be stored in the refrigerator for short periods. Soft-fleshed varieties keep this way for about one week; firm-fleshed varieties keep for two to three weeks.
• Do not plant cherries between other kinds of fruit trees. They bear fruit early in the season, while spraying is still going on with other fruit. Plant them a safe distance away.

'Montmorency' sour cherry.

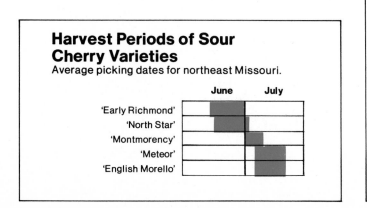

Harvest Periods of Sour Cherry Varieties
Average picking dates for northeast Missouri.

	June	July
'Early Richmond'	▓	
'North Star'	▓	
'Montmorency'		▓
'Meteor'		▓
'English Morello'		▓

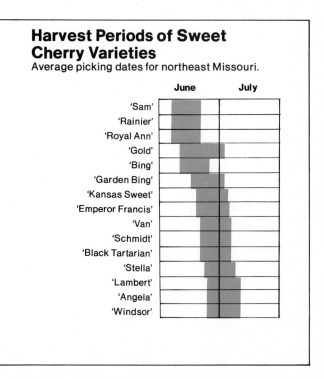

Harvest Periods of Sweet Cherry Varieties
Average picking dates for northeast Missouri.

	June	July
'Sam'	▓	
'Rainier'	▓	
'Royal Ann'	▓	
'Gold'	▓	
'Bing'	▓	
'Garden Bing'	▓	
'Kansas Sweet'	▓	
'Emperor Francis'	▓	
'Van'	▓	
'Schmidt'		▓
'Black Tartarian'		▓
'Stella'		▓
'Lambert'		▓
'Angela'		▓
'Windsor'		▓

'Van' sweet cherry in bloom adds beauty to roadside.

Sour Cherries

Variety	Origin	Zones	Harvest Season	Pollinator	Fruit	Remarks
'EARLY RICHMOND'	Unknown	4-7	Early	Self-fertile	Fruit small, round. Skin red. Flesh yellow with clear juice. Tree vigorous, cold-hardy.	Use for pies, jam and preserves. Small growth habit of 15 to 20 feet.
'ENGLISH MORELLO'	Unknown	4-7	Late	Self-fertile	Fruit medium. Skin dark red. Flesh dark red with red juice. Tree small, cold-hardy with drooping branches. Moderately vigorous and productive.	Use for pies. Good pollinator for other cherries.
'METEOR'	Minnesota	4-7	Late	Self-fertile	Fruit large. Skin bright red. Flesh yellow with clear juice. Tree cold-hardy and vigorous.	Use for pies and preserves. Ideal home-garden tree for all cherry climates. Genetic dwarf growing to only 10 feet high. Thrives in mild climates.
'MONTMORENCY'	France	4-7	Midseason	Self-fertile	Fruit large. Skin bright red. Flesh yellow with clear juice. Tree medium to large, vigorous, spreading.	Use for pies and canning. Fruit resists cracking. Different strains ripen at different times.
'NORTH STAR'	Minnesota	4-7	Early	Self-fertile	Fruit medium. Skin red. Flesh yellow with clear juice. Tree small, attractive, vigorous, cold-hardy.	Use for pies and canning. Fruit resists cracking and brown rot. Fruit ripens early, but hangs on tree for up to two weeks. Especially recommended for home gardens—the tree is a genetic dwarf.

Sweet Cherries

Variety	Origin	Zones	Harvest Season	Pollinator	Fruit	Remarks
'ANGELA'	Utah, 1974	5-7	Late	'Lambert'	Fruit large. Skin black, glossy. Flesh sweet, dark red, almost as firm as 'Bing'. Tree medium-upright, productive, vigorous.	Hardier than 'Lambert'. Resists splitting. Blooms late, along with 'Lambert', so usually escapes spring frosts.
'BING'	Oregon, 1875	5-7	Midseason	'Black Tartarian', 'Sam', 'Van'	Fruit large. Skin deep mahogany-red. Flesh firm, juicy. The standard for black sweet cherries. Tree spreading, heavy producer.	Use for canning and eating fresh. Fruit subject to cracking and doubling. Tree subject to bacterial attack in humid climates.
'BLACK TARTARIAN'	Russia	5-7	Early	Any sweet cherry	Fruit medium. Skin black. Flesh firm at harvest but softens quickly. Tree vigorous, erect, heavy bearer.	Early cherry. Use for canning, preserves or eating fresh. Cracks, spurs and doubles badly.
'EMPEROR FRANCIS'	Europe	5-7	Midseason	'Rainier', 'Gold',	Fruit large, high-quality 'Royal Ann' type. Skin slightly more red and dark. Tree productive and cold-hardy.	Less subject to cracking than 'Royal Ann'. One of the best main-crop sweet cherries.
'GARDEN BING'	Dave Wilson Nursery, California	Not fully tested	Midseason	Self-fertile	Fruit large, similar to 'Bing'. Skin dark red. Flesh firm, sweet, juicy. Tree grows approximately 6 feet high with 4-foot spread.	Ornamental tree, a genetic dwarf. Light bearing. Use on patio or terrace in warm areas only.
'GOLD'	Nebraska	5-7	Midseason	Any sweet cherry	Fruit medium. Skin yellow. Flesh firm and sweet. Tree cold-hardy and productive.	Some strains bear larger fruit. Resists cracking. Adapted to cold regions of Zone 5.
'KANSAS SWEET'	Wichita, Kansas	5-7	Midseason	'Black Tartarian', 'Sam', 'Van'	Fruit larger than 'Bing'. Skin red. Flesh firm and sweet. Tree and blossoms are quite cold-hardy.	Use for pies. Fairly palatable fresh, but 'Bing' is sweeter. Plant in cold regions of Zone 5.
'LAMBERT'	Summerland, British Columbia, Canada, 1964	5-7	Late	'Van', 'Sam'	Fruit large, similar to 'Bing'. Skin dark. Flesh sweet, firm, high quality. Tree more widely adapted than 'Bing', but bears erratically in many Eastern areas.	A connoisseur's cherry. Subject to cracking, but resists doubling in hot areas.
'RAINIER'	Washington, 1960	5-7	Early	'Royal Ann', 'Emperor Francis', 'Bing', 'Sam', 'Van'	Fruit large. Skin yellow with pink blush. Flesh light yellow, firm, low acid, high quality. Tree vigorous, productive, early bearing. Cold-hardy in bud and wood.	Fruit resists cracking, spurs and doubling.
'ROYAL ANN' ('NAPOLEON')	Europe	5-7	Midseason	'Van', 'Windsor',	Fruit medium. Skin yellow, blushed. Flesh firm, juicy. Tree large, wide-spreading. Productive.	Fruit used to make maraschino cherries. Use fresh or for canning. Cracks and spurs badly. Relatively cold-tender. Best for Zones 6 and 7.
'SAM'	Summerland, British Columbia, Canada	5-7	Early	'Van', 'Lambert', 'Bing'	Fruit medium to large. Skin black. Flesh firm and juicy. Tree vigorous, cold-hardy, heavy bearer.	Fruit high quality. Resists cracking.
'SCHMIDT'	Germany	5-7	Midseason	'Bing', 'Lambert', 'Royal Ann'	Fruit large. Skin thick, mahogany color. Flesh wine-red, sweet but somewhat tart. Tree large, vigorous, upright, spreading. Cold-hardy but fruit buds are fairly cold-tender.	Excellent quality fruit. Resists cracking.
'STELLA'	Summerland, British Columbia, Canada, 1968	5-7	Midseason	Self-fertile	Fruit large. Skin black like 'Lambert'. Flesh firm and sweet. Tree vigorous, bears early.	First self-fertile sweet cherry developed. Fruit buds can be tender to cold after severe winters. Suitable pollinizer for all other cherries. Resists cracking after rain.
'VAN'	Summerland, British Columbia, Canada	5-7	Midseason	'Bing', 'Lambert', 'Royal Ann' any others.	Fruit medium. Skin dark and shiny. Flesh sweet and firm. Tree cold-hardy, bears 1 to 3 years before 'Bing'.	Tends to overset so may produce a crop when other cherry varieties fail.
'WINDSOR'	Unknown	5-7	Late	Any sweet cherry except 'Van' and 'Emperor Francis'	Fruit small. Skin dark. Flesh not as firm as 'Bing' or 'Lambert'. Tree medium, vigorous with wide spread. Bears heavily.	Standard late commercial cherry in the East. Very cold-hardy, a good choice for difficult borderline areas where other cherries may fail.

'Kadota' fig, almost ready for harvest.

Fig

Fig trees are a common sight in back yards of urban ethnic neighborhoods. People of Mediterranean origin have been growing figs in Chicago, New York, Boston and as far north as Montreal for well over a century. You can spot the trees during winter when they are wrapped, braving the cold temperatures.

Figs are best suited to warm climates. But with proper winter protection, they can thrive in colder Northern climates. If you are not willing to provide protection against cold temperatures, do not grow figs. Your trees will freeze and die. If you are willing to provide the extra effort, you'll enjoy a bonanza of this tropical fruit at harvest time.

VARIETIES
'Black Mission'—Fruit large with purplish black skin. Use fresh or canned.

'Kadota'—Fruit medium to large with tough, yellow-green skin. Tree is vigorous.

'Osborne Prolific'—Fruit medium size, purplish brown with strong flavor.

CULTURAL REQUIREMENTS
Fig trees thrive in a wide range of soils, but do not grow well in alkaline or salty soil. Give trees an annual dose of general-purpose fertilizer. Follow label directions. Water regularly during periods of dry weather.

PRUNING
The primary consideration in pruning fig trees is to keep them manageable for winter protection. The larger the tree grows, the more difficult it will be to provide protection. If you are interested in harvesting large quantities of fruit, plant more than one tree. Two or three small trees are easier to manage than one large one.

Train and prune to a vase shape. See page 29. If long, vertical shoots develop, head them back. Rather than trying to develop plants as trees, train to a shrub-like form.

POLLINATION
All fig trees are self-fertile and do not require a cross-pollinator.

WINTER PROTECTION
There are two recommended ways to provide winter protection. One way is to bury the tree alive. After leaf drop, pull branches tightly together and tie them with rope or twine. Form tree into a narrow column. Be careful when handling limbs. Dig a trench near one side of the tree. Make the trench 2 to 3 feet deep and as wide and as long as the wrapped tree. Push the tree toward the trench. Cut the main roots on the near side of the tree. On the opposite side, the side away from the trench, slice straight down with a spade, about 1 foot deep, severing the roots. Gradually pull the tree into the trench and cover with earth.

Another method is to protect the tree by wrapping and insulating the branches. Bind branches together with rope or twine. Push dry leaves or wads of newspaper into the middle of the bound branches. Wrap tree with an insulating material such as old rugs, burlap, sheets of paper or fiberglass insulation. Tie in place with string or wire.

Finally, wrap entire tree in tar paper, plastic or other water-resistant material, and tie again. Wrap from the bottom and work up toward the top. Place a small bucket or can over the top of the tree. Pile leaves around the tree's base.

With either method, unearth the tree or remove the protective covering after all danger of frost has passed.

PROPAGATION
Propagating fig trees is simple. Cut off a branch and place it in a jar of water. Keep the jar in a shady location, and change the water about once each week. In about one month, the cutting will produce roots.

Fig	Standard	Dwarf
Height at maturity (feet)		
Unpruned	40	N/A
Pruned	6-25	
Spread at maturity with no competition (feet)	25-60	
Recommended planting distance (feet)	20-40	
Years to reach bearing age	2-3	
Life expectancy (years)	100	
Chilling requirement (hours)	100-350	
Pollinator required	No	
Good for espalier	Yes	
Good for containers	Yes	

Comments: Can be pruned to fit small space.

N/A = Not Available

When sufficient roots are formed, plant as you would new stock.

HARVESTING AND STORAGE
When the neck of the fig wilts and bends over on the stem, the fruit is ready to pick. But if a milky, latex substance oozes out of the stem end when the fruit is picked, it is not ready to eat. You can allow such fruit to ripen at room temperature, but the flavor will not be as good. For eating fresh and for freezing, pick fruit when fully ripe. For pickling or canning, pick when firm-ripe.

PESTS AND DISEASES
Figs are relatively free of diseases and pests in Northern regions. Bacterial diseases and mold are occasional problems. See page 54 for more information.

GARDENER'S TIPS
• If you have neighbors who are successful with figs, consult with them about their winter protection methods. They can tell you the best way to protect figs in your particular area.
• Bring container-grown figs indoors before first frost. Water sparingly during winter. When growth begins in spring, move to sunny window and water regularly. Move outdoors to sunny spot when danger of frost has passed.

'Black Mission' fig, with new growth in background.

Protecting Figs Against Cold

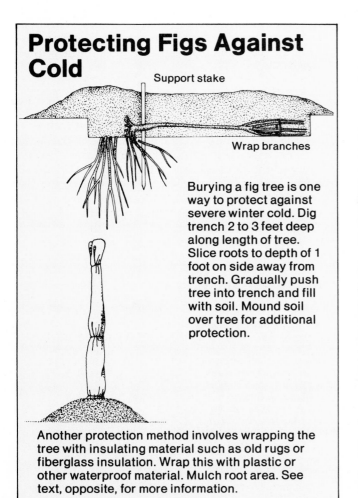

Support stake

Wrap branches

Burying a fig tree is one way to protect against severe winter cold. Dig trench 2 to 3 feet deep along length of tree. Slice roots to depth of 1 foot on side away from trench. Gradually push tree into trench and fill with soil. Mound soil over tree for additional protection.

Another protection method involves wrapping the tree with insulating material such as old rugs or fiberglass insulation. Wrap this with plastic or other waterproof material. Mulch root area. See text, opposite, for more information.

Leaves of figs are large, tropical in appearance.

'Elberta' peach.

Peach and Nectarine

Next to the apple, the peach is the most widely grown of all home fruit. Its cousin, the smooth-skinned nectarine, is increasing in popularity.

Peaches and nectarines are often categorized as *freestone* or *clingstone*. Freestone means the flesh does not adhere to the pit or stone when the fruit is broken open. Clingstone means that the flesh sticks to the pit.

Peaches and nectarines prefer hot weather during their growth period. Because of this, they are well suited to hot, inland areas. In cooler regions of the North, select early ripening varieties. Most peaches and nectarines cannot tolerate extreme winter cold or late frosts of the northern Plains states or northern New England. They are not recommended for these areas. If you live in one of these regions, you could experiment by planting cold-hardy varieties in a protected microclimate.

Nectarines are susceptible to the fungus disease brown rot. If you are not prepared to battle this disease, do not plant nectarines. See page 54.

SAVING SPACE
More varieties of peaches and nectarines become available in genetic-dwarf forms every year. The variety charts list several recommendations. You can also graft different varieties of peach and nectarine on one tree.

POLLINATION
Most peaches and nectarines are self-fruitful and do not need cross-pollinators present. 'J. H. Hale' peach is an exception. It produces sterile pollen and needs another peach or nectarine variety nearby to pollinate it.

NUTRIENT REQUIREMENTS
After several years of bearing, you may find quality and yield of fruit have deteriorated. If this is the case, your trees are probably in need of nitrogen. Peaches and nectarines are vigorous growers and heavy feeders. Mix in 1 to 1-1/2 pounds of nitrogen fertilizer annually.

PRUNING
Prune peach and nectarine trees to a vase shape. See page 29. These trees produce new wood at a surprisingly fast rate. This is an attribute, because all fruit are produced on new wood that has grown during the preceding season.

In late winter or early spring, remove at least one-third of the previous year's growth. If you do not prune, your tree will set far more fruit than it can possibly produce. Even with substantial pruning, you will have to thin fruit after it has formed.

Mature trees can produce anywhere from 15 to 50 inches of new growth per season. If your tree is especially vigorous, you might prune up to one-half of the previous year's growth each year.

Should you neglect to prune a tree one year, the subsequent fruit will be small and numerous. In following years, fruit set is reduced, as well as new growth.

Every few years, eliminate old branches entirely. This allows sunlight to enter the tree's interior, and forces new, vigorous, bearing growth. All long, upright-growing shoots should be pruned to an outward-pointing bud.

Genetic dwarf peaches are much more conservative in their growth habit than standard trees. Little pruning is necessary.

THINNING FRUIT
Under normal conditions, peaches and nectarines set heavy crops every year. A large number of fruit drop from the tree naturally. But if you do not hand-thin fruit, the fruit crop is often small and poor quality. Thinning improves quality and flavor. The weight of the fruit may break limbs. Growth of the tree can also be retarded, because so much of the tree's energy goes into developing fruit rather than top growth.

After fruit are positively set, when they are about the size of a thumbnail, the tree goes into a rest period.

Peach and Nectarine

	Standard	Dwarf
Height at maturity (feet)		
Unpruned	25	6
Pruned	15	5-6
Spread at maturity with		
no competition (feet)	25	4-6
Recommended planting		
distance (feet)	18-22	5-8
Years to reach bearing age	3	1-2
Life expectancy (years)	20	20
Chilling requirement (hours)	600-900	600-900
Pollinator required	See charts, pages 94 to 99.	
Good for espalier	Informal	Yes
Good for containers	No	Yes

Comments: Wide selection of genetic dwarfs are available.

This is the best time to hand-thin. Thin fruit until they are about 4 to 6 inches apart, depending on how much fruit are on the tree. If the tree does not have an abundance of fruit, thin to 4 inches apart. If the tree is heavily laden with fruit on all of its branches, thin to 6 inches apart.

Early bearing varieties should be thinned to 8 inches apart. The fruit has less time to ripen than later-maturing varieties. As the season progresses and your tree is still heavy with fruit, thin some more.

The most important principle when thinning is to maintain a good ratio of leaf surface to the number of fruit. For example, if a late frost has destroyed most of your crop, leave all the rest, even if the fruit are clustered or mostly in the top of the tree.

PESTS AND DISEASES

Peach-leaf curl is a disease almost certain to attack your peaches and nectarines. Mildew, rust, blight and brown rot are other common problems. All are relatively easy to control with a regular spray program.

HARVESTING AND STORAGE

Harvest peaches and nectarines when they are firm-ripe. This is just before they are ready to eat. Do not squeeze fruit or press your finger into it. Hold fruit and twist it gently. If ripe, it will come loose from the stem.

Fruit picked when soft-ripe on the tree may be sweeter but deteriorates rapidly.

White-fleshed peaches signal ripeness when the greenish skin turns yellow-white. Yellow-fleshed peaches are ripe when skin turns an orange tint. Some varieties develop a red blush. Nectarines take on an orange or red cast.

After you harvest fruit, store at or below room temperature about 60F to 70F (16C to 21C). Fruit should be ripe and ready to eat or process in 24 hours. You can enjoy fruit immediately after picking, or store in the refrigerator until ready to use.

GARDENER'S TIPS

● Peaches thrive in temperate climates such as those near the Great Lakes. Select a warm site that is sheltered and sunny. Avoid sites in low basins where cold air collects during winter.
● Peaches and nectarines peel more easily after softening slightly. If fruit are to be processed, they are more appetizing when peeled.
● When canning clingstone varieties, harvest fruit when it breaks away from the stem easily when picked. Freestone peaches can be picked when hard-ripe. Allow to soften for a day or two.

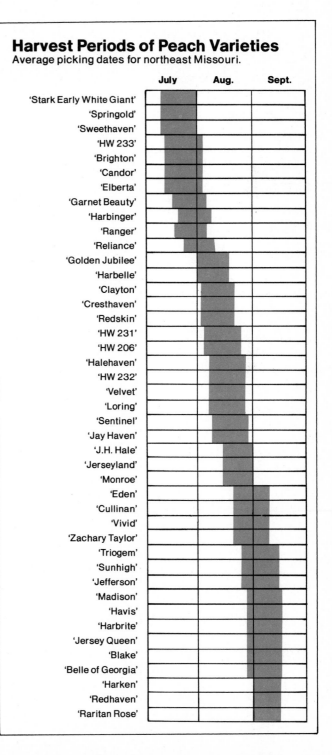

Harvest Periods of Peach Varieties
Average picking dates for northeast Missouri.

	July	Aug.	Sept.
'Stark Early White Giant'	■		
'Springold'	■		
'Sweethaven'	■		
'HW 233'	■		
'Brighton'	■		
'Candor'	■		
'Elberta'	■		
'Garnet Beauty'	■		
'Harbinger'	■		
'Ranger'	■		
'Reliance'	■		
'Golden Jubilee'	■		
'Harbelle'		■	
'Clayton'		■	
'Cresthaven'		■	
'Redskin'		■	
'HW 231'		■	
'HW 206'		■	
'Halehaven'		■	
'HW 232'		■	
'Velvet'		■	
'Loring'		■	
'Sentinel'		■	
'Jay Haven'		■	
'J.H. Hale'		■	
'Jerseyland'		■	
'Monroe'		■	
'Eden'			■
'Cullinan'			■
'Vivid'			■
'Zachary Taylor'			■
'Triogem'		■	
'Sunhigh'		■	
'Jefferson'		■	
'Madison'			■
'Havis'			■
'Harbrite'			■
'Jersey Queen'			■
'Blake'			■
'Belle of Georgia'			■
'Harken'			■
'Redhaven'			■
'Raritan Rose'			■

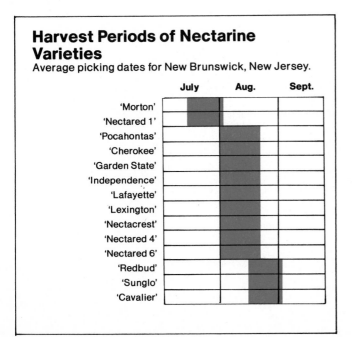

Harvest Periods of Nectarine Varieties
Average picking dates for New Brunswick, New Jersey.

	July	Aug.	Sept.
'Morton'	■		
'Nectared 1'	■		
'Pocahontas'		■	
'Cherokee'		■	
'Garden State'		■	
'Independence'		■	
'Lafayette'		■	
'Lexington'		■	
'Nectacrest'		■	
'Nectared 4'		■	
'Nectared 6'		■	
'Redbud'		■	
'Sunglo'		■	
'Cavalier'		■	

'Golden Jubilee' peach.

Peaches

Variety	Origin	Zones	Harvest Season	Fruit and Tree	Remarks
'BELLE OF GEORGIA'	Georgia	5-7	Late	Fruit large. Skin red over creamy white. Flesh white and freestone, firm. Tree vigorous, cold-hardy, productive, frost tolerant.	Use for eating fresh. Mediocre if frozen. Highly susceptible to brown rot.
'BLAKE'	New Jersey	5-7	Late	Fruit large. Skin red, slightly fuzzy. Flesh yellow, freestone, firm, melting. Tree vigorous, productive, although occasionally erratic.	Use for freezing and canning. Fruit hangs well on tree. Susceptible to bacteriosis.
'BRIGHTON'	Geneva, New York	5-7	Early	Fruit uniformly medium, attractive, roundish. Skin bright red on yellow. Flesh semicling stone, high quality, yellow, medium-firm. Slightly fibrous, juicy and slow to brown. Tree vigorous, productive, medium to average cold-hardiness.	Use for eating fresh or for canning. Use varieties in cold regions of Zone 5.
'CANDOR'	North Carolina, 1965	5-7	Early	Fruit small, oval. Skin 80% red on yellow. Flesh medium-firm, slightly coarse, semicling stone, juicy and non-browning with sweet, mild flavor. Tree vigorous, productive, average cold-hardiness.	Excellent quality for an early season peach. Not recommended for cold regions of Zone 5.
'CLAYTON'	North Carolina, 1976	5-7	Midseason	Fruit attractive, roundish. Skin yellow, flushed with bright-red blush. Flesh freestone, medium-firm, juicy, almost smooth, with sweet, rich flavor. Tree sets heavily. Requires heavy thinning to produce good-size fruit.	Flesh does not brown when exposed to air.
'CRESTHAVEN'	Michigan	5-7	Midseason to late	Fruit medium to large, roundish. Skin gold with red blush. Flesh freestone, firm, yellow, clear and juicy. Tree self-fertile and has above average cold-hardiness.	Use for canning and freezing, as well as for eating fresh. Fruit holds well on tree.
'CULLINAN'	Beltsville, Maryland, 1977	5-7	Late	Fruit roundish. Skin 70% bright red on yellow. Flesh yellow, moderately firm, juicy and smooth with sweet, rich flavor. Freestone. Tree moderately cold-hardy.	Excellent for canning. Tree's blossom buds are less tolerant of low winter temperatures than those of 'Redhaven'. Not recommended for cold regions of Zone 5.
'EDEN'	Geneva, New York, 1972	5-7	Late	Fruit large and round. Skin 60% red on creamy white. Flesh freestone, thick, firm and almost smooth texture. Sweet, rich flavor. A white-fleshed peach that oxidizes slowly. Tree vigorous, productive, cold-hardy.	Good for eating fresh. Especially good for canning.
'ELBERTA'	Georgia	5-7	Early	Fruit large. Skin deep gold with red cheek. Flesh freestone, yellow, with slight bitterness around pit. Tree spreading with large, pink flowers.	Old variety that is still quite popular. Resists brown rot. Thrives in hot-summer areas.

Compare difference between white, left, and yellow, right, peach varieties.

Peaches

Variety	Origin	Zones	Harvest Season	Fruit and Tree	Remarks
'GARNET BEAUTY'	Ontario, Canada	5-7	Early	Fruit medium to large. Skin yellow, streaked with red. Flesh freestone, yellow, firm, slightly fibrous. Tree vigorous and cold-hardy.	Excellent for eating fresh or cooking. Fruit hang on tree until overripe. Heavy bearer, producing excellent fruit well inside the tree. Susceptible to bacterial spot.
'GOLDEN JUBILEE'	California	5-7	Early	Fruit medium to large, oblong and flattened. Skin mottled bright red. Flesh freestone, yellow, coarse, soft with melting texture. Tree sets heavily, but thins itself naturally.	Average for canning and freezing. Fruit drop early from tree. Flowers small, not very showy.
'HALEHAVEN'	Michigan	5-7	Midseason	Fruit medium to large. Skin 25% to 50% red over greenish yellow, turning to yellow when ripe. Sweet flesh, freestone, yellow, juicy sweet. Tree vigorous, productive.	Excellent all-purpose peach for home gardens. Medium, non-showy flowers. Fruit and leaf buds are winter-hardy.
'HARBELLE'	Harrow, Ontario, Canada, 1968	5-7	Early	Fruit large and attractive. Skin almost smooth, deep yellow with bright-red blush. Flesh semifreestone, golden yellow, medium-firm, juicy, melting, slow to brown. Tree moderately cold-hardy and vigorous.	Fair to good quality. Semifreestone. Select other varieties for cold regions of Zone 5.
'HARBINGER'	Harrow, Ontario, Canada, 1971	5-7	Early	Fruit small to medium, roundish. Skin 90% red blush over yellow. Flesh clingstone, juicy, coarse, soft, yellow, with sweet, mild flavor. Tree vigorous, moderately cold-hardy.	Excellent, early peach. Somewhat tolerant of bacterial spot.
'HARBRITE'	Harrow, Ontario, Canada, 1969	5-7	Late	Fruit medium roundish. Skin almost smooth, 80% bright-red blush on yellow. Flesh freestone, yellow, medium-firm, juicy, melting. Tree productive, moderately vigorous.	Excellent all-around peach.
'HARKEN'	Harrow, Ontario, Canada, 1970	5-7	Late	Fruit large. Skin yellow, 80% covered with dark-red blush. Flesh freestone, firm, juicy, almost smooth with sweet, rich flavor. Slow to brown. Tree moderately vigorous, productive and cold-hardy.	Similar to 'Redhaven'.
'HAVIS'	Beltsville, Maryland, 1977	5-7	Late	Fruit about 2-3/8 inches in diameter, oblate. Skin 30% red blush on yellow. Flesh freestone, yellow, juicy, slightly fibrous, firm, with sweet, slightly tart flavor. Tree similar to 'Elberta'.	High quality, all-around peach. Resists bacterial spot. Blossom buds less resistant to low winter temperatures than those of 'Redhaven'. Select 'Redhaven' in cold regions of Zone 5.
'HW 206'	Harrow, Ontario, Canada	5-7	Midseason	Fruit medium. Skin attractive, smooth, 60% red blush on yellow. Flesh freestone, yellow, firm and melting. Good flavor and texture. Tree cold-hardy.	Tree has good tolerance to bacterial spot and brown rot.

Close-up photos show difference between peach blossoms, left, nectarine blossoms, right.

Peaches

Variety	Origin	Zones	Harvest Season	Fruit and Tree	Remarks
'HW 231'	Harrow, Ontario, Canada	5-7	Midseason	Fruit large, exceptionally attractive. Skin 75% red blush on yellow. Flesh freestone, firm, melting, yellow except around pit cavity where it is red. Tree medium in vigor, productive.	Tree has good tolerance to bacterial spot and brown rot. Excellent dessert peach.
'HW 232'	Harrow, Ontario, Canada	5-7	Midseason	Fruit large, almost smooth, attractive. Skin red blush covering 60% of yellow. Flesh freestone, firm, melting, yellow. Tree vigorous, cold-hardy and productive.	Tree has good tolerance to bacterial spot and brown rot, as well as some resistance to canker.
'HW 233'	Harrow, Ontario, Canada	5-7	Early	Fruit medium. Skin has red blush covering 75% of skin surface. Flesh freestone, firm, yellow, melting, good quality. Tree is productive with medium vigor.	Tree moderately resistant to bacterial spot.
'JAYHAVEN'	Michigan, 1977	5-7	Midseason	Fruit medium to large, round. Skin has bright-red color at full maturity. Flesh freestone, yellow, melting. Tree medium in vigor with strong scaffolds. Consistent bearer.	Good choice for cold Midwestern areas. More resistant to bacterial spot than 'Redhaven'.
'J.H. HALE'	Connecticut	5-7	Midseason	Fruit extra large. Skin deep crimson over yellow. Flesh freestone, golden yellow. Little fuzz. Tree not vigorous. Pollinator required.	Large fruit are good for eating fresh. Best for warmer areas of recommended zones.
'JEFFERSON'	Virginia, 1960	5-7	Late	Fruit medium-large, attractive. Skin about 50% red blush on bright yellow. Flesh freestone, yellow. Tree moderately vigorous.	Approaches 'J.H. Hale' in quality. Blossom buds moderately resistant to mid-winter cold. Adapted to cold areas of Zone 5.
'JERSEYLAND'	New Jersey	5-7	Midseason	Fruit large, skin dark red over greenish yellow. Flesh semifreestone, yellow, melting. Tree vigorous and productive.	Excellent all-around peach.
'JERSEY QUEEN'	New Jersey	5-7	Late	Fruit large. Skin bright red over yellow. Flesh freestone, yellow, firm. Tree productive.	Flowers are showy. Fine landscape specimen tree.
'LORING'	Missouri	5-7	Midseason	Fruit large, roundish and attractive. Skin has red blush. Flesh freestone, yellow, firm and melting with medium texture. Moderately juicy. Tree is vigorous, bears well even if spring weather is unpredictable.	Not good for canning or freezing. Tolerates adverse spring weather. Fruit does not color well.
'MADISON'	Virginia	5-7	Late	Fruit medium. Skin bright red over orange. Flesh freestone, orange-yellow and bright red near pit. Firm, fine texture with rich flavor. Non-stringy, non-browning qualities. Tree produces heavily.	Blossom buds have considerable resistance to spring frosts. Adapted to cold regions of Zone 5.

'Redhaven' peach.

Peaches

Variety	Origin	Zones	Harvest Season	Fruit and Tree	Remarks
'MONROE'	Virginia	5-7	Late	Fruit large. Skin red over orange-yellow. Flesh cling stone, yellow-orange, firm, fine texture. Tree moderately productive.	Flowers are showy pink. Above-average tolerance to frost during blossom season. Disease resistant.
'RANGER'	Maryland	5-7	Early	Fruit medium-large. Skin mottled red over greenish yellow to yellow-gold. Flesh freestone, yellow, flecked with red, firm, melting. Tree moderately vigorous, consistently productive.	Cans and freezes well. Resists bacterial rot.
'RARITAN ROSE'	New Jersey	5-7	Late	Fruit medium-large. Skin red over yellow. Flesh freestone, white, fine texture, melting, juicy. Tree spreading, vigorous, cold-hardy, productive.	Flowers are showy. Tolerant to bacteriosis.
'REDHAVEN'	Michigan	5-7	Midseason	Fruit medium. Skin bright red over yellow. Flesh semifreestone, yellow, juicy, sweet with fine grain. Tree medium, vigorous, spreading.	Flowers not showy. Often requires heavy thinning. Excellent fresh. Very good for canning. Adapts well to cold climates. Adapted to cold regions of Zone 5.
'REDSKIN'	Maryland	5-7	Midseason	Fruit medium. Skin yellow with deep-red blush. Flesh freestone, firm, yellow, slightly fibrous. Tree upright, vigorous, productive.	Early blooming, large flowers have showy pink petals. Excellent quality fruit. Keeps well. Use fresh, canned or frozen. Tree resistant to bacterial spot.
'RELIANCE'	New Hampshire, 1964	5-7	Early to midseason	Fruit medium. Skin dark red over yellow. Flesh freestone, firm, yellow, good to fair flavor. Tree cold-hardy, productive, self-fertile.	Showy bloom. Adapted to cold regions of Zone 5.
'SENTINEL'	Georgia, 1966	5-7	Midseason	Fruit medium, roundish. Skin 80% dark-red blush on yellow. Flesh semiclingstone, medium-firm, juicy, slightly coarse with sweet flavor.	Blossom survival in winter is erratic, but normally sets good crops. Resists bacterial spot. In years of light crops, tends to have many split pits.
'SPRINGGOLD'	Fort Valley, Georgia, 1966	5-7	Early	Fruit round. Skin striped 90% red on yellow. Flesh is clingstone, more than most early peaches. Tree is as resistant to low winter temperatures as 'Redhaven'. Adapted to cold regions of Zone 5.	Good flavor. Less prone to split pits than most early varieties.
'STARK EARLY WHITE GIANT'	Missouri	5-8	Early	Fruit large, white flushed. Clingstone. Tree vigorous, relatively cold-hardy.	Excellent for pies, cobblers and fresh eating. One of the earliest to ripen.

Fresh and canned peaches and peach preserves are proof of gardening success.

Peaches

Variety	Origin	Zones	Harvest Season	Fruit and Tree	Remarks
'SUNHIGH'	New Jersey	5-7	Late	Fruit medium to large. Skin bright red on yellow. Flesh freestone, yellow, firm. Tree vigorous, spreading.	Good-quality fruit but tree is susceptible to bacteriosis. Requires thorough summer spraying.
'SWEETHAVEN'	Michigan, 1977	5-7	Early	Fruit small to medium, oblate. Skin 80% red on yellow. Flesh semifreestone, juicy, slightly fibrous, soft with sweet, rich flavor. Tree vigorous and productive.	Blossom buds not as cold-hardy as 'Redhaven'.
'TRIOGEM'	New Jersey	5-7	Late	Fruit medium, oval. Skin 70% red over bright yellow. Flesh freestone, juicy, non-browning, with sweet flavor. Tree productive and cold-hardy.	Use for canning. Ripens slowly. Sets heavily and produces good crop under adverse weather conditions.
'VELVET'	Ontario, Canada, 1966	5-7	Midseason	Fruit large, roundish to oblate. Skin 80% red on yellow. Flesh freestone, thick, moderately firm, juicy with sweet, rich flavor. Tree moderately vigorous.	Not recommended for northern regions of Zone 5. Blossom buds less hardy to winter cold than 'Redhaven'.
'VIVID'	Ontario, Canada, 1974	5-7	Late	Fruit medium to large. Flesh freestone. Skin bright red. Tree moderately vigorous.	Productive. Completely freestone.
'ZACHARY TAYLOR'	Virginia, 1972	5-7	Late	Fruit medium. Skin 50% red stripes on yellow. Flesh clingstone, medium-firm, nearly smooth, non-browning with sweet, rich flavor. Tree vigorous.	Excellent all-around peach.

Genetic Dwarf Peaches

Variety	Origin	Zones	Harvest Season	Fruit and Tree	Remarks
'BONANZA II'	California	5-7	Midseason	Fruit large. Skin orange blushed red. Flesh yellow, freestone, sweet. Tree grows to about 6 feet high. Plant in containers and give substantial winter protection.	Better tasting than 'Bonanza'. Flowers are showy, pink and semi-double.
'COMPACT REDHAVEN'	Orondo, Washington	5-7	Midseason	A chance sport of 'Redhaven'. Exactly like it in all ways except size.	Accepts colder temperatures than other genetic dwarfs.

Nectarines

Variety	Origin	Zones	Harvest Season	Fruit and Tree	Remarks
'CAVALIER'	Virginia	5-7	Late	Fruit medium to large, attractive. Skin dark red over orange-yellow. Flesh freestone, yellow, firm. Tree vigorous, cold-hardy, productive.	Fruit slightly bitter. Flowers showy. Resists spring frost and brown rot.
'CHEROKEE'	Virginia	5-7	Midseason	Fruit medium to large. Skin highly colored with slight gloss. Flesh semifreestone, yellow, rich flavor. Tree moderately vigorous, productive.	Excellent fruit. Flowers showy. Above-average tolerance to brown rot infection and spring frost.

Photos show how much to thin peaches and nectarines. If tree has large amount of fruit, thin to 6 inches apart.

Nectarines

Variety	Origin	Zones	Harvest Season	Fruit and Tree	Remarks
'GARDEN STATE'	New Jersey	5-7	Midseason	Skin red blush over greenish yellow. Flesh freestone, firm, yellow, juicy. Tree vigorous, productive, spreading.	Light-pink showy flowers.
'INDEPENDENCE'	Fresno, California, 1965	5-7	Midseason	Fruit large, attractive. Skin almost completely dark red over yellow. Flesh freestone and non-browning, yellow, firm, juicy, slightly coarse texture with sweet, rich flavor. Tree vigorous, spreading.	Blossom buds are fairly cold-hardy.
'LAFAYETTE'	Virginia Polytechnic Institute	5-7	Midseason	Fruit medium to large. Skin smooth, bright red. Flesh freestone, white, juicy, with excellent flavor. Tree has average vigor, above-average cold-hardiness.	Flowers showy. Heavy producer of fruit.
'LEXINGTON'	Unknown	5-7	Midseason	Fruit medium to large. Skin medium red over deep yellow. Flesh freestone, deep yellow, medium-firm. Tree vigorous and cold-hardy.	Flowers showy. Resists brown rot and frost in blossom season.
'MORTON'	New York, 1965	5-7	Early	Fruit somewhat small. Skin attractive dark red. Flesh semiclingstone, white, juicy, slightly coarse and medium-firm. Tree cold-hardy.	Early bearing season makes this tree worth planting.
'NECTACREST'	New Jersey, 1947	5-7	Midseason	Fruit large. Skin red on yellow. Flesh freestone, white, fairly firm. Tree vigorous and cold-hardy.	Preferred for fine flavor. Flowers showy.
'NECTARED 1'	New Jersey, 1962	5-7	Early	Fruit about 2-1/4 inches in diameter, slightly oval. Skin 95% covered with dark-red blush. Flesh clingstone, yellow, juicy, slightly coarse, moderately soft with sweet, good flavor. Tree vigorous, spreading.	Blossom buds are moderately cold-hardy. The New York State Fruit Testing Association says, "The best very early, yellow-fleshed nectarine that we have tested."
'NECTARED 4'	New Jersey, 1962	5-7	Midseason	Fruit medium. Skin 90% dark red on yellow. Flesh mostly freestone, yellow, medium-firm, juicy, slightly fibrous. Sweet, rich flavor. Tree moderately vigorous, productive.	Blossom buds moderately resistant to low winter temperatures.
'NECTARED 6'	New Jersey, 1962	5-7	Midseason	Fruit medium and slightly oval. Skin 85% dark red over bright yellow. Flesh freestone, yellow, slightly soft, juicy and fibrous. Sweet flavor. Tree vigorous.	Blossom buds resistant to low winter temperatures.
'POCAHONTAS'	Virginia	5-7	Early	Fruit medium-large. Skin highly colored with red and yellow. Flesh semifreestone, yellow, slightly stringy. Tree vigorous.	Flowers showy. Resistant to brown rot and frost damage during blossom season.
'REDBUD'	Virginia	5-7	Midseason	Fruit medium. Skin smooth, bright red over yellow. Flesh freestone, white with bright red. Tree moderately vigorous.	Flowers showy. Tree sets heavily. Resists brown-rot infection and blossom season frost.
'SUNGLO'	California	5-7	Midseason	Fruit medium. Skin bright red over golden orange. Flesh freestone, firm, melting. Tree moderately vigorous, upright, spreading.	Heavy bearer. Requires heavy thinning and extra nitrogen for best performance. One of the high-quality nectarines.

'Dr. Jules Guyot' pear.

Pear

If apple trees grow in your area, pear trees will thrive as well. Pears are excellent for the home garden. White blossoms grace trees in spring. Handsome foliage and fruit are attractions in summer and fall. Even in winter, the framework of the bare branches adds interest to the landscape.

Pears extend the fresh-fruit season. Most finish ripening in storage during late fall and early winter, when fresh, home-grown fruit is not usually available.

Pears are easy to grow and begin to bear fruit a few years after planting. They require little pruning after they reach bearing age.

Three kinds of pears are commonly grown, but only two are appropriate for the regions discussed in this book. *European* pears are the most common. *Asian* pears are grown in many parts of the West, but are not recommended for the East, Midwest or Mid-Atlantic areas. *Hybrid pears* are a cross between the European variety and Asian pears. They are suited to both warm and cool regions.

CULTURAL REQUIREMENTS

Like all deciduous fruit trees, pears require regular amounts of water. During periods of summer drought, apply water equal to of 1 inch of rain each week.

Deep, well-drained soil is ideal, but trees grown in moderately drained soils usually survive. Bedrock, compact subsoil or poor drainage reduce growth and productivity. Pears planted in areas with poor drainage rarely grow to reach bearing age, if they survive at all.

POLLINATION

Plant at least two different pear varieties for pollination. Any combination is fine except 'Bartlett' with 'Seckel'. These do not cross-pollinate. Cold, wet, windy, spring weather, particularly during bloom period, reduces bee activity. If bee flights are curtailed, less pollen is transferred, thus reducing fruit set. If you live in an area that usually has this kind of spring weather, plant three varieties.

PRUNING

Most pear trees have an upright growth habit. Pear wood that grows vertically seldom bears much fruit. Multiple-leader training is recommended so that branches grow more horizontally. It helps to head or cut all leaders to an outward-pointing leaf bud each year. This promotes strong growth and branching. Doing this spreads the risk of fireblight among three or four leaders. If fireblight infects a branch, you can remove it. The others continue to grow and bear fruit.

Trees that bear young, 'Bartlett', 'Bosc' and 'Duchess', are also heavy bearers. The weight of fruit can cause limb breakage. To prevent, tie vertical scaffold limbs with a piece of rope or strap. After fruit has set, thin ends of secondary branches to an upright shoot or bud. Fruit develop on sturdy wood rather than on the ends of fragile branches. Or simply remove fruit that set on branch ends.

'Anjou' and 'Comice' can be stimulated to set fruit by heading branches to a flower bud just before bloom.

After trees bear, prune lightly, if at all, except when a branch is infected with fireblight. Remove it to prevent spread of the disease.

SIZE CONTROL

Dwarf pears from reliable nurseries are recommended if your space is limited. However, the quince rootstock commonly used in dwarfing is not cold-hardy in Northern zones. In addition, some pears are not compatible with quince rootstock. An *interstem* must be grafted between the quince rootstock and stock. See page 46.

Many of the same techniques of growing apples are applicable to pears. Grow them as an espalier, hedge or garden divider trained on wires. They readily adapt to a

Pear	Standard	Dwarf
Height at maturity (feet)		
Unpruned	40	25
Pruned	15	12-15
Spread at maturity with no competition (feet)	25	15
Recommended planting distance (feet)	18-25	12-15
Years to reach bearing age	4-8	3-5
Life expectancy (years)	75	60
Chilling requirement (hours)	600-900	600-900
Pollinator required	Yes	Yes
Good for espalier	Yes	Yes
Good for containers	No	Yes

Comments: Can be pruned to fit small space.

Gallery of Pear Varieties

'Anjou'

'Aurora'

'Bartlett'

'Bosc'

'Comice'

'Duchess'

'Kieffer'

'Max Red Bartlett'

'Seckel'

trellis or to containers as single *cordons*—short, straight stems. Grafting additional varieties expands selection if space is too limited for more trees.

THINNING FRUIT
Pears rarely require thinning unless the crop is unusually heavy. If this is the case, thin out small and imperfect fruit about three weeks before harvest.

HARVESTING AND STORAGE
With a few exceptions such as 'Duchess', pears reach their best flavor when ripened *off* the tree, so pick them before they become fully ripe. Fruit left to ripen on the tree do not develop the characteristic, buttery texture or peak flavor. Instead, they become soft and turn brown at the core.

Usually, you can begin to pick pears when the first few fruit drop from the tree. At this time, the more mature fruit are changing from green to yellow. Others have attained full size, but are green and hard.

Pears, like apples, bear on the same spurs every year. When you harvest, do it carefully. Do not break the spur off the branch. Lift the fruit gently. Do not pull or twist. Fruit will separate from the stem if it is ready to pick. 'Bartlett' and 'Kieffer' are exceptions. They should be picked while it still takes a twist to loosen them. If fruit does not separate easily from the spur, allow it to ripen a few more days, then try again.

Pears require one or two days to several weeks to ripen after they are picked. It depends on the variety. Summer pears ripen more quickly than late-fall or winter pears.

To store, wrap each pear in a sheet of paper toweling. Arrange in shallow boxes or flats one layer deep. If you wish to eat them within several weeks, store in a cool, dark place. To hold pears for a longer period, refrigerate them at 32F to 40F (0C to 5C). Bring out to room temperature about one week before you wish to eat them.

Pears ripen faster if they are kept in a poorly ventilated storage area. If you want them to ripen quickly, place several in a plastic bag and seal. Check for ripeness after one week. Try adding a ripe apple to the bag. The ethylene gas produced by the apple promotes ripening. Summer varieties such as 'Clapp's Favorite' and 'Bartlett' should be stored below 75F (25C). Generally, the lower the temperature, the longer fruit will keep. Check fruit every few days to determine ripeness.

PESTS AND DISEASES
Healthy leaves are essential for vigorous tree growth. *Fireblight,* pear's most lethal disease, is often transmitted by sucking insects such as aphids, plant bugs and leaf hoppers. Signs of the disease are terminal shoots and blossoms that look like they have been scorched by fire.

Remove fireblight damage just below infection and paint wound with a product containing fixed copper. See page 55. Burn or dispose of infected branch. Afterward, disinfect all pruning tools used.

A number of wild plant species commonly found in the Midwest and East harbor fireblight and other pests.

These include wild apple and wild pear seedlings, mountain ash, hawthorn and thorn apple. Removing these plants that grow near your fruit trees will significantly reduce the risk of fireblight.

Damage from pear psylla, an insect that attacks pears, can be infected by the fireblight bacteria. A regular and thorough spray program must be carried out during the growing season.

Pear scab is another scourge of pear trees. It too requires a meticulous spray program of both insecticide and fungicide.

Insects attacking pears also include codling moth, mites, pear slug, scale and flathead borer. Check the variety charts for resistance.

GARDENER'S TIPS
• When pears have ripened to perfection in storage, place them in plastic bags in the refrigerator to maintain peak quality. They will keep about one week.
• Fresh pears are not at their best eaten cold. For full, glorious flavor, eat them at room temperature.

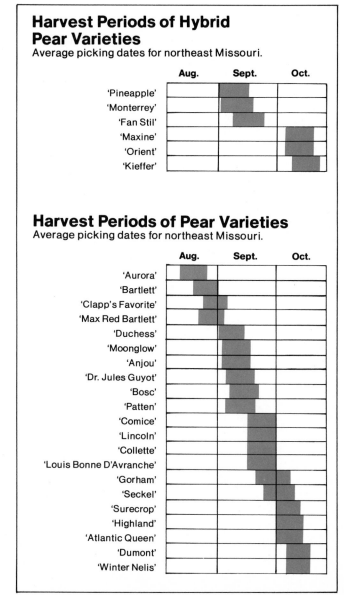

Harvest Periods of Hybrid Pear Varieties
Average picking dates for northeast Missouri.

	Aug.	Sept.	Oct.
'Pineapple'		▓	
'Monterrey'		▓	
'Fan Stil'		▓	
'Maxine'			▓
'Orient'			▓
'Kieffer'			▓

Harvest Periods of Pear Varieties
Average picking dates for northeast Missouri.

	Aug.	Sept.	Oct.
'Aurora'	▓		
'Bartlett'	▓		
'Clapp's Favorite'	▓		
'Max Red Bartlett'	▓		
'Duchess'		▓	
'Moonglow'		▓	
'Anjou'		▓	
'Dr. Jules Guyot'		▓	
'Bosc'		▓	
'Patten'		▓	
'Comice'		▓	
'Lincoln'		▓	
'Collette'		▓	
'Louis Bonne D'Avranche'		▓	
'Gorham'			▓
'Seckel'			▓
'Surecrop'			▓
'Highland'			▓
'Atlantic Queen'			▓
'Dumont'			▓
'Winter Nelis'			▓

'Seckel' dwarf pear, heavy with abundant crop.

Pears

Variety	Origin	Zones	Harvest Season	Fruit and Tree	Remarks
'ANJOU'	Belgium	5-7	Midseason	Fruit large. Skin light green at harvest, cream to green after ripening. Flesh white, fine texture, somewhat bland, juicy. Tree vigorous, upright.	Use for dessert or for fresh eating. Ripens after one month of storage when refrigerated. Susceptible to cork spot in warm-summer regions. Slow to begin bearing. 'Red Anjou' is a red-skin variation. Good keeper.
'ATLANTIC QUEEN'	France, 18th Century	5-7	Late	Fruit large, up to 1-1/2 pounds. Skin yellow with red blush, sweet, juicy, fine aroma. Tree vigorous, particularly along the East Coast.	Highly resistant to fireblight. Excellent eating pear.
'AURORA'	Geneva, New York, 1964	5-7	Early	Fruit large, with regular pear shape. Skin bright yellow overlaid with russet, slightly blushed with pink. Flesh smooth, melting, juicy, sweet with good aroma. Tree is vigorous spreader.	Keeps well in storage until December. Not resistant to fireblight.
'BARTLETT'	England	5-7	Early	Fruit medium to large. Skin green at harvest, yellow when ripened in storage. Flesh white, sweet and tender. Tree vigorous.	Use for eating fresh and for canning. Thrives in warm-summer areas. Cool summers produce inferior fruit. Ripens without cold storage. Subject to fireblight. Standard pear in many areas of the world.
'BOSC'	Belgium, 1807	5-7	Late	Fruit large. Skin green to dark yellow with light-brown blotch. Distinctive narrow shape with long neck. Flesh white, tender, juicy, sweet. Tree large, vigorous, with upright growth habit.	Use for canning or for eating fresh. Ripens at room temperature. Highly susceptible to fireblight. Stores well.
'CLAPP'S FAVORITE'	Massachusetts	5-7	Early	Fruit large. Skin yellow with red blush. Flesh much like 'Bartlett', but breaks down at core if picked too late. Tree cold-hardy, productive, bears annually.	Use for canning or for eating fresh. Softens quickly after picking. Susceptible to fireblight.
'COMICE'	France	5-7	Midseason to late	Fruit large. Skin greenish yellow when harvested, yellow with russet specks when ripe. Flesh buttery, sweet, tender, juicy and highly aromatic. Tree large, vigorous and slow to bear.	Considered by many to be the best pear. Often included in fruit gift packs under the name Royal Riviera. Requires low chilling and cold storage to ripen.

Pears

Variety	Origin	Zones	Harvest Season	Fruit and Tree	Remarks
'COLETTE'	Unknown	5-7	Midseason to late	Fruit and tree are similar to 'Bartlett'.	Excellent for eating fresh and cooking. Fruit mature over a period of 6 to 8 weeks. First are ready to pick in late August. Others continue to ripen until frost.
'DR. JULES GUYOT'	Unknown	5-7	Midseason	Fruit large. Skin lemon-yellow with pink blush. Flesh fine texture, melting, sweet and juicy. Tree upright, slow growing.	Not available in markets. Only available in home gardens. Excellent dessert pear.
'DUCHESS' ('DUCHESSE DE'ANGOULEME')	Europe	5-7	Midseason	Fruit large. Skin green to yellow blushed with red. Flesh juicy, buttery, lightly spiced. Tree slow growing, bears early. Self-fruitful, acts as pollinator for all other pears.	Superb dessert pear. A good selection for the home garden because it is a good pollinator.
'DUMONT'	Europe, 1867	5-7	Late	Fruit medium to large. Skin subtle yellow with slight pink blush. Flesh firm, juicy, smooth texture, sweet and rich. Tree tends to alternate-bear when mature.	Excellent winter pear. Stores for 6 to 8 weeks.
'GORHAM'	Geneva, New York, 1923	5-7	Midseason	Fruit medium. Skin bright yellow with touch of russet around stem. Flesh juicy, melting and sweet.	Use for dessert or canning. Keeps in cold storage 4 to 6 weeks longer than 'Bartlett'. Slightly more resistant to fireblight than 'Bartlett'. Tree may need additional doses of nitrogen.
'HIGHLAND'	Geneva, New York, 1974	5-7	Late	Fruit large. Skin fairly smooth, yellow covered with light russet. Flesh melting, juicy, smooth, sweet and rich. Tree moderately vigorous, productive.	Use for dessert or canning. Susceptible to fireblight. Quality improves by being stored at room temperature 1 month before ripening. Picked 4 weeks after 'Bartlett'.
'LINCOLN'	Unknown	4-7	Midseason	Fruit large. Skin medium yellow flecked with russet. Flesh melting, sweet, aromatic. Tree extremely cold-hardy and blight resistant.	Use for dessert or canning. Abundant producer. Perhaps the most dependable pear for cold, Midwestern climates.
'LOUIS BONNE D'AVRANCHE'	France	5-7	Midseason	Fruit medium, elongated, red and yellow. Top-quality flesh. Tree strong, upright.	Rarely seen in home gardens, but should be planted more often. Highly productive.
'MAX RED BARTLETT'	Washington	5-7	Early	Fruit medium. Skin striped russet-red changing to bright red when ripe. Tree similar to 'Bartlett'. Growth is weak.	Reasonable fruit quality for eating fresh and for canning. Tree susceptible to fireblight. Attractive red foliage.
'MOONGLOW'	Maryland	5-7	Midseason	Fruit medium, resembling 'Bartlett'. Skin yellow with pink blush when ripe. Flesh soft, juicy, low acid with little grit. Tree vigorous, upright, bearing when young.	Use for eating fresh or for canning. Stores well. Heavy cropper resistant to fireblight. Produces many spurs.
'PATTEN'	Charles City, Iowa	4-7	Midseason	Fruit large. Skin yellow with pink blush. Flesh juicy, melting, with quality taste and aroma. Tree especially cold-hardy.	Excellent fresh. Fair for canning. Cold-hardiness allows it to be grown in areas where 'Bartlett' and 'Anjou' fail.
'SECKEL'	Pennsylvania 1775	5-7	Late	Fruit small. Skin reddish brown over yellow-brown with russet. Flesh creamy white, sweet, superb flavor. Tree naturally semidwarf, productive.	Not much to look at but considered the standard of taste quality by many. Use in preserves. Tree somewhat fireblight resistant. Extensive thinning helps produce medium-size fruit.
'SURECROP'	Arkansas	5-7	Late	Fruit large. Skin yellow. Resembles 'Bartlett' in appearance and taste. Blooms for long period, good for late-frost areas. Bears annually on vigorous, upright tree.	More resistant to fireblight than any other variety.
'WINTER NELIS'	Belgium	5-7	Late	Fruit medium. Skin yellow-green to russet. Flesh buttery, melting but has grit near core. Tree vigorous, heavy bearer.	Use for baking. Susceptible to fireblight. Recommended for warm-summer areas. Tends to alternate-bear. Requires another variety nearby for cross-pollination. Stores well.

Well-pruned pear tree, decked out in springtime blossoms, is attractive addition to home landscape.

Hybrid Pears

Variety	Origin	Zones	Harvest Season	Fruit and Tree	Remarks
'FAN STIL'	Texas	5-7	Midseason	Fruit medium. Skin yellow with red cheek. Flesh white, crisp, juicy. Tree vigorous and upright.	Low chilling requirement. Recommended for warm areas of Zone 7.
'KIEFFER'	Pennsylvania	5-7	Late	Fruit medium to large. Skin yellow with red blush. Flesh white, crisp, coarse, juicy with some grit. Tree vigorous, upright.	Use for cooking and canning. Low chilling requirement. Recommended for warm areas of Zone 7. Stores well. Poor to fair flavor.
'MAXINE', ('STARKING DELICIOUS')	Ohio	5-7	Late	Fruit large. Skin yellow. Flesh moderately firm, some grit, sharp flavor. Tree vigorous.	Use for eating fresh and canning. Resists fireblight. Better than average quality for a hybrid pear.
'MONTERREY'	Mexico	5-7	Midseason	Fruit large, shaped like an apple. Skin yellow. Flesh soft, smooth, little grit. Tree vigorous.	Use for eating fresh or canned. Highly resistant to fireblight. Recommended for warm areas of Zone 7. Stores well.
'ORIENT'	Chico, California	5-7	Late	Fruit large. Skin yellow with russet blush. Flesh white, smooth, sugary. Tree strong, easy to train, heavy cropper.	Tree bears early. Produces regularly. Highest resistance to fireblight of any hybrid pear. Requires another variety nearby for cross-pollination. Recommended for warm areas of Zone 7.
'PINEAPPLE'	Texas	5-7	Midseason	Fruit large. Skin heavily russeted. Tree vigorous and productive.	Flesh tastes similar to pineapple.

'Burbank' Japanese plum.

Plum

Of all stone fruit, plums offer the widest variety of tastes, colors, sizes and forms. They are perhaps the most versatile of the home-garden fruit. Plums can be eaten fresh or preserved as jellies, jams and butters. They can be used whole, baked in cakes, pastries and pies and dried as prunes.

Plums are also adaptable. Varieties are available for almost every climate region in North America, whether they are cultivated or domestic, wild varieties.

Plums belong to the genus *Prunus,* and are com-prised of four groups. There are two European types called *European* and *Damson,* one Japanese species and several wild, native North-American varieties.

European plums have been cultivated for centuries, and probably originated in the area of Russia's Caucasus Mountains. They are usually the sweetest plums, and are commonly dried and eaten as prunes. Their high sugar content allows them to be dried in the sun without fermenting the pit. Fruit are oval, with predominately blue skin. There are also green, yellow and reddish varieties. Fruit flesh is firm.

Damson plums are oval, usually blue or purple, but yellow varieties are grown as well. Like European plums, they are of ancient origin. Trees of Damson are fairly small, making them highly suitable for residential gardens. They are not as versatile as European plums because they are not as sweet. For that reason, they are used primarily as cooking plums. Damson preserves are regarded highly.

As a rule, both European and Damson plums ripen in late summer or early fall.

Japanese plums, which trace their origin to China, are primarily red or reddish orange, although some are yellow, green or deep purple. They are softer and juicier than the European varieties, but less sweet. They excel as dessert fruit. Most varieties are suited to warmer areas, such as the West. However, many varieties are available that thrive in the cooler climates of the Northeast, Midwest and Mid-Atlantic areas. Japanese plums ripen earlier than European or Damson varieties.

As a rule of thumb, if pears grow well in your area, European and Damson plums will also do well. They are not suited for the warm areas of the South or Southwest.

If peaches thrive locally, so will the hardier varieties of Japanese plums.

CULTURAL REQUIREMENTS
European and Japanese plums thrive in loamy, well-drained soil. Wet, soggy soil promotes root rot. Water young trees regularly during dry spells. After trees are established, a thick layer of organic mulch should make watering unnecessary.

POLLINATION
Plums vary greatly in pollination requirements. Most

European Plum	Standard	Dwarf
Height at maturity (feet)		
Unpruned	30	15
Pruned	15	8
Spread at maturity with no competition (feet)	25	12
Recommended planting distance (feet)	20-22	10-12
Years to reach bearing age	4-5	3-4
Life expectancy (years)	40	40
Chilling requirement (hours)	700-1,000	700-1,000
Pollinator required	See chart, page 109.	
Good for espalier	Yes	Yes
Good for containers	Yes	Yes

Japanese Plum	Standard	Dwarf
Height at maturity (feet)		
Unpruned	30	15
Pruned	15	8
Spread at maturity with no competition (feet)	25	12
Recommended planting distance (feet)	18-22	10-12
Years to reach bearing age	3	3
Life expectancy (years)	40	40
Chilling requirement (hours)	500-900	500-900
Pollinator required	See chart, page 110.	
Good for espalier	Yes	Yes
Good for containers	Yes	Yes

'President' European plum.

European plum in bloom.

'Green Gage' European plum.

need specific varieties nearby to set adequate amounts of fruit. Requirements are included in the variety charts.

PRUNING

Train European and Damson plums the same as apple trees—in a cone shape with a central leader. Remove vigorous, vertical growth. If preferred, you can pull the tree down to a more horizontal position. Because fruit are borne on 4- to 6-inch spurs, do not thin these out. Rather, cut back annual shoot growth. Fruit are borne on spurs that live for many years. After they are established, trees require little pruning.

Train Japanese plums in a vase shape. This is because yearly growth is extremely vigorous. These must be pruned rather severely through their bearing lives. Remove shoots, watersprouts and suckers each year. Prune vertical-growing varieties such as 'Santa Rosa' to outward-growing branches. Prune spreading varieties to inside branches. Japanese plums are also borne on long-lived spurs, as well as on 1-year-old shoots. To avoid fruit from oversetting and thus producing inferior fruit, remove 1-year-old shoots and promote fruit bearing on spurs only.

In later years, prune out non-bearing wood and spurs to make room for new, bearing growth.

THINNING FRUIT

Unless fruit set is exceptionally heavy, it is not necessary to thin most European plums. Damson plums are never thinned. Japanese plums overbear occasionally. Hand-thin as soon as fruit are large enough to handle comfortably. Thin to 4 to 6 inches apart, and divide all clusters. Doing this will result in larger fruit of better quality.

HARVESTING AND STORAGE

A plum that is ready to be picked separates easily from the tree when given a little twist. Ripe plums are slightly soft when squeezed lightly. A *bloom,* or powdery coating, covers the skin. Fruit should not be picked when firm.

Harvest European plums when dead-ripe. Japanese plums are picked just as they begin to soften. Allow them to ripen in a cool, 60F (16C) room.

Harvest early season plums in two or three pickings as they ripen. Pick later-maturing varieties at one time, or make two pickings about 7 to 10 days apart.

Pick and store early plums when they are not quite dead-ripe. They will keep in a cool place for several weeks. Later-maturing varieties can be stored this way for one to three months, depending on variety.

PESTS AND DISEASES

As with all fruit, a number of pests and diseases attack plum trees. Few are serious pests. Plum curculio, peach borer, San Jose scale and aphids are easy to control with a regular spray program. Brown rot, yellow leaf and black knot may also infect plants. See pages 52 to 55.

GARDENER'S TIPS

• Damson plums are used primarily for preserves. Pick after they have developed full color.
• An easy way to harvest plums is to shake the tree vigorously, then gather the fallen plums.
• Like cherries, plums can be piled into containers without fear of bruising them, unless they are overly ripe and soft.

Plums are ready to harvest when they separate from stem with a light twist. These are 'Mirandy'.

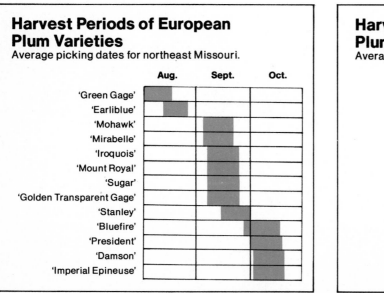

Harvest Periods of European Plum Varieties
Average picking dates for northeast Missouri.

Variety	Aug.	Sept.	Oct.
'Green Gage'	■		
'Earliblue'	■		
'Mohawk'		■	
'Mirabelle'		■	
'Iroquois'		■	
'Mount Royal'		■	
'Sugar'		■	
'Golden Transparent Gage'		■	
'Stanley'		■	
'Bluefire'		■	■
'President'			■
'Damson'			■
'Imperial Epineuse'			■

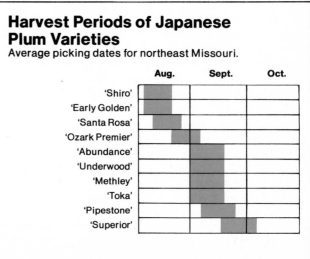

Harvest Periods of Japanese Plum Varieties
Average picking dates for northeast Missouri.

Variety	Aug.	Sept.	Oct.
'Shiro'	■		
'Early Golden'	■		
'Santa Rosa'	■		
'Ozark Premier'	■		
'Abundance'		■	
'Underwood'		■	
'Methley'		■	
'Toka'		■	
'Pipestone'		■	
'Superior'		■	■

European Plums

Variety	Origin	Zones	Pollinator	Harvest Season	Fruit and Tree	Remarks
'BLUEFIRE'	Europe	5-7	Self-fertile	Late	Fruit large. Skin blue. Flesh freestone, yellow. Tree vigorous, bears young. Fruit hang on tree after ripening.	Susceptible to brown rot. Fruit tend to double.
'DAMSON'	Europe	Warm areas of Zone 4, 5-7	Self-fertile	Late	Fruit small. Skin blue. Flesh golden yellow, melting, juicy, slightly tart. Tree vigorous, but small.	Improved varieties include 'Blue Damson', 'French Damson', and 'Shropshire Damson'. Use for canning and preserves.
'EARLIBLUE'	Unknown	5-7	'Mohawk'	Early	Fruit medium. Skin blue. Flesh greenish yellow, tender, similar to 'Stanley' but softer. Tree cold-hardy. Moderate production.	Takes longer than most to bear.
'GOLDEN TRANSPARENT GAGE'	England, 1894	5-7	Self-fertile	Midseason	Fruit medium. Skin clear yellow with small, red dots. Flesh firm, sweet with rich flavor. Tree has dwarf growth habit.	Choice dessert plum. Use fresh.
'GREEN GAGE'	Europe	5-7	Self-fertile	Midseason	Fruit medium, round to oval. Skin greenish yellow. Flesh amber, aromatic, sweet, mild and juicy. Tree medium .	Use for canning, preserves and eating fresh.
'IMPERIAL EPINEUSE'	France	5-7	Other late European plum.	Late	Fruit large. Skin reddish purple. Flesh greenish yellow. Tree vigorous.	Use fresh or for canning or drying.
'IROQUOIS'	New York, 1966	5-7	Self-fertile	Midseason	Fruit medium, oval. Skin blue. Flesh amber. Tree medium, bears early and annually. Productive.	A prune-type plum. Use fresh or for preserves.
'MIRABELLE'	France	5-7	Self-fertile	Midseason	Fruit small. Skin yellow. Flesh yellow, sweet and juicy. Tree vigorous, spreading.	An excellent plum. Favored above all others in France, but rarely grown in the United States or Canada.
'MOHAWK'	New York, 1966	5-7	Any European plum.	Midseason	Fruit large. Skin blue. Flesh amber. Blue-prune type. Tree vigorous, bushy.	Use fresh or for cooking.
'MOUNT ROYAL'	Unknown	Warm areas of Zone 4, 5-7	'Stanley'	Midseason	Fruit medium. Skin deep blue. Flesh freestone, amber. Tree cold-hardy and vigorous.	The most cold-hardy of all European plums. Will withstand all but the most severe Northern winters.
'PRESIDENT'	England	5-7	Other late European plum.	Late	Fruit large. Skin dark blue. Flesh amber. Tree moderate in growth habit.	Does not have outstanding flavor, but ripens late. Use for cooking or canning.
'STANLEY'	New York	5-7	Self-fertile	Midseason	Fruit large. Skin dark blue. Flesh firm, richly colored yellow. Tree large, spreading, productive. Bears heavily every year.	Highly susceptible to brown rot. Fruit doubles in hot climates. This variety replacing 'Italian Prune' throughout Northeast and Midwest. Sometimes cold-hardy in warm regions of Zone 4.
'SUGAR'	California	5-7	Self-fertile	Midseason	Fruit fairly large. Skin dark blue. Flesh purple, sweet, highly flavored. Tree bears alternate years. Heavy cropper.	Use for home drying and canning.

Cluster of plums, ready for harvest.

Japanese Plums

Variety	Origin	Zones	Pollinator	Harvest Season	Fruit and Tree	Remarks
'ABUNDANCE'	California	5-7	'Methley', 'Shiro'	Midseason	Fruit medium. Skin reddish purple. Flesh tender, yellow, softens rapidly. Tree tends to alternate-bear.	Use for desserts or cooking.
'EARLY GOLDEN'	Canada	5-7	'Burbank', 'Shiro'	Early	Fruit medium, round. Skin yellow. Flesh freestone, tender, flavorful, fair quality. Tree vigorous, but tends to alternate-bear.	Use for desserts or cooking.
'METHLEY'	South Africa	5-7	Self-fertile	Midseason	Fruit small to medium. Skin reddish purple. Flesh red with excellent flavor. Tree upright with cold-hardy flower buds.	Ripens over long period. Needs several pickings. Good pollinator.
'OZARK PREMIER'	Missouri	5-8	'Methley'	Midseason	Fruit large. Skin red. Flesh yellow. Tree cold-hardy, productive, vigorous.	Use for eating fresh, canned or in preserves and sauces.
'PIPESTONE'	Minnesota	Warm regions of Zone 4, 5-7	'Toka', 'Superior'	Midseason	Fruit large. Skin deep red with purple blush. Flesh yellow. Tree cold-hardy and vigorous.	Flesh somewhat stringy. Use for eating fresh or for cooking. Adapted to cold-winter areas.
'SANTA ROSA'	California, 1906	5-7	Self-fertile or any early or midseason plum	Early	Fruit large. Skin deep crimson. Flesh purple near skin and yellow, streaked pink near pit. Tree prolific bearer.	One of Luther Burbank's triumphs. Almost all characteristics of tree surpass 'Abundance'. Use fresh, canned or for desserts. Widely adapted.
'SHIRO'	California	5-7	'Santa Rosa', 'Methley', 'Early Golden'	Midseason	Fruit medium to large, roundish. Skin yellow. Flesh yellow, good flavor. Tree low growing, cold-hardy, prolific.	Use for cooking, canning and desserts. Considered one of the best yellow plums.
'SUPERIOR'	Minnesota	Warm regions of Zone 4, 5-7	'Toka'	Late	Fruit large, conical in shape. Skin red with russet dots. Flesh yellow and firm, excellent for eating fresh. Tree vigorous, early bearer.	Good dessert quality. Tends to overbear and needs thinning. Adapted to warm regions of Zone 4.
'TOKA'	Minnesota	Warm regions of Zone 4, 5-7	'Superior'	Midseason	Fruit large, pointed. Skin medium red with apricot hue. Flesh firm, yellow with rich, spicy flavor. Tree medium, spreading. Heavy producer.	Use fresh or for canning. Tree may be short-lived. Adapted to warm regions of Zone 4.
'UNDERWOOD'	Minnesota	Warm regions of Zone 4, 5-7	'Superior'	Midseason	Fruit large. Skin red. Flesh freestone, golden yellow. Tree vigorous, among the most cold-hardy.	Good dessert quality, although sometimes stringy. Ripening extends over long season starting in July. Adapted to warm regions of Zone 4.

'Smyrna' quince.

Quince

Quince used to be grown more often. This is a shame, because jams and jellies made from the fruit are exceptional. In addition, trees are attractive ornamentals, with dark, glossy green leaves and delicate, pinkish-white blossoms. Fruit are large, often reaching 5 inches in diameter, weighing more than 1 pound.

Do not confuse flowering quince with fruit-bearing varieties. Each is a different plant. Flowering quince is a handsome shrub but does not produce fruit.

Quince		
	Standard	**Dwarf**
Height at maturity (feet)		
Unpruned	12-15	N/A
Pruned	8-10	
Spread at maturity with		
no competition (feet)	12-15	
Recommended planting		
distance (feet)	10-15	
Years to reach bearing age	3-5	
Life expectancy (years)	40	
Chilling requirement (hours)	100-450	
Pollinator required	No	
Good for espalier	Informal only	
Good for containers	Yes	
N/A = Not Available		

VARIETIES

'Champion'—Fruit are large, yellow and shaped like pears. Flesh is tinged green. Tree bears early and produces heavily. Ripens late in the season.

'Orange', also 'Apple'—Fruit are round, golden, with orange-yellow flesh. Old-fashioned fruit quality. Ripens early in the season.

'Pineapple'—Fruit are round with light-golden skin and white flesh. Aroma is similar to a pineapple. Developed by Luther Burbank.

'Smyrna'—Large fruit, round to oblong with bright-yellow skin. Strong fragrance. Many consider this the best variety.

'Van Deman'—Fruit are large, yellow. Fruit retain flavor when cooked. Developed by Luther Burbank.

All varieties except 'Orange' are cold-hardy in Zones 5 to 7. It is cold-hardy in Zones 6 and 7.

CULTURAL REQUIREMENTS

Quince adapt to a wide range of soils. They are more tolerant of heavy or wet soils than most fruit trees. A reasonably fertile soil supplies necessary nutrients, with little fertilizing recommended. Water regularly during drought, although trees are drought resistant after they are established.

PRUNING

Train trees to a vase shape. See page 29. Prune trees lightly, because fruit are borne on wood grown the same year. Branches tend to droop and become leggy. Head them to maintain full foliage and productivity. Remove suckers and watersprouts from mature trees. Trees can also be trained to a shrub form.

Thinning fruit is seldom required unless an exceptionally heavy fruit set threatens to break branches.

POLLINATION

Quince is self-fruitful. A single tree is able to set adequate crops.

HARVESTING AND STORAGE

When fruit turn yellow, they are ready to harvest. Handle with care because they bruise easily and do not store well.

Quince is inedible raw. Cook and use in desserts, jams and jellies.

PESTS AND DISEASES

Few pests bother quince, but fireblight is an occasional problem. Black knots commonly appear on trunk and branches of old trees. Do not confuse them with fireblight. The knots are normal and should not be removed.

GARDENER'S TIPS

● Do not store quince with other fruit. Quince's aroma is so strong it can affect the taste of other fruit nearby.

● The fuzz on the skin of fruit can be rubbed off easily with your hands.

BERRIES

'Heritage' raspberry.

Zone Adaptation

	Zone 4	Zone 5	Zone 6	Zone 7
Blackberry	●*	●	●	●
Blueberry	●*	●	●	●
Currant	●	●	●	●
Gooseberry	●	●	●	●
Grape	●*	●	●	●
Raspberry, Black	●	●	●	●
Raspberry, Red	●	●	●	●
Strawberry	●	●	●	●

* See variety chart for cold-hardy varieties for this zone.

Blackberries ready for harvest.

Blackberry

There are two basic types of blackberries: those that have an *erect* growth habit, and those that have a *trailing* growth habit. Some varieties are thornless and some have thorns. All bear similar fruit.

Berries labeled as 'Boysenberry', 'Loganberry' and 'Dewberry' are cultivars of blackberry. They are suited to the warm climates of the South and the warmer areas of Zone 7.

CULTURAL REQUIREMENTS

Like most fruit and berries, blackberries thrive in deep, fertile loam with regular moisture. They do not like slow-draining clay soil or waterlogged soil. Each year during late spring, apply 1/4 pound actual nitrogen per plant. To determine how much actual nitrogen is in a bag of commercial fertilizer, multiply the first number of the fertilizer formula, the percentage of nitrogen, by the number of pounds in the bag. A 100-pound bag of 5-10-10 (.05 x 100) would contain 5 pounds actual nitrogen.

PRUNING

The best time to prune depends on where you live. If you live in the Northeast or Midwest, prune in late March to early April. Farther south, early to mid-March is the best time.

Prune lateral-growing branches of the previous year's canes so they are about 8 inches long. These branches will bear fruit later in the season. Near the end of June, new shoots will be about 3-1/2 feet high. Pinch tips at this time to encourage branching. Remove weak canes, roughly half of planting, leaving only strong canes.

Trailing varieties may need support. An easy way to provide support is to tie a clump of canes to a single post. Or you can string two wires at the same level from crossbars on top of posts. Canes do not have to be secured to supports because they will drape over the wires. See illustration, page 114.

POLLINATION

Blackberries are self-fruitful and do not need another variety for cross-pollination.

HARVESTING AND STORAGE

Pick blackberries when they develop their characteristic color. Fruit turn from pinkish or red to deep, blackish red. They are ready to harvest when they part easily from the stem.

Blackberries normally ripen over a two-week period. Early varieties are ready for harvest around mid-June. Late varieties are harvested in late fall. Handle fruit with care because they are fragile and bruise easily. Plan to use them soon after picking.

PESTS AND DISEASES

If plantings are not crowded and the garden is kept clean, blackberries are usually free of pests and diseases. Plants are susceptible to orange rust, anthracnose, leaf spot and verticillium wilt. Your best protection is to buy certified, disease-resistant varieties. Specify that you want only certified varieties when you buy plants from a mail-order source or from a nursery.

Blackberry	Standard	Dwarf
Height at maturity (feet)		
Unpruned	Cane trails	N/A
Pruned	5-6	
Spread at maturity with no competition (feet)	20-40	
Recommended planting distance (feet)		
Between plants	4-8	
Between rows	6-9	
Years to reach bearing age	2	
Life expectancy (years)	6-25	
Pollinator required	No	
Good for espalier	No	
Good for containers	Yes	

N/A = Not Available

If disease infects plants, remove damaged canes and burn or dispose of them. If your entire stand of bushes becomes infected, you have no choice but to remove all plants and start a new planting elsewhere.

Place netting over plants as harvest time approaches to prevent birds from eating your crops.

GARDENER'S TIPS
• 'Thornfree' produces a sparse number of branches and does not require pruning.
• When making jelly, include a hefty handful of *half-ripe* berries. They give the jelly an appetizing sheen.

Fresh cream over blackberries is a supreme taste treat.

How to Prune Blackberries

Follow these four steps when pruning blackberries.

1. Remove old canes after bearing.

2. Remove suckers as they appear.

3. In early spring, cut back laterals to 18 inches, which will result in larger fruit.

4. Cut cane tips when they reach 3 feet high to encourage branching, resulting in a larger crop.

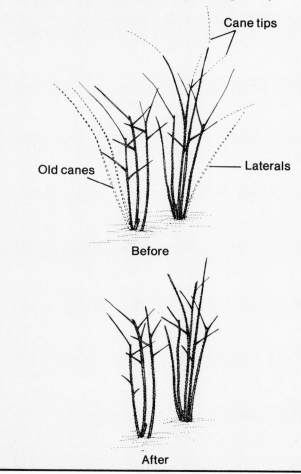

How to Train Blackberries

Training blackberries to a trellis or other support makes them more manageable and easier to harvest. Erect-growing plants are trained to a one-wire support. Trailing plants are best trained to a two-wire support.

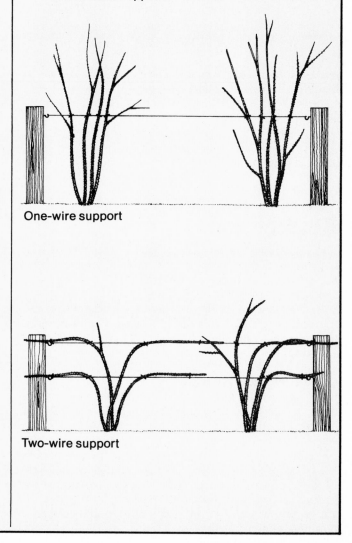

One-wire support

Two-wire support

Post-and-wire supports work well for blackberry training.

Blackberries

Variety	Zones	Harvest Season	Fruit and Plant	Remarks
'BAILEY'	5-7	Midseason	Fruit large, glossy, black. Plant tall, vigorous, cold-hardy, productive.	Use fresh or for processing.
'BRAINERD'	5-7	Early	Fruit large, high flavor, tart. Plant vigorous, thorny.	Trailing type of blackberry.
'DARROW'	5-7	Early to midseason	Fruit black, glossy, irregular size with firm flesh. Slightly tart. Plant vigorous, erect.	Not necessary to support canes. Subject to winter damage unless heavily mulched.
'EBONY KING'	5-7	Early	Fruit purplish, glossy, with sweet, tangy taste. Plant upright and cold-hardy.	Resists orange rust.
'ELDORADO'	5-7	Early to midseason	Fruit medium to large, firm, good quality, sweet. Plant upright, cold-hardy, vigorous and productive.	Extremely cold-hardy. Recommended for cold regions of Zone 5. Resists orange rust.
'EVERGREEN'	5-7	Late	Fruit only fair quality. Plant vigorous and productive.	A satisfactory thornless variety.
'HEDRICK'	Warm areas of Zones 4, 5-7	Early	Fruit large, medium-firm, glossy. Plant cold-hardy, productive, vigorous.	Cold-hardy but susceptible to orange rust.
'JERSEYBLACK'	5-7	Midseason	Fruit large, good quality. Plant vigorous, semitrailing.	Use for eating fresh or for processing.
'LAWTON'	5-7	Midseason	Fruit large, soft, good quality. Bush vigorous, productive.	Originated in New York. Better suited to the Southwest.
'RAVEN'	5 only	Early	Fruit large, high quality. Plant upright, vigorous, productive.	Use fresh or process. Plant can be damaged by frost in cold areas of Zone 5. Mulch heavily.
'SMOOTHSTEM'	5-7	Late	Fruit large, firm, tart. Plant erect, canes thornless. More productive than 'Thornfree', another thornless variety.	Recommended for Atlantic coastal areas. Resistant to leaf spot.
'THORNFREE'	5-7	Late	Fruit medium-large, glossy, black, blunt in shape. Canes thornless, but unlike other thornless varieties, bush canes grow semiupright. Bush productive, moderately cold-hardy.	Canes grow 7 to 8 feet high. Some trellis support is necessary. Fruiting laterals bear 20 to 30 berries. Low winter temperatures may damage plants unless they are heavily mulched.

Blueberries ready for harvest.

Blueberry

Blueberries are excellent for most of the Northeast, Midwest and Mid-Atlantic areas. Many varieties are cold-hardy to −25F (−32C). Plants adapt well to different climatic conditions.

Blueberries are handsome, compact plants. Their glossy green foliage turns bright yellow, then orange and red in the fall. Plants are easy to train into a manageable shrub form.

One of the most important cultural requirements of blueberries is acid soil. If in doubt about your soil's pH, a soil test may be in order. Consult your local county extension office or the nearest state university for advice. Blueberries do best with the soil pH between 5.0 and 5.5. If soil pH is above 5.5, add sulfur or aluminum sulfate to make the soil more acid. Mix one of these additives 6 inches deep into the soil at least one year before planting.

CULTURAL REQUIREMENTS

Blueberries grow best in well-drained soils rich in organic matter. They do poorly in heavy clay soil or in dry, gravelly soil.

After a plant is established, which takes about one year, mix 4 ounces of ammonium sulfate (21-0-0) into the soil around plant before growth starts in early spring. Increase amount of ammonium sulfate by 1 ounce each year until bushes are mature. After they reach maturity in about five years, increase the annual dosage to 8 ounces per year.

Roots of blueberries grow shallow, so be careful when cultivating around plants. Plants require considerable moisture. Water thoroughly during dry periods in summer.

Plants do better with a thick mulch around their base. This helps conserve moisture, cools the soil and reduces weeds that compete for moisture and nutrients.

PRUNING

Blueberries require little pruning. Experts at Cornell University recommend that all blossoms be removed during the plant's first year so vigor will go into vegetative growth.

A fully grown bush consists of seven to nine main branches and two or three new branches. In late March, cut back all new branches by one-third and remove weak or damaged branches. Remove one or two of the oldest branches from mature bushes each year. See illustration on page 117.

POLLINATION

Blueberries require cross-pollination. For best fruit set, plant at least two different varieties near each other.

PROPAGATION

Blueberry cuttings do not root easily, so it is probably best to purchase stock. If you want to try to propagate your own plants, here's how.

Select root cuttings of shoots that have grown the previous season. Pick shoots that bear *leaf buds*. These are smaller than fruit buds. Cut shoots in early spring, making a slanting 45° cut. Each cutting should be about 4 inches long. Place peat moss in a flat and moisten. Insert cutting in peat moss so that only the top one-third of cutting is above the ground. Store flat in a shady spot. Keep peat moss moist through the rooting process. Cuttings should root in about three months.

You can also propagate by layering. Using stakes, peg down a few lower branches and cover them with soil. Making a cut half through the underside of the branch before covering with soil may hasten rooting. Rooting hormones to increase your success are available at nurseries.

Blueberry

	Standard	Dwarf
Height at maturity (feet)		
Unpruned	7-8	N/A
Pruned	6-8	
Spread at maturity with		
no competition (feet)	8	
Recommended planting		
distance (feet)	3-4	
Years to reach bearing age	3-4	
Life expectancy (years)	Indefinite	
Pollinator required	Yes*	
Good for espalier	Yes	
Good for containers	Yes	

*Best production with cross-pollination.

N/A = Not Available

How to Prune Blueberries

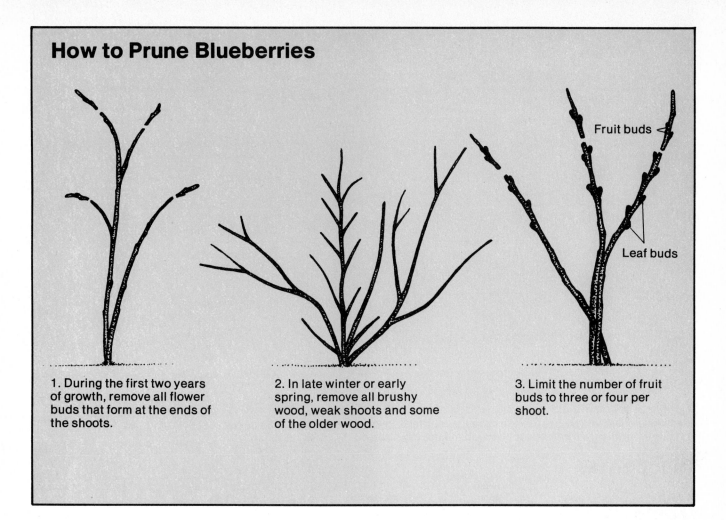

Fruit buds

Leaf buds

1. During the first two years of growth, remove all flower buds that form at the ends of the shoots.

2. In late winter or early spring, remove all brushy wood, weak shoots and some of the older wood.

3. Limit the number of fruit buds to three or four per shoot.

HARVESTING AND STORAGE
Plants reach full production in 6 to 10 years. Berries ripen over a period of 6 or 7 weeks. Do not pick berries when they first acquire their characteristic blue color. They will be sweeter and better tasting if left on the plant 7 to 10 days longer. Handle berries with care, because they bruise easily. Berries keep in the refrigerator for about one week.

PESTS AND DISEASES
Blueberries are generally free of insects and diseases. Blueberry maggots sometimes attack plants. A fungus disease called *mummy berry* is known to infect blueberries.

Perhaps the most serious pests are birds. Unless you cover bushes with netting, you will probably have no blueberries for yourself. Select a coarse netting, perhaps 3/4- to 1-inch mesh, and cover the entire bush. If the whole bush is not covered, birds will find any unprotected spots and strip fruit from plants.

For best flavor, pick blueberries about one week *after* they attain their rich, blue color.

Birds love blueberries. To keep the crop for yourself, cover plants with netting as harvest time approaches. This fencepost-and-wire form does a good job of keeping birds out.

Blueberries

Variety	Zones	Harvest Season	Fruit and Plant	Remarks
'BERKELEY'	4-7	Midseason	Fruit large with loose clusters. Berry has faint aroma. Skin pale blue. Bush vigorous, spreading, productive.	Use for pies or eating fresh. Less acid than most. Fruit stores well and resists cracking.
'BLUECROP'	4-7	Early midseason	Fruit large. Skin light blue. Flesh firm. Bush medium height, upright, vigorous, productive.	Use for cooking or for eating fresh. Good keeper. May require pruning to curb production. Tolerates drought.
'BLUEHAVEN'	4-7	Early midseason	Fruit large. Skin light blue. Flesh firm. Bush tall and upright.	Ripens over a long season.
'BLUERAY'	4-7	Early midseason	Fruit very large. Skin medium blue. Flesh firm. Bush grows tall, upright, productive, cold-hardy.	Good flavor, aromatic. More tart than most. Fruit resists cracking.
'COLLINS'	4-7	Early	Fruit large. Skin light blue. Flesh firm. Bush vigorous, upright and moderately productive.	Good flavor.
'COVILLE'	4-7	Late	Fruit large. Skin light blue. Flesh firm. Bush vigorous, spreading, productive, with large leaves.	Remains tart until ripe. Does not drop fruit. Not a consistent bearer.
'EARLIBLUE'	5-7	Very early	Fruit medium. Skin light blue. Flesh firm. Bush vigorous, upright and productive.	Good flavor, aromatic. Sweeter than most. Excellent dessert quality.
'HERBERT'	4-7	Late midseason	Fruit large. Skin medium blue. Flesh firm. Bush vigorous, upright, productive.	Resists cracking. Flavor reminiscent of huckleberries.
'JERSEY'	4-7	Late midseason	Fruit medium. Skin light blue. Flesh firm. Bush vigorous, upright, productive, with large leaves.	Fair flavor, no aroma.
'KEEWEENAW'	Warm areas of Zone 3, 4-7	Midseason	Fruit medium. Skin medium blue. Flesh firm. Bush upright.	Excellent for cold, Northern climates with a short growing season.
'NORTHLAND'	4-7	Early	Fruit small. Skin medium blue. Flesh firm. Bush spreading, semidwarf, reaching only 4 feet high at maturity.	Useful where space is limited. Good flavor. Adapts well to container planting. Cold-hardy.

Red currants, ready for harvest.

Currant and Gooseberry

Currants and gooseberries, both members of *Ribes* species, are largely ignored in the United States and Canada. Rarely, if ever, are they available in markets. This is unfortunate, because these luscious berries are prized for jams, jellies, tarts and pies. With the exception of European gooseberries, they cannot be eaten fresh. They must be cooked to be consumed.

Food connoisseurs know that a gooseberry tart is one of the triumphs of the art of pastry-making. Currant jelly is also prized, widely used as a glaze on pastry or spread on fresh-baked bread.

In addition to their value as a taste treat, both of these bush-type fruit are easy to grow and are almost maintenance-free. Because of their bushy, non-spreading growth habit and attractive foliage, they make handsome additions to the landscape. Their compact growth makes them excellent as foundation plantings. Plants are adaptable, thriving in full sun, or on the shady, north side of a house. They are *self-fruitful,* meaning they require no companion planting for cross-pollination. But chances are, after you've enjoyed their bounty, you will want more than one plant of each.

Some gardeners are reluctant to plant currants or gooseberries because they can be host plants to white-pine blister rust. This is a disease that spends part of its life cycle on certain, old-time varieties before infecting nearby white pine and other five-needled pine species.

During the past few decades, progress has been made in developing disease-free varieties of red and white currants and gooseberries. Black currant is still banned in most areas of the United States, although there are reports of varieties developed in Canada that are disease resistant.

The United States Department of Agriculture has mapped out districts called *White-Pine Blister Control Areas* in states where these pine trees grow. These areas are localized and comprise a small part of the country. In most areas there are no regulations forbidding cultivation of *Ribes* species. If you have any doubts, check with a reputable nursery or with your local county extension agent. They should be able to tell you if you live in a control area. More important, reputable mail-order houses sell plants free of disease and certified to be immune. If you do live in a control area, and plant currants and gooseberries 900 feet away from white pines, you are beyond the legal limit.

RECOMMENDED VARIETIES

'Red Currant', also 'Red Lake'—This variety is the most common red currant, and with good reason. Fruit are large, growing in large clusters with long stems, which makes them easy to pick. Berries have a slightly lighter color than other varieties. Taste is excellent. Plant is vigorous, cold-hardy, disease resistant, productive and not prone to sprawling as other varieties. Berries ripen from mid-June to mid-July in most areas.

'Cascade'—Ripens about one week later than 'Red Lake'. Berries are larger but clusters are smaller. This cultivar originates in Minnesota, so is recommended for northern plantings as well as farther south.

Older varieties, which are considered to be more disease-prone by some, are 'Cherry', 'Victoria', 'Fay', 'Wilder' and 'Perfection'.

White or Yellow Currant—'White Grape' has plant characteristics similar to red varieties, but fruit are ivory-white. This is the most widely available cultivar.

'White Imperial'—Considered to have superior-quality berries, but is difficult to find.

Currant and Gooseberry

	Currant	Gooseberry
Height at maturity (feet)		
Unpruned	4-6	6-8
Pruned	3-4	5-7
Spread at maturity with		
no competition (feet)	2-4	2-4
Recommended planting		
distance (feet)	3-4	2-1/2 to 5
Years to reach bearing age	3	3
Life expectancy (years)	15-30	15-30
Pollinator required	No	No
Good for espalier	Yes	Yes
Good for containers	Yes	Yes

Comments: Dwarf currants or gooseberries are not available.

Gooseberries can remain on bush up to two weeks after ripening.

Plastic netting is relatively inexpensive way to protect currant crop against birds. Netting is usually available at nurseries and home-center outlets.

Black Currant—This variety is not recommended or is not available in most of the United States because of its association with white-pine blister rust. Do not import these plants from neighboring states, where they are grown legally, into a White-Pine Blister Control Area.

American Gooseberry—'Pixwell' is the most readily available of the American gooseberries, and the most highly recommended. American strains produce smaller berries than European or English strains, but are less prone to diseases. Plants are medium size, have few thorns and are cold-hardy. Fruit hang away from the stems, making them easy to pick. The name 'Pixwell' is derived from this characteristic. Berries turn pink to purple when ripe. Bears midseason.

'Welcome'—Has no spines on the fruit and few on the plant, but it is not readily available. Medium-size berries are dull red with pink flesh. Bears midseason.

'Poorman'—Plants are medium to large, vigorous, with fruit ripening to a rich red. Fruit are perhaps the sweetest of all available American varieties. Bears midseason.

European or English Gooseberry—'Chatauqua' plants are relatively small, but fruit are substantially larger than fruit of American varieties listed previous-

ly. Fruit are pale yellow-green when ripe and possess a more tart taste than the American varieties. 'Chatauqua' is subject to mildew. Bears midseason.

'Fredonia'—Another European variety. It has a rather open, bush-type growth. Red fruit are larger than American varieties and are good quality. They ripen somewhat later than other European or English gooseberries.

PLANTING

The best time to plant currants and gooseberries is fall or early spring. They are among the first plants to leaf out in spring. Plant as soon as ground can be worked. This is usually about the time that you plant onions and peas in your vegetable garden.

When your bare-root stock arrives by mail, or when you bring it home from the nursery, prune off broken branches and broken roots. Cut back tips of all shoots so they are 6 to 8 inches long.

Plants are not fussy about soil, but prefer a well-drained soil with a neutral pH—7.0. Set plants about 1 inch deeper than the *soil line*. This is the dark area visible on the main stem of a plant. It indicates the original depth that the plant was positioned in the soil when it was grown. Space plants about 4 feet apart. Mulch with

Gooseberries ready for harvest.

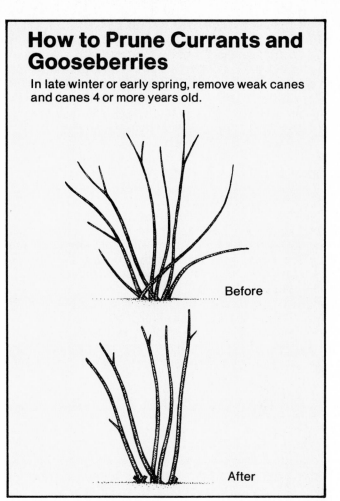

How to Prune Currants and Gooseberries

In late winter or early spring, remove weak canes and canes 4 or more years old.

Before

After

rotted manure or compost, and water well during dry periods.

If leaves turn yellow, this indicates a need for nitrogen. Supply with an application of general-purpose fertilizer. Follow package instructions.

PRUNING CURRANTS

Prune currants each year. Generally, more canes are formed than are needed for a balanced, attractive bush. During the dormant season—late winter to early spring—remove weak canes at ground level. Canes 4 years old or older should be removed at ground level. After they reach about 4 years old, canes often become weak and produce few fruit. Remove low-growing branches that might bend to the ground when heavy with fruit.

Ideally, a well-pruned bush should have about five 1-year-old shoots, four 2-year-old shoots, three 3-year-old shoots and two or three 4-year-old shoots, if they are still producing fruit.

Shoots that are 1 year old should be pinched back to encourage branching. If your currant bush produces too many 1-year-old shoots, prune several from the interior of the plant. This allows better air and light penetration, which discourages mildew.

PRUNING GOOSEBERRIES

Pruning gooseberries is done essentially the same way as currants. If growing conditions are ideal, you might find that your plants produce a substantial number of low-growing lateral branches. Remove some of these during the dormant period, as well as any low-hanging branches. To encourage vigorous production, remove all 4-year-old canes at the base of the plant. Try to maintain a ratio of three 1-year-old shoots, three 2-year-old shoots and three 3-year-old shoots.

PROPAGATING CURRANTS

Propagate currants by taking 8- to 10-inch-long cuttings from vigorous growth on 1-year-old shoots. Do this in late fall or early winter. Take cuttings that are about the diameter of a pencil or a little smaller. Store in moist sand, sawdust or peat moss. If you choose to take more than one cutting from any one shoot, cut the bottom end at an angle and the top straight across. By doing this, you will know which end should be sunk in the ground. Leave cuttings in a cool, shady place until early spring, then plant about 6 inches apart. Let them grow for one to two years before placing them in a permanent spot. When planting cuttings, cover all but the two upper buds with soil.

PROPAGATING GOOSEBERRIES

Gooseberries are easy to propagate. You simply bend a low branch to the ground, secure it with a brick or stone and bury along its length. Allow the tip of the branch to stick out of the ground. This method of propagation is called *layering*. Eventually, the branch will put down roots. About one year later, you can cut the branch from the bush and transplant it.

To keep your gooseberry plants tidy, remove low-growing lateral branches so the bushes won't spread and propagate on their own.

PESTS AND DISEASES

Currants and gooseberries are resistant to diseases and pests. But birds have a definite appetite for currants. Given the opportunity, they will strip fruit from the bushes. Cover your plants with 3/4- to 1-inch netting as crops begin to show. Remove netting after you harvest your crop.

White-pine blister rust is an occasional problem. If you've followed the precautions mentioned on page 119, you should have no problem with this disease.

Anthracnose, mites, borers and aphids sometimes bother currants and gooseberries. See pages 52 to 55 for control methods.

HARVESTING AND STORAGE

These are among the first of the bush berries to ripen in summer. Depending on the variety, gooseberries turn plum-purple or lime-green blushed with pink. Currants turn bright red. When you pick currants, keep in mind that berries just short of being ripe produce a finer-tasting jelly. Picked at this stage, they have more pectin for jelling. Pick currants by the bunch the same as with grapes.

Gooseberries can remain on the bush for almost two weeks at the ripe stage. Bushes tend to be thorny, so wear gloves when you harvest. An easy way to pick gooseberries is to hold a branch in one hand and strip the berries off with the other.

GARDENER'S TIPS
• Prepare soil and plant currants and gooseberries properly. Plantings will last for 20 years or more.
• After you have harvested currants, run the bunches through the tines of a kitchen fork to separate the berries from the stems.
• To prepare gooseberries for cooking, baking or processing, remove both the stem from one end and the blossom collar from the other. A pair of small, sharp, cuticle scissors work well for this.

Currant blossoms are self-fertile and do not require additional plants nearby for cross-pollination.

Currants and gooseberries are underrated for their culinary qualities. Above: Fresh gooseberries and gooseberry jam set stage for a special breakfast. Below: Currants make exceptional jams and syrups.

'Suffolk Red' American seedless grape.

Grape

Four types of grapes are available to fruit growers in Zones 4 to 7. These are *American* and *American hybrids, French hybrids, vinifera (Vitus vinifera)* and *muscadine.*

American hybrid grapes are the most cold-hardy—to −10F (−24C). They are called *slip skin* because the pulp of the grape slips out of the skin easily.

French hybrids were developed in Europe by crossing vinifera grapes with cold-hardy American varieties and wild species.

Vinifera grapes, also known as *European grapes* or *California grapes,* are the most cold-tender. They should be grown only in the mildest section of Zone 7.

Muscadine grapes were developed in the South. They are tolerant of high temperatures and mildew disease. They are fairly resistant to attacks from insect pests.

Experimental plantings of European wine grapes such as 'Cabernet Sauvignon', 'Chenin Blanc', 'White Riesling' and others have been successful. In a few, small, isolated areas such as eastern Long Island, Cape Cod, eastern shore of Maryland and tidewater Virginia and North Carolina, cultivation has surpassed the most optimistic expectations. But unless you live in a temperate climate with a moderating influence, such as the Atlantic Ocean, vines will probably not survive. For more information, see page 61.

PLANTING
Plant grapes in spring, as soon as the soil can be worked. You can also plant in the fall when vines are dormant. If you do, be sure to protect against winter damage by mounding soil over crown of plant.

Plant at the same depth that the vine grew in the nursery. Remove all but one stem with two or three buds. Space plants 8 to 10 feet apart, between wood or metal posts for supports.

Mulch soil beneath grapes to help control weeds. After the first growing season, fertilize in early spring with 1 pound of 5-10-10 fertilizer per vine. Remove flower clusters during the first and second growing seasons to encourage vigorous root and vine growth.

CULTURAL REQUIREMENTS
Grapes prefer a fertile, deep, well-drained, loamy soil, but accept sandy or clay soil. Dry or wet soils do not suit them.

Roots of mature vines can grow to 20 feet deep. Except during drought, you probably won't have to water. But be sure vines are getting sufficient moisture when fruit begin to mature.

PRUNING
If you want to grow quality grapes, you must learn how to prune vines. There are two reasons for pruning. One is to train the vine to suit available space and to maintain manageability. Second, mature vines are pruned to maintain proper balance between fruiting and vegetative growth.

Pruning is done in the spring, before the sap begins to flow. There are two ways to prune: *spur pruning* and *cane pruning.* Few grape varieties grown in the Midwest and East require spur pruning. See variety charts for specifics.

To spur prune, select healthy canes and cut back to two or three buds. These buds will produce fruit during the season. Use this method with grapes that produce fruit close to the main trunk.

To cane prune, select a cane and reduce it to 6 to 18 buds, depending on the vigor and maturity of the vine.

Step-by-step instructions on how to prune and train grapevines are shown in the illustrations on page 125.

Grape		
	Standard	**Dwarf**
Height at maturity (feet)		
Unpruned	Canes trail	N/A
Pruned	4-5	
Spread at maturity with		
no competition (feet)	100	
Recommended planting		
distance (feet)	6-12	
Years to reach bearing age	3	
Life expectancy (years)	40-60	
Pollinator required	No	
Good for espalier	Yes	
Good for containers	Yes	
N/A = Not Available		

Training to the Four-Arm Kniffen System

The most popular system used to train grapes is the four-arm Kniffen system. Build a trellis of two wires supported by posts. Posts should stand 6 feet *above* ground. String No. 9- or 10-gage wire at the 2-1/2-feet level and the 5-1/2-feet level.

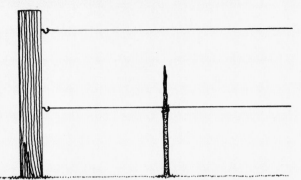

1. Plant grapevine. As the vine grows during the first year, tie it to the bottom wire so a straight trunk develops.

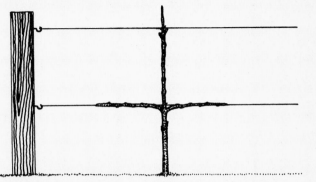

2. As growth continues, tie vine to top wire. Shoots will grow at the level of the first wire. Train one shoot in each direction along the lower wire.

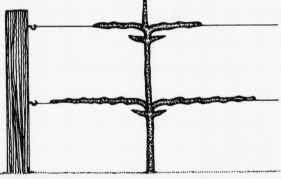

3. When shoots develop near top wire, train one shoot in each direction the same as the bottom wire. In late winter or early spring of the following year, select four canes for arms. Remove other shoots.

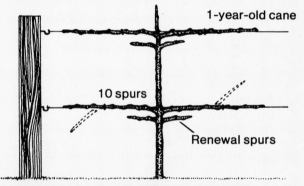

1-year-old cane

10 spurs

Renewal spurs

4. Prune canes on top wire to 10 buds. Secure to wire. Cut four other canes back to two or three buds for renewal spurs. Remove all other canes. Each subsequent year, replace arms with canes from renewal spurs and leave new renewal spurs for following year.

Variation: The Umbrella Kniffen System

Instead of training canes *along* wires, the umbrella Kniffen system allows canes to drape *over* wires.

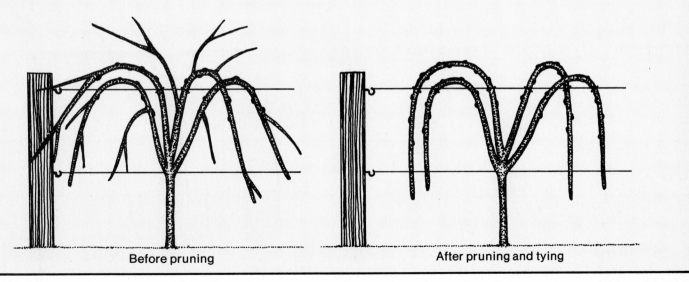

Before pruning

After pruning and tying

PROPAGATION

You can propagate grapes by taking cuttings during the dormant season from the previous season's growth. *Mallet cuttings*—those of the previous season's growth with a small portion or heel of the season *prior* to the previous season—root more easily.

Select wood that is at least 1/3 inch in diameter. Make the basal cut below a bud. Canes should have at least three buds. Plant so that one bud is above the ground. Set 4 to 6 inches apart in rows 2 to 4 feet apart. Leave cuttings in soil through complete growing season. Mulch to prevent *heaving,* alternate freezing and thawing of the soil, during winter.

The following spring, when cuttings are well rooted, dig up and replant in a permanent position.

POLLINATION

Grapes are self-fertile and do not require another variety for cross-pollination, except muscadine varieties.

HARVESTING AND STORAGE

The best way to determine if grapes are ready to eat or process is to taste them. If they are sweet, juicy and have attained characteristic flavor, pick them. Cut bunches of grapes from vines with a knife. Do not pull the bunches off the vines.

PESTS AND DISEASES

To control insects and diseases, spray grapes with an all-purpose spray at least three times during the season. Spray at pre-bloom stage, petal fall and 10 to 14 days later.

Disease problems that are known to occur include black rot, downy mildew, anthracnose, leaf spot, dead arm and powdery mildew. Insects that may attack are grape-berry moth, leaf hopper, curculio, mealybug and Japanese beetle. See pages 52 to 55 for control information.

GARDENER'S TIPS

● In Zone 4, select a cold-hardy variety such as 'Concord'. If 'Concord' does not survive, a last resort is 'Beta', the most cold-hardy of all grapes. It survives temperatures to about −20F (−29C). 'Blue Jay' and 'Red Amber' are additional cold-hardy varieties. Adding a thick, organic mulch around plants and over the soil helps to protect against winter cold.

Harvest grapes with pruning shears or knife, the same as done commercially.

'Concord'

'Ontario'

American and American Hybrid Grapes

Variety	Zones	Season	Pruning	Remarks
'ALDEN'	5-7	Midseason	Cane	Fruit reddish black, juicy with fine aroma. They grow in large clusters. Skin does not slip. Thin when vine overbears. Slightly tender to cold.
'ALWOOD'	5-7	Early	Cane	Fruit blue-black, sweet, resembles 'Concord'. Colors and ripens more evenly than 'Concord' in Southern areas. Reported to be resistant to diseases.
'BATH'	5-7	Midseason	Cane	Fruit black, juicy, sweet. Vine as cold-hardy as 'Concord'. Prune severely or thin clusters to prevent overbearing. Use fresh or process.
'BUFFALO'	5-7	Early	Cane	Fruit slipskin, juicy, sweet, spicy-tart and vinous. Vine vigorous and productive. Considered by many to have finest dessert quality of early season black grapes.
'CATAWBA'	5-7	Midseason	Cane	Fruit large, round, deep copper-red. Aromatic. Light, musky winelike flavor. Use for wine or juice.
'CONCORD'	5-7	Late	Cane	Fruit large, oblong, blue-black, slipskin. Widely planted. Often the standard of quality in judging new varieties. Tolerates cold, resists powdery mildew. When flavor of grape is described as "foxy," it refers to 'Concord' flavor.
'DELAWARE'	5-7	Early	Cane	Fruit and bunches small, excellent for dessert and wine. Light-red color with lilac bloom. Vines subject to mildew. An American hybrid.
'FREDONIA'	5-7	Midseason	Cane	Fruit black, larger than 'Concord', thick, tough skin. Vines cold-hardy and vigorous. Allow to set heavily because pollination is sometimes a problem.
'GOLDEN MUSCAT'	5-7	Late	Cane	Fruit large, compact, a beautiful golden yellow. Clusters large and compact. Excellent quality when well ripened. Vine vigorous. An American hybrid.
'NEW YORK MUSCAT'	Warm areas of Zones 4, 5-7	Midseason	Cane	Fruit reddish black to black, sweet, with rich muscat flavor. Not foxy. Cold-hardy. Recommended for warm areas of Zone 4. Makes an excellent wine.
'NIAGARA'	5-7	Midseason	Cane	Fruit white, more productive than 'Concord'. The most widely planted white grape. Vine vigorous, moderately cold-hardy. Use for juice and wine.

'Suffolk Red'

American and American Hybrid Grapes

Variety	Zones	Season	Pruning	Remarks
'ONTARIO'	5-7	Early	Cane	The best early season white grape available. Ripens two weeks before 'Niagara'. Vine vigorous and productive.
'SCHUYLER'	5-7	Very early	Spur or cane	American hybrid that possesses more European grape characteristics than most hybrids. Fruit black, high quality, sweet. Does not have slipskin character. Musky flavor. Vine is productive and vigorous. Prune severely to avoid overbearing.
'SENECA'	5-7	Early	Cane	Fruit large, white, uniform, firm, tender skin. Flavor sweet, vinous, aromatic. Vine vigorous, productive, moderately cold-hardy. Mildew must be controlled to ensure maximum cold-hardiness.
'SHERIDAN'	5-7	Late	Cane	Fruit large, with tough, black skin. A 'Concord' type. Requires long season to mature. Vine is cold-hardy.
'STEUBEN'	5-7	Midseason	Cane	Fruit large, bluish black, sweet with distinctive, spicy tang. Clusters long, tapering and compact. Vine cold-hardy, vigorous, productive.
'VAN BUREN'	5-7	Very early	Cane	Fruit large, black, a 'Concord' type. Vine cold-hardy, vigorous, productive. Protect against mildew.
'YATES'	5-7	Late	Cane	Fruit red, large, juicy, sweet, vinous, extremely tasty. Clusters large, conical, medium compact. Stores well. Vine vigorous, productive.

American Seedless Grapes

Variety	Zones	Season	Pruning	Remarks
'CANADICE'	5-7	Very early	Cane	Berries medium, red, well-filled clusters, similar flavor to 'Delaware'. One of the most cold-hardy of the seedless varieties.
'CONCORD SEEDLESS'	5-7	Midseason	Cane	Fruit resembles 'Concord' in color and flavor, but clusters and berries are smaller. Seeds occasionally present but fruit is generally seedless. Use as pie grape.
'HIMROD'	5-7	Very early	Cane	Fruit medium-oval, sweet, yellow, with good flavor. Clusters large but loose. Not cold-hardy. Not recommended for cold regions of Zone 5.
'INTERLAKEN SEEDLESS'	5-7	Very early	Cane	Berries small, golden, good quality. Clusters medium. Vines not overcropped are reasonably cold-hardy.
'REMAILY SEEDLESS'	5-7	Very early	Cane	Berries small, golden, good quality. Clusters medium. Vines not overcropped are reasonably cold-hardy. Clusters should be thinned.
'SUFFOLK RED'	5-7	Early	Cane	Fruit large, red, excellent quality. Average cold-hardiness. In Zone 5, grow only in warm regions.

'September' red raspberry

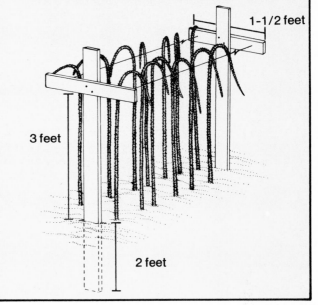

How to Train Raspberries

One way to train raspberry bushes is to a trellis. Note that the two-wire system on the crossbar keeps the canes from bending to the ground.

1-1/2 feet

3 feet

2 feet

Raspberry

Raspberries are one of the best investments available to the home gardener. Fruit are perishable and do not ship well, so they are rarely seen in markets. But with a minimum of care and by selecting several varieties with a range of maturity dates, you can harvest all the raspberries you can use from June until first frost.

Raspberries vary in color, size and quality. Red raspberries are the most popular, although black, purple and gold varieties are also available. See variety charts for more information.

Most regions covered in this book are suitable for raspberry cultivation. Exceptions are Zones 2 and 3, and the coldest areas of Zone 4. By choosing a good site location, planting cold-hardy varieties and using winter protection, you may be able to succeed in these areas.

To avoid problems with diseases, buy only plants that have been inspected and tagged as disease-free by your state department of agriculture. Do not set out plants that have been dug from an abandoned patch or a non-inspected planting.

CULTURAL REQUIREMENTS

Raspberries thrive in moderately fertile soil that has adequate drainage. Sandy loam is the best, but gravelly soil or well-drained clay soil is satisfactory.

Plants tolerate some shade, but growth and yields are better in full sun. Water thoroughly during dry summer periods.

Plants can be damaged by too much fertilizer applied too late in the season. The fertilizer encourages a flush of new, tender growth that is easily damaged by cold. The first year, use a complete fertilizer such as 5-10-10. Apply at a rate of 5 pounds per 100 linear feet. Thereafter, add 10 pounds of 10-10-10 per 100-foot row. Broadcast fertilizer over soil around plants in early spring, before buds emerge.

POLLINATION

Raspberries are self-fertile and do not require another variety for cross-pollination.

PRUNING

The popular red raspberry is available in two general growth habits: *standard* and *everbearing*. Both are *biennial,* meaning their canes live and bear for two years. Standard varieties produce fruit the second year. Everbearing varieties produce fruit in the fall of the first year and again the following summer.

Canes of both types die during the second year after

Raspberry		
	Red	**Black**
Height at maturity (feet)		
Unpruned	6-10	6-7
Pruned	6-10	4-5
Spread at maturity with	Indefinite	
no competition (feet)	suckers	6
Recommended planting		
distance (feet)		
Between plants	2-4	2
Between rows	6-7	6
Years to reach bearing age	2	2
Life expectancy (years)	6-30	6-30
Pollinator required	No	No
Good for espalier	No	No
Good for containers	Yes	Yes

they fruit. New canes emerge at the plant's base, or as suckers from an underground network of rootlike stems.

To prune standard types, remove canes that have borne fruit. To prune everbearing types, remove only summer-fruiting canes. Fall-fruiting canes fruit again the following summer, so leave them on the vine. You will have no difficulty determining which are which. The canes to be removed look obviously dead. Those that should remain look alive. At the same time, remove damaged or diseased canes. Prune small or weak canes and leave only two or three of the stronger canes per linear foot of row.

Cornell University experts recommend that pruning of spur or cane types be done between November and early April, preferably in March.

Black and purple raspberries are pruned differently. In June, when new canes are 18 to 24 inches high, remove growing points. This encourages vigorous lateral growth. The following spring, remove all old fruiting canes. Shorten laterals on black raspberries to 6 inches. Shorten laterals on purple raspberries to 10 inches. Leave only three or four of the largest canes in each hill.

PROPAGATION

Red and black raspberries are propagated differently. Red raspberries send up root suckers. In early spring, dig them up along with a piece of root and replant.

Black raspberries arch their canes to the ground. They then send roots from the tips where they touch the ground to form new plants. If you wish to increase your plantings, allow a few canes to go unpruned. Late in summer, peg cane to the ground at the tip with a clothespin or wire. When it has rooted, dig up and replant. See illustrations, page 38.

WINTER PROTECTION

Although raspberries are cold-hardy, surviving in the colder areas of Zone 4, winter protection may be necessary. Canes can be protected by covering them with an insulating mulch. Taking care not to break canes, bend them to the ground and secure with clothespins or wire. Secure portions between base of plant and tip of cane. Cover with several inches of straw or newspaper. Cover mulch with chickenwire to keep it from blowing away.

If rodents are a problem, bury canes in the earth to a depth of 2 inches. Remove soil from canes as the buds swell in early spring, before they begin to leaf out. If you wait too long, the cold-tender buds may be damaged by a late frost.

HARVESTING AND STORAGE

Pick raspberries when they are dead-ripe. They separate easily from the stem when they are ready to pick. Fruit are perishable and can be stored in the refrigerator for only a few days. Eat or process them right away.

PESTS AND DISEASES

Prevent problems before they become established. A clean, well-maintained planting is the best protection against pests and diseases. Full sunlight, good air drainage and cultivation helps maintain a healthy planting.

Occasionally, spur blight, anthracnose, tarnished plant bugs, sap beetles, cane borers and Japanese beetles attack plants. See pages 52 to 55 for control methods.

Birds love raspberries. To protect maturing berries, cover the entire bush with coarse netting, 3/4- to 1-inch mesh. Or, plan to grow enough fruit for yourself and the birds.

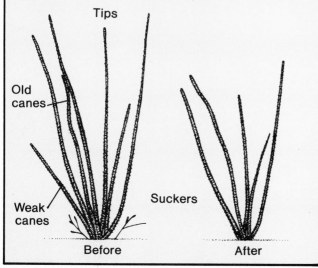

How to Prune Red Raspberries

In late winter or early spring, remove old canes, thin out weak canes, remove suckers and cut back tips of plants to 4-1/2 feet. In early summer, remove canes of everbearing varieties after they bear. This makes way for new canes that will bear in fall.

Tips

Old canes

Weak canes

Suckers

Before   After

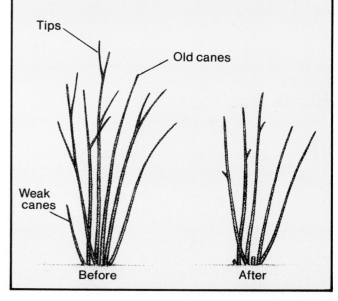

How to Prune Black Raspberries

In late winter or early spring, remove old canes and thin out weak canes. When canes are about 2 feet tall, pinch tips to encourage branching. When canes are about 6 feet tall, cut off growth at top.

Tips

Old canes

Weak canes

Before   After

Red Raspberries—Single Crop

Variety	Zones	Harvest Season	Fruit and Plant	Remarks
'CANBY'	5-7	Midseason	Fruit large, bright red. Flesh thick, delicious flavor. Thornless canes. Bush vigorous.	Use for desserts. One of the best. Requires good soil drainage.
'CHEROKEE'	4-7	Early to midseason	Fruit medium, slightly conic, deep red. Flesh moderately firm. Bush vigorous.	Produces over a long season.
'HILTON'	5-7	Late	Fruit large, long, conic, medium red. Flesh thick. Bush vigorous, erect, highly productive.	Seldom requires support.
'NEWBURGH'	4-7	Midseason	Fruit large, bright red. Flesh firm, excellent flavor. Bush vigorous and cold-hardy.	Easy to grow. Cold-hardy. Good home-garden berry.
'TAYLOR'	4-7	Late	Fruit large, long, conic, medium red. Flesh firm, somewhat tart, excellent quality. Plant highly productive, vigorous, erect, suckers freely.	Suited to Eastern gardens, but may be susceptible to mosaic.

Red Raspberries—Everbearing

Variety	Zones	Harvest Season	Fruit and Plant	Remarks
'HERITAGE'	4-7	Midseason and late August through October	Fruit medium to large, deep red. Flesh firm, good to fair quality. Bush erect, vigorous, highly productive.	Reliable. Large fall crop.
'LATHAM'	4-7	Midseason and early fall	Fruit medium-round, light red. Flesh moderately firm but poor quality. Bush vigorous, productive, suckers freely.	An old cultivar. May not bear in fall some seasons. Outstanding because of cold-hardiness and adaptability to wide range of climates and soils.
'SEPTEMBER'	4-7	Midseason and late August, early September	Fruit medium to large. Flesh firm, good flavor. Bush vigorous.	Cold-hardy and productive. Grows tall.

Black Raspberries

Variety	Zone	Harvest Season	Fruit and Plant	Remarks
'ALLEN'	4-7	Midseason	Fruit large and attractive. Flesh firm. Bush vigorous, productive.	Most of crop can be picked at one time.
'BRISTOL'	4-7	Midseason	Fruit large, glossy, attractive. Flesh firm, good quality. Bush cold-hardy, vigorous, productive.	Excellent for eating fresh.
'HURON'	4-7	Midseason	Fruit large, glossy, attractive, almost black. Flesh firm. Bush vigorous, productive, hardy.	Not susceptible to anthracnose.
'JEWEL'	5-7	Midseason	Fruit large, glossy black, slightly woolly. Flesh firm and high quality. Bush vigorous, productive.	Resistant to all serious diseases. Slightly susceptible to mildew.

Strawberry at peak ripeness.

Strawberry

Strawberries are easy to grow and a practical crop in all but the most extreme Northern climates. Almost everyone loves fresh strawberries, and fruit are loaded with Vitamin C. Properly maintained, a patch of 25 plants will supply a family of four with fresh fruit. A patch of 50 plants provides ample amounts for fresh use, plus enough for jams, jellies and freezing.

There are three kinds of strawberries: *June-bearing* kinds produce a single, bountiful crop over a few weeks, beginning in June. *Everbearing* kinds produce a more sparse crop throughout the season. A third kind, European in origin, is called *fraise des bois,* which means "strawberries of the woods." They produce small, intensely flavored berries. They do not send out runners and can be used as edging for walks, patios, foundation plantings or gardens. *Fraise des bois* adapt well to container growing. They prefer semishade, making them useful in areas where domestic strawberries, which prefer sun, will not thrive.

PLANTING

Plant strawberries in early spring or late fall. Early spring is preferred in Zone 4 and the colder areas of Zone 5. Before setting out plants, add a 2-inch layer of organic matter over the soil and dig to a depth of 4 to 6 inches. Well-rotted manure, sawdust, peat moss, compost and grass clippings are commonly used.

Strawberries are usually purchased *bare root*—roots do not have soil around them. Purchase stock that is not dried out. Before planting, remove dead and yellow leaves and cut roots so they are about 4 inches long.

Set plants about 12 inches apart in rows 12 to 15 inches apart. Proper planting depth is important. Place plants just above the root line and just below the crown. If you plant too shallow, some of the root system will be exposed and the plant will dry out and die. If you plant too deep, some of the crown will be buried and the plant will rot and die. Spread and extend roots into the soil vertically when planting. See illustrations on page 133.

If you plant June-bearing varieties, remove all flowers that develop during the first year. With everbearing types, remove all flowers until July 1. This increases plant vigor, promoting earlier production of runners. The result is a greater fruit yield the following summer.

As plants develop, they send out runners. When runners reach 12 to 15 inches long, arrange them in a row, spaced about 6 to 9 inches apart. Gently press runners into the soil about 1/2 inch deep. Or cover with 1/2 inch of soil and place a stone on each runner to hold it in position until roots develop. Do not sever runner from mother plant.

The bearing life of a strawberry plant varies. Generally, new, everbearing varieties should be planted from runners every year or at least every other year.

Depending on conditions and varieties, some June-bearing types may bear for up to five years. This is true if plants are vigorous, productive and the bed is reasonably free of weeds. But renovation is still recommended. Each year after harvest, run a rotary lawn mower set to cut 2 to 3 inches high over the strawberry bed. This rejuvenates plants, creating new productive growth. Cultivate between rows. Remove excess plants so that remaining plants are spaced 6 to 9 inches apart. After about five years, purchase new stock and move the bed to a new site.

Strawberry

	Standard	Dwarf
Height at maturity (feet)		
Unpruned	1/2-1	N/A
Pruned	1/2-1	
Spread at maturity with no competition (feet)	1/2-1	
Recommended planting distance (inches)		
Between plants	12	
Between rows	12-15	
Years to reach bearing age	1	
Life expectancy (years)	1-10*	
Pollinator required	No	
Good for espalier	No	
Good for containers	Yes	

*Low yields, poor vigor and greater likelihood of pest and disease problems after 3 years.

N/A = Not Available.

Planting Bare-Root Strawberries

When planting strawberries, crown of plant should be level with soil and roots spread out evenly. If crown is planted below soil surface, crown is kept too moist and will rot. Planted too high, roots are exposed. If roots are not straightened they tend to be too close to the soil surface, and plant grows lopsided.

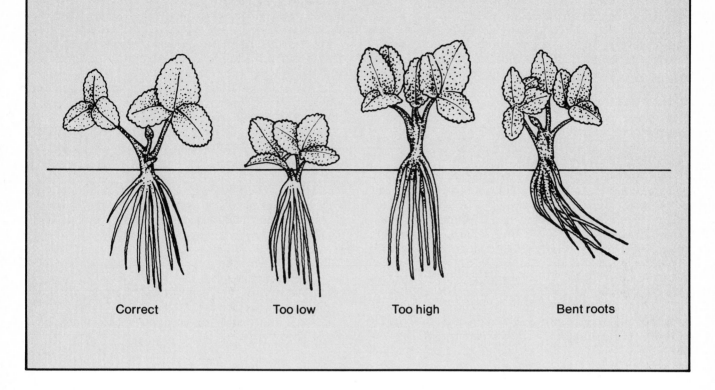

Correct   Too low   Too high   Bent roots

Using Plastic Mulch—To keep strawberry beds free from weeds, to retain moisture and to keep fruit off the ground, lay down plastic mulch over the planting area before planting. The mulch also warms the soil earlier in the spring. Clear plastic warms the soil more than black plastic, but weeds will grow underneath, so it is probably best to use black plastic. Secure the plastic by mounding soil over the edges. If you live in a particularly windy area, place stones or bricks along the edges. Cut holes in the plastic and plant the strawberry plants.

STRAWBERRIES FROM SEED
'Sweetheart' strawberry is an everbearing variety that can be grown from seeds started indoors, the same as many common vegetable crops. Sow seeds in a flat filled with seed-starting mix such as potting soil. Sow early in the season—January or February. Place flat in a cool, 65F (19C) location under fluorescent lights for 14 hours a day. Keep soil moist. Seedlings emerge in about 30 days. After they reach a size that allows them to be handled, and have about five leaves, transplant them from flat to individual containers to grow them to transplant size. Keep soil moist and feed with a dilute solution of liquid house-plant fertilizer. Con-

tinue to grow seedlings under lights, or move them to a sunny windowsill. After danger of frost has passed, plant outdoors in permanent beds.

Fertilize plants with a complete fertilizer once each month during the growing season. Plants bear about 120 days after sowing seeds. They are everbearing, and are reported to produce fruit right up until the first frost.

Remove runners the first year for best fruit production. In subsequent years, cultivate as you would everbearing varieties.

CULTURAL REQUIREMENTS
Strawberries thrive in a sandy loam soil. Soil pH of 6.0 is ideal, but strawberries can be productive in clay loam to coarse, sandy soil, with a pH of 5.5 to 7.5. Good drainage is essential to vigorous, healthy growth.

Strawberries are well suited to all areas except Zones 2 and 3. When you select a planting site, avoid areas infested with perennial weeds. This makes maintenance of the strawberry bed much easier. To protect against diseases, select a site that has not been planted with potatoes, tomatoes, peppers or eggplant within the two previous years. These plants are hosts of diseases that also infect strawberries.

Before you set out plants, apply 5 pounds of 10-10-10 or 10-6-4 fertilizer per 100 linear feet of row. Cultivate into the top 4 inches of soil. Apply a second application in early July and again in late August. Do not fertilize again until after the following year's harvest.

Strawberries prefer full sun, except *fraise des bois,* which does best in partial shade.

Because they have shallow roots, strawberries should receive regular water, about 1 inch per week, either from rainfall or irrigation. Watering is crucial during early bloom period to the end of harvest.

POLLINATION
Strawberries are self-fertile and do not need a second variety for cross-pollination.

WINTER PROTECTION
In some areas, alternate freezing and thawing of soil can cause *heaving* of plants. Plant roots are pushed out of the soil, causing plants to die. A mulch in winter helps prevent heaving. Straw is one of the best mulch materials. Before the soil is frozen hard, cover plants with 3 or 4 inches of straw. Hold straw in place with chicken wire or other covering. In the spring, when plants acquire a fresh, yellow-green color, remove most of the mulch.

Leave straw mulch on plant rows during summer. It helps reduce weeds and cuts down on moisture loss by slowing evaporation.

HARVESTING AND STORAGE
Strawberries are ready to pick when they turn bright red. Tasting a few fruit is the best indication of ripeness. If the berries are sweet, juicy and have characteristic flavor, they are ready for harvest.

Flavor generally improves if fruit are allowed to remain on the plant for about two days after they have turned red. But check fruit often, because ripe fruit deteriorate rapidly.

Most plants ripen fruit over a period of 10 to 15 days. Fruit will keep in the refrigerator for about one week.

Remove all rotted or stunted fruit from plants each time you pick. These sap plant vigor, which is put to better use in ripening more fruit.

Berries are usually picked with the green *calyx,* leafy stem, attached. Remove the calyx at picking time to save tedious work later.

PESTS AND DISEASES
The tarnished plant bug is common in many growing areas. It causes malformed berries unless controlled. Red stele or root rot may infect plants, particularly if drainage is poor.

Birds like strawberries. As with raspberries, currants, blueberries and cherries, cover strawberry plants with 3/4- to 1-inch mesh netting. Or grow enough strawberries for yourself and the birds. For additional information on pest and disease control, see pages 52 to 55.

Fraise des bois are simple to propagate by division. Dig up mature plant, divide and replant.

Strawberries

Variety	Origin	Zones	Harvest Season	Fruit and Plant	Remarks
'ARDMORE'	Missouri	4-7	Late midseason	Fruit large. Skin bright red with yellow-red flesh. Plant produces best when grown in heavy silt loam.	Good flavor. Use for eating fresh or freeze.
'CANOGA'	Geneva, New York, 1979	4-7	Midseason	Fruit large, wedge-conic shape. Skin intense red, tough. Flesh firm, seeds bright yellow.	No data yet as to resistance to red stele and verticillium wilt.
'CATSKILL'	New York	4-7	Midseason	Fruit large, good dessert quality. Plant vigorous, cold-hardy.	Particularly good for freezing. Grown in a wide range of soil types, from New England to southern Minnesota.
'DUNLAP'	Illinois, 1890	4-7	Early to midseason	Fruit medium. Skin dark crimson, flesh deep red. Fruit highly perishable, so handle with care to avoid bruising. Regular cropper, quite cold-hardy.	Sometimes referred to as the domestic strawberry with the wild strawberry flavor.
'FAIRFAX'	Maryland, 1923	4-7	Early to midseason	Fruit medium, bright red outside, deep red inside. Plant cold-hardy, productive.	Plant is cold-hardy if runners are removed late in the season.
'FLETCHER'	New York, 1959	5-7	Midseason	Fruit medium to large. Glossy, medium red. Tender skin, medium-firm flesh is low acid. Plant vigorous, productive, produces runners freely.	Flowers somewhat resistant to frost. Preferred over 'Sparkle' for freezing.
'GARNET'	New York, 1965	4-7	Midseason	Fruit large, remain same size well through season. Medium red, attractive, moderately firm. Plant vigorous, productive.	Promising variety.
'HOLIDAY'	New York, 1972	4-7	Early to midseason	Fruit large, firm, bright red, glossy, oblate to round oblate. Distinctive, aromatic flavor. Plants productive, vigorous, producing matted rows of well-spaced plants.	Promising introduction. Fruit freezes well.
'HONEOYE'	New York, 1979	4-7	Early midseason	Fruit large, conic in shape, bright red. Skin and flesh firm. Plant vigorous and productive.	No data yet on resistance to root disease.
'MIDWAY'	Maryland, 1951	4-7	Midseason	Fruit large, good dessert quality. Plant vigorous, cold-hardy.	Planted widely in Michigan but susceptible to leaf spot, leaf scorch and verticillium wilt.
'OZARK BEAUTY'	Arkansas, 1955	4-7	Everbearing	Fruit large, sweet, flavorful, bright red. Plant vigorous.	Produces on mother plant, but not on runner plants during summer and fall.
'POCAHONTAS'	Maryland, 1946	4-7	Early	Fruit large. Plant vigorous.	Use fresh, freeze or preserve. Plants resist leaf scorch.
'RARITAN'	New Jersey, 1968	4-7	Midseason	Fruit large, firm. Good flavor. Plant medium in vigor.	Highly productive.
'SPARKLE'	New Jersey, 1942	4-7	Midseason	Fruit large, firm. Good flavor. Plant medium in vigor.	Highly productive.
'STARK RED GIANT'	Minnesota, 1967	4-7	Midseason	Fruit large, firm, juicy with burgundy-red flesh, good flavor. Plants have large leaves and are sturdy and healthy.	Use for eating fresh, preserving, canning and freezing.
'SURECROP'	Maryland, 1956	4-7	Midseason	Fruit large, good flavor, round, glossy, rich and sweet. Plant thrives on soil too dry or nutrient-poor for some varieties. Vigorous, production of runners must be curbed.	Use for freezing, eating fresh, canning and preserves. Resists red stele, verticillium wilt, leaf spot, leaf scorch and drought.
'TRUMPETER'	Minnesota, 1960	4-7	Late	Fruit medium, soft, glossy with good flavor. Plant cold-hardy.	Recommended for cold areas of upper Mississippi Valley and Plains States.

NUTS

Mixed harvest of chestnuts, hazelnuts and walnuts.

Zone Adaptation

	Zone 3	Zone 4	Zone 5	Zone 6	Zone 7
Chestnut, Chinese			●	●	●
Hazelnut, American	●	●	●	●	
Hazelnut, Hybrid			●	●	●
Walnut, Persian		●*	●	●	●
Walnut, Eastern Black	●	●	●	●	●
Butternut	●	●	●	●	●

* See text under Varieties heading for cold-hardy selections for this zone.

Chestnuts have interesting burred hulls. Inset: chestnuts without the husks.

Chestnut

During the past century, the native American chestnut has just about disappeared from North America. There was a time when extensive forests of this beautiful tree covered the land.

Chestnut blight has been responsible for killing many trees. In some cases, it has reduced full-size trees to shrub stature. Horticulturists have spent considerable effort trying to find resistant species, or to produce a hybrid resistant to the disease. The most promising is the Chinese chestnut, or a hybrid called *Oriental-American chestnut.*

The tree is medium size, round-headed, and grows to about 40 feet high. Nuts are quite similar in flavor to the native chestnut. They are smaller than the imported European chestnuts available in markets.

CULTURAL REQUIREMENTS
Chestnut trees prefer a deep, fertile, well-drained, slightly acid soil. They are subject to oak-root fungus, prevalent in soggy soils. Avoid planting them in low, slow-draining areas. If the soil has been properly prepared at planting time, additional fertilizer is usually not necessary.

POLLINATION
Chinese and Oriental-American chestnuts are not self-fertile. Plant two trees of the same variety or two different varieties nearby for cross-pollination.

HARVESTING AND STORAGE
In late summer, nuts begin to drop to the ground. Gather them each day. Nuts can be eaten raw. For storage, remove nuts from burrs and dry in the sun for one or two days. Store in a cool, dry place at 32F (0C). Nuts keep for several months.

Chestnut		
	Chinese	**European**
Height at maturity (feet)		
Unpruned	30-40	50
Pruned	20	25
Spread at maturity with		
no competition (feet)	30-50	40-50
Recommended planting		
distance (feet)	25-30	40
Years to reach bearing age	3-4	4
Life expectancy (years)	50	50
Chilling requirement (hours)	Low	Low
Pollinator required	Yes	Yes
Good for espalier	No	No
Good for containers	No	No

Hazelnuts without husks.

Hazelnut

You have a choice of three kinds of hazelnuts, or *filberts,* as they are sometimes called. These are European, American and hybrids, a cross between American and European. Native American varieties, known as *American hazelnuts,* are the most cold-hardy, but the nuts do not have the fine quality of the Europeans or the hybrids. They are recommended for Zones 4 to 7 and the warmer areas of Zone 3.

Hybrids such as 'Bixby', 'Buchanan', 'Potomac' and 'Reed' are recommended for Zones 5 to 7. Hybrids have similar growth habits and produce medium-size nuts.

European varieties produce larger nuts of finer quality. Varieties such as 'Barcelona', 'New Royal' and 'Davianna' are recommended for Zones 6 and 7.

CULTURAL REQUIREMENTS
Hazelnuts do best in deep, well-drained soil, but adapt to a wide range of soil types, from clay to sand. Avoid planting in waterlogged soil.

If growth is vigorous and foliage is healthy and dark green, do not fertilize. If foliage pales and growth slows, add 1/2 to 1 pound of actual nitrogen around tree each year. See page 113. Water thoroughly during periods of extreme drought.

PRUNING
Hazelnuts are shrublike rather than treelike. You can train them to a tree form, although yields are smaller. Train to a central-leader system for a tree form. See page 30.

For a shrub form, prune out excessive sucker growth every year at base of bush. Because nuts are formed on 1-year-old growth, prune moderately to stimulate new growth.

POLLINATION
Hazelnuts are not self-fertile and must be planted near another variety for cross-pollination. If you plant hybrids, plant another, different variety. If you plant a European variety, plant another European variety. Any two native American hazelnuts will cross-pollinate each other.

PROPAGATION
Hazelnut is the only nut that can be propagated by layering suckers that grow close to the trunk. Select a sucker that can be bent to the ground. Make a cut on the soil side of the sucker to speed up the rooting process. Cover with 3 inches of soil, allowing one or two buds to project beyond the soil level. Place a brick or stone on top to secure the sucker. If layering is done in summer, roots form by November.

Large suckers with roots already formed can be dug and replanted.

HARVESTING AND STORAGE
When nuts begin to turn brown, they are almost ready for harvest. Soon after, they begin to drop. Gather nuts from the ground every few days. Spread them out in a well-ventilated place for several weeks to allow them to dry. Husk and store in a cool, dry place. Nuts keep for several months in the shell. Shelled nutmeats can be stored for several weeks at room temperature, or for more than a year when frozen.

Hazelnut		
	Standard	**Dwarf**
Height at maturity (feet)		
Unpruned	20	N/A
Pruned	15	
Spread at maturity with		
no competition (feet)	15-20	
Recommended planting		
distance (feet)	20	
Years to reach bearing age	4	
Life expectancy (years)	50	
Chilling requirement (hours)	Medium to high	
Pollinator required	Yes	
Good for espalier	No	
Good for containers	No	
N/A = Not Available		

Black walnut.

Walnut

Mature walnut trees make excellent specimen shade trees, as well as providing an ample harvest of choice nuts. Many varieties are available. Some are native to North America. Others are European or Asian in origin. Persian walnuts, usually called *English walnuts,* include many varieties with varying degrees of cold-hardiness.

Until their introduction about 40 years ago, little success was reported with Persian walnuts in the East. Trees are extremely cold-hardy, withstanding temperatures from −35F to −40F (−37C to −40C). They can be grown in Zones 3 to 7.

VARIETIES OF PERSIAN WALNUTS

'Broadview'—Perhaps the most prolific producer of nuts. Bears annually. Shells are long and oval, 47% kernel by weight. Slightly bitter flavor.

'Fickes'—Medium-size nuts, 51% kernel. Recommended for Illinois and Iowa.

'Hansen'—Small tree. Annual bearer of small, thin-shelled nuts, 60% kernel. Self-pollinating, cold-hardy and adaptable to a wide range of growing conditions. Late-spring frost may damage blossoms.

'Lake'—Medium to large nuts, good flavor, 50% kernel. Recommended for Illinois and Missouri.

'McKinster'—Medium-size nut, 48% kernel. Self-pollinating. Yields well in Ohio and Michigan.

'Metcalfe'—Annual bearer of high-quality nuts, 52% kernel. Recommended for New York state.

EASTERN BLACK WALNUT

This native American species is a beautiful tree that grows rapidly, ultimately reaching 150 feet. It needs plenty of room because it spreads up to 60 feet wide. It makes an excellent lawn tree, providing high shade that is not too dense to interfere with grass growth.

Do not plant where roots will compete with flowers or vegetables or with foundation plantings. Roots are toxic to tomatoes and some other plants. Try to keep such plantings at least 150 feet away from trees.

PRUNING

Train walnut trees to a modified central-leader system. See page 30. After they are established, trees require little pruning except to remove damaged or dead limbs.

HARVESTING AND STORAGE

When nuts begin to fall to the ground, they are ready for harvest. Rather than wait for all nuts to fall, shake trunk or limbs vigorously to cause nuts to drop. Nuts can be stored in or out of their shells. To store nutmeats, remove hulls and rinse them in water. This removes *tannin,* a black chemical substance that can discolor nutmeats. After washing, dry nutmeats in the sun for several days. Shelled nutmeats keep in the refrigerator for several months. If frozen, they keep for more than a year.

Store nuts in the shell in a cool, dry place. They will keep for several months.

GARDENER'S TIPS

● In the fall, rake up fallen walnut leaves from around trees. Burn or dispose of them. *Do not* add them to compost or use them as a mulch. Toxic elements in the leaves can affect the growth of some plants.

● If you order a walnut tree through a mail-order supplier, check to see if the long taproot has been pruned. If it has not, cut the end of the taproot back a few inches. This helps encourage early bearing.

● Baking soda can be used to remove black tannin stains from hands. Better yet, wear rubber gloves to avoid the stain.

● "A tough nut to crack" applies to black walnuts and butternuts. Crack by standing them on end and hitting the end with a hammer.

Walnut

	Black	English
Height at maturity (feet)		
Unpruned	70	60
Pruned	40	50
Spread at maturity with no competition (feet)	50-60	50-70
Recommended planting distance (feet)	50-60	60-70
Years to reach bearing age	5	5-8
Life expectancy (years)	100	100
Chilling requirement (hours)	Medium	Medium
Pollinator required	Yes	No*
Good for espalier	No	No
Good for containers	No	No

*Better yields with a pollinator.

VARIETIES OF EASTERN BLACK WALNUT

'Hare'—Heavy nut with good kernel percentage. On a par with 'Thomas'. Easy to propagate by budding. Well adapted to the Midwest.

'Myer'—Thin shell with good cracking quality. Vigorous, upright growth. Regular yield. Thrives in Northeast and along the East Coast.

'Ohio'—High kernel percentage. Vigorous, upright growth. Regular yields.

'Stabler'—Thin shell. Variable producer of nuts. Recommended for East Coast.

'Thomas'—High kernel weight and percentage. The standard for comparison. Vigorous, early bearing, but tends to *alternate-bear,* produce nuts every other year. Widely adapted.

'Victoria'—Vigorous but tends to alternate-bear. Shells are thicker than most. Resists leaf spot.

BUTTERNUT

This is the hardiest walnut tree. It produces elongated nuts that have exceptional flavor. They are prized in many areas of the United States and Canada. Fungus infections are prevalent in certain areas, and can shorten the life of the tree.

Nuts of grafted varieties, available in nurseries, are superior to native wild species. Usually, entire halves of nuts can be removed from hulls if cracked from the ends.

Superior varieties include: 'Craxeasy', 'Thill', 'Johnson', 'Van Dyckle' and 'Ayers'.

CULTURAL REQUIREMENTS

All walnuts prefer deep, well-drained, fertile soil with ample moisture. They do not do well in waterlogged soil. Water thoroughly during extremely dry periods in summer.

POLLINATION

English walnuts, black walnuts and butternuts produce crops without a pollinator. However, you will have a more bountiful crop if another tree is located about 50 feet away.

Comparison of black walnut, top, and English walnut, bottom.

Walnuts are impressive, long-lived landscape trees.

Catalog Sources

The Adams Country Nursery Inc.
P.O. Box 108
Aspers, PA 17304
Dwarf and standard fruit trees. Free catalog.

Ahrens Strawberry Nursery
Route 1
Huntingburg, IN 47542
Strawberry, raspberry, gooseberry, blueberry and blackberry plants. Currants and grapes. Free catalog.

W.F. Allen Co.
P.O. Box 1577
Salisbury, MD 21801
Specializes in strawberry plants. Also carries blueberries, raspberries, blackberries and grapes. Free catalog.

Bountiful Ridge Nurseries Inc.
P.O. Box 250
Princess Anne, MD 21853
Dwarf and standard fruit trees, grapes, berries and nut trees. Free catalog.

Brittingham Plant Farms
P.O. Box 2538
Ocean City Road
Salisbury, MD 21801
Strawberries, blueberries, raspberries, thornless blackberries and grapes. Free catalog.

Bunting's Nurseries Inc.
Drawer 306-OG
Selbyville, DE 19975
Strawberries and other fruit and nuts. Free catalog.

Burgess Seed and Plant Co.
905 Four Seasons Road
Bloomington, IL 61701
Dwarf and standard fruit trees, nut trees and berries. Free catalog.

W. Atlee Burpee
300 Park Ave.
Warminster, PA 18974
Fruits, berries and nut trees. Catalog free upon request.

The Conner Co.
P.O. Box 534
Augusta, AR 72006
Arkansas-certified strawberry plants. Free information.

Cumberland Valley Nurseries
P.O. Box 430
McMinnville, TN 37110
Peaches, plums and nectarines. Free price list.

J.A. Demonchaux Co.
827 N. Kansas Ave.
P.O. Box 8330
Topeka, KS 66608
Fraise des bois strawberry seeds. Catalog free. Send 50¢ for handling.

Emlong Nurseries
Stevensville, MI 49127
Dwarf and standard fruit trees, nut trees and berries. Specializing in fruit trees. Free catalog.

Farmer Seed & Nursery
818 N.W. 4th St.
Faribault, MN 55021
Northern-grown vegetable seeds, fruit trees and small fruit. 64-page color catalog free.

Henry Field Seed & Nursery Co.
Dept. 87, 2176 Oak St.
Shenandoah, IA 51602
Fruit trees, nut trees and berries. Free catalog.

Dean Foster Nurseries
Route 2, OG-L
Hartford, MI 49057
Fruit and berries and nut trees. Specializes in strawberries. Free catalog.

Gurney Seed & Nursery Co.
Dept. 98, 1910 Page St.
Yankton, SD 57079
Fruit trees, berries and nut trees. Free catalog.

J.W. Jung Seed Co.
Randolph, WI 53956
Fruit trees, berries, shrubs, vegetable and flower seeds. Free catalog.

Kelly Brothers Nurseries Inc.
Dansville, NY 14437
Dwarf and standard fruit trees, nut trees, berries and grapes. Free catalog.

Lawson's Nursery
Route 1, P.O. Box 294
Yellow Creek Road
Ball Ground, GA 30104
Specializes in old-fashioned and unusual fruit trees. Free catalog.

Henry Leuthardt Nurseries
Montauk Highway
P.O. Box 666
East Moriches, NY 11940
Dwarf and semidwarf fruit trees, espaliered fruit trees, hybrid grapes and berry plants. Descriptive price list.

Earl May Seed & Nursery Co.
100 N. Elm St.
Shenandoah, IA 51601
Fruit trees, berries and grapes. Free catalog.

McConnell Nurseries Inc.
Port Burwell, Ontario CANADA
NOJITO
Dwarf and standard fruit trees and berries. Free catalog.

J. E. Miller Nursery
5060 W. Lake Road
Canandaigua, NY 14424
Fruit and nut trees, grapevines, small fruit and berry bushes. Free catalog.

Neosho Nurseries
900 North College
Neosho, MO 64850
Dwarf and standard fruit trees, nut trees and small fruit. Free catalog.

New York State Fruit Testing Cooperative Association
Geneva, NY 14456
Free 32-page fruit catalog. Membership fee $5, levied on first order.

Nourse Farms Inc.
Box 485 RFD
South Deerfield, MA 01373
Strawberry and raspberry plants. Free catalog.

L.L. Olds Seed Co.
P.O. Box 7790
Madison, WI 53707
Northern-grown fruit and berries. Free catalog.

Geo. W. Park Seed Co. Inc.
Highway 254N
Greenwood, SC 29647
Berries, grapes and dwarf fruit trees. Free catalog.

Ponzer Nursery
Route 1, P.O. Box 313C
Lecoma, MO 65540
Fruit trees. Free price list.

Rayner Bros. Inc.
P.O. Box 1617G
Salisbury, MD 21801
Specializes in strawberry plants. Also raspberries, blueberries, bush fruit, fruit and nut trees. Free catalog.

Savage Farm Nursery
P.O. Box 125
McMinnville, TN 37110
Fruit trees and berry plants. Free catalog.

Spring Hill Nurseries
Catalog Reservation Center
P.O. Box 1758
Peoria, IL 61658

Stark Bro's Nurseries & Orchards
P.O. Box A3441A
Louisiana, MO 63353
Dwarf and standard fruit trees, grapes, berries, cherries and nut trees. Free catalog.

Stern's Nurseries Inc.
Geneva, NY 14456
Small fruit. Free catalog.

Van Bourgondien Bros.
245 Farmingdale Road, Route 109
Babylon, NY 11702
Fruit and nut trees and berries. Free catalog.

Waynesboro Nurseries
P.O. Box 987
Waynesboro, VA 22980
Fruit and nut trees and small fruit. Free catalog.

Wolf River Nurseries
Route 67, P.O. Box 73
Buskirk, NY 12028
Grapes, berry plants, dwarf fruit trees and hybrid Chinese-American chestnut trees. Free catalog. Offers mail-order course in propagation.

Index

Index